WELCOME TO NEW YORK

Welcome To New York

HOW TO SETTLE AND SURVIVE

IN NEW YORK

SECOND EDITION

By Roberta Seret, Ph.D.

HARPER COLOPHON BOOKS
Harper & Row, Publishers
New York, Cambridge, Philadelphia, San Francisco, London
Mexico City, São Paulo, Singapore, Sydney

FOR MY HUSBAND, MICHEL, MY VERY BEST FRIEND

Library of Congress Cataloging in Publication Data

Seret, Roberta.
  Welcome to New York.

  Bibliography: p.
  Includes index.
  1. New York (N.Y.)—Description—1981–   —Guide-
books. 2. New York (N.Y.)—Directories. I. Title
F128.18.S42   1985   974.7'1   84-48620
ISBN 0-06-091238-3 (pbk.)

85 86 87 88 89 RRD 10 9 8 7 6 5 4 3 2 1

Acknowledgments

I would like to show my appreciation to my friends Selene Levin and Hilary Becker for their talents and ideas.

Special thanks to Janet Wilkens Manus, whose unfaltering enthusiasm and support encouraged me.

In appreciation of my editor, Carol Cohen, and her assistant, Cathy Guigui, of Harper & Row, whose expertise helped shape this book.

Table of Contents

vii

Introduction

ESTABLISHING oneself and one's family in a new country, new city, and new language can be difficult. Where do you begin, and how do you begin? When you relocate to any new city or country, it is inevitable that protocol and social customs and traditions mix together in confusion. You may wonder for many months: "Will I ever really understand this new city? Will I ever be able to enjoy it?"

It takes time, patience, and effort to understand any new city. It takes knowledge, skill, and a sense of humor to live in New York City. But once you understand her and know where the pleasant places are, how to get there, what customs are important, what etiquette and traditions to follow, and how to go about getting what you want, life in New York City can be truly exciting. One morning you may wake up and resent her noises and unpleasantries. Yet, on another morning, you will wake up excited to begin your day as you begin to discover how to live in New York.

But before you start your struggle with this city, you must learn about its customs and traditions. You must study its corners, walk its streets, meet its people, and take advantage of every new thing it can offer you. Don't stay apart from the city's life.

This handbook will help you learn how to do it all. The information, the advice, the facts—they are the answers to actual questions asked by the hundreds of newcomers we have consulted in our seminars and workshops. What has previously been available to the participants of our seminars is now available to all readers of *Welcome To New York*. Our organization, the American Welcome Services, has documented and put in written form guidelines for understanding the practical aspects of daily life in New York City. The information will be most useful during your first months in New York City. These months are

xiii

probably the most difficult, but they are also the most challenging. This handbook will help make those days seem less frustrating. Each chapter offers you data that was gathered from many sources and from many people. The most detailed information has been acquired by experts in specific areas who have lived and worked in this city for many years. We offer you practical advice, facts, and valuable names and addresses. We will try to save you time by directing you to proper sources and recommending the most efficient way to proceed. We want you to have more time to see the wonderful parts of New York and to enjoy the wide range of cultural events, the unending artistic expressions, and the unlimited exhibitions of creativity that make New York City the unique city it is. Our aim is to help you find what you need as quickly as possible, to understand New York City *and New Yorkers* as easily as possible, so that you will have both enough energy and desire to enjoy the pleasure of living in New York City.

Read each section carefully, one by one, little by little. Afterward, you will reach out to New York with eagerness and excitement. We believe this handbook will help you understand New York City and enjoy her so you can love her as we do.

Above all, WELCOME!

DR. ROBERTA SERET
President
American Welcome Services

PART I

Settling In

CHAPTER 1

How To Rent an Apartment in New York City

Map of Leading Residential Neighborhoods
Descriptions of Leading Residential Neighborhoods in New York City
Temporary Quarters: Furnished Apartments; Furnished Rooms; Hotels
*   with Efficiencies; Bed and Breakfast; Roommates*
Steps To Follow When You Look To Rent an Apartment:
*   Names of Renting Agencies*
What Is the Procedure Once You Find the Apartment You Want?
What Legal Rights Do Tenants Have? Lease; Rent-Stabilization
Steps To Follow Once the Apartment Is Yours
Housing Price Ranges for Eighty-Two Communities (see Appendix A)
Public High Schools in the Five Boroughs (see Appendix D)
Private High Schools in New York City (see Appendix E)

RENTING an apartment in New York City is not easy. Many people want to live in New York City, and there are a limited number of apartments available. No matter how many tall buildings go up, or how much construction is being done, finding an apartment, especially the right apartment, in New York City still takes time, patience, persistence, and money.

The concept of supply and demand dictates the movement of New York's real estate market. Those tenants who are already in modestly priced rental apartments do not usually move unless they must. They realize that to move elsewhere within the City could mean a very large increase in their rent. To complicate matters even more, many old rental apartment buildings in New York are being converted to co-operatives and condominiums, which decrease the already limited number of rental apartments available. Each year, more and more people want to live in Manhattan. Due to the increase in costs of gasoline and transportation, and rising real estate taxes, many suburbanites are moving back into the city. As a result, there are not enough reasonably priced apartments for

3

all those who want to live in New York City. Have courage, however. It is not impossible to find an apartment in New York. We say what the French say: the word impossible does not exist. This chapter will give you some useful hints and practical advice on how to go about finding your apartment.

Before you look for an apartment, you must answer some important questions. In which section of New York City do you want to live? (Take into consideration the safety and security of the neighborhood, the ambiance of the community, the type of people who generally live in that area, as well as such practical aspects as closeness to your work, proximity to public transportation, proximity to public and private schools and parks if you have children, and proximity to friends and relatives.) What type of apartment do you want (terrace, fireplace, old building, new building, large rooms, small rooms, townhouse, 24-hour doorman, walk-up, view, tranquility, sunshine, garage in building, etc.)? What size apartment do you want? What size apartment would be adequate? Can you get a smaller or larger apartment in the same building at a later date? How much rent can you afford to pay? What size apartment can you get for that rent (this is the most delicate question)? Don't base your expected rent on what your friends pay. They may have an old lease. The prices of apartment rentals are forever increasing. You may have to compromise on the size you originally wanted, or you may be obliged to pay more rent. This will depend upon the neighborhood you choose. Not all neighborhoods in New York City are the same; the most desirable neighborhoods are more expensive. The rents of the Upper East Side (60's, 70's, 80's, and 90's from Fifth Avenue to East End Avenue) are the most expensive in Manhattan. One of the reasons for their high costs is that the two best public elementary schools in Manhattan are located in these neighborhoods. P.S. #6 is located at Madison Avenue and 82nd Street, and P.S. #158 is located at York Avenue and 77th Street. If your child is aged five to eleven years old (grade Kindergarten to Sixth Grade) and you live in one of these school districts, your child has the option of attending one of these free, public schools. This may be an influencing factor in choosing to live in one of these neighborhoods.

However, there are many other lovely communities in New York City which are equally agreeable to live in. Remember, before you begin looking for an apartment, you will have to know in which neighborhood you would prefer to live.

The following breakdown will describe for you many of the major residential areas of the city. We will take into consideration safety elements, transportation, availability, proximity to public and private schools, access to recreational activities, and the general ambiance and description of each neighborhood. It is important to understand that New York City, in spite of its great size and overwhelming population, can be a very "homey" place in which to live. Each neighborhood of New York City is similar to a small village—independent, self-functioning, and very friendly. Each community has its own flavor. Within your neighborhood, you will most likely frequent the same shops, see the same faces, and make friends with the people of your community in the same way you would if you moved into a new village or town anywhere in the world.

DESCRIPTIONS OF LEADING RESIDENTIAL AREAS IN NEW YORK CITY

1. *The Upper East Side* is an area which includes the 60's, 70's, 80's and 90's from Fifth Avenue to York Avenue and East End Avenue. This is probably the most expensive section of New York City. Many of the best co-ops and luxurious rental buildings are located in this area, as are the most fashionable boutiques and most elegant shops. The public schools, such as P.S. #6 at Park Avenue and 82nd Street and P.S. #158 at York Avenue and 77th Street, are very good. The private schools are excellent in this community. This neighborhood, world renowned for its expensive rents and fancy cars, has many playgrounds (especially at the Carl Schurz Park at East End Avenue and 84th Street), recreational activities, schools, cosmopolitan boutiques, and gourmet shops. In spite of its chic and opulence, this neighborhood is a family-oriented community. There may be a good number of young singles who live on First, Second, and Third Avenues, and you may observe them float from one night spot to another, but the atmosphere of this neighborhood is predominantly well-established family. It is not uncommon to see many elegant mothers pushing baby carriages and lively young children playing ball in front of their expensively guarded buildings. From this neighborhood, transportation is excellent to all parts of the city. There is an express bus to Wall Street, and the Lexington Avenue subway line can be reached by buses from each main avenue of the Upper East Side.

2. *Sutton Place* is a very small section of New York City, but it is very choice and expensive due to its mid-town location and proximity to Bloomingdale's and major shopping. It is one of the few enclaves left in New York that is unknown to the boisterous crowds and traffic jams. Geographically, it extends from 53rd Street to 59th Street, and maybe as far west as York Avenue or even First Avenue. Most of the buildings are

HOW TO RENT AN APARTMENT IN NEW YORK CITY

Key

1. The Upper East Side
2. Sutton Place
3. The United Nations
4. Murray Hill
5. Gramercy Park
6. Greenwich Village
7. Soho
8. Chelsea
9. Lincoln Center
10. The Upper West Side
11. Columbia University
12. Yorkville
13. Ukrainian
14. Little Italy
15. Chinatown

co-ops; rentals are possible to find but are very costly. Many of the tenants work in the 50's or low 60's and have the privilege of walking to work from home. The 57th Street crosstown bus can take you to Fifth Avenue and the West Side within minutes. The age group of this area tends to be mature.

3. The *United Nations* area is a quiet area on the East Side of Manhattan in the 40's. For those who work at the United Nations or in the 40's, this is an excellent place to live. The most residential area is around Tudor City (off First Avenue and the low 40's), where you have a true international flavor of the city. Rents in this area are not as expensive as in the more northerly section, but there are fewer residential apartments available, and they are more difficult to find. Most of the tenants in this area have been here for a very long time.

4. The *Murray Hill* section of New York City is a lovely area in which to live and not as "discovered" as other sections of Manhattan. This area is centered in the East 30's. On Third Avenue are a varied number and styles of restaurants, cafés, and after-work meeting spots, especially popular with the young professionals in the area. On Second Avenue are such new highrise buildings as Kips Bay Plaza (30th to 33rd Streets on First and Second Avenues). On First Avenue is New York University Medical Center. The side streets have some beautiful townhouses and small residential buildings. 34th Street and Second Avenue is the center for several movie houses, and transportation is good to all parts of Manhattan and Queens. This Murray Hill section is an interesting area in which to live, for it is practically located and aesthetically designed.

5. *Gramercy Park*, like Sutton Place and East End Avenue, is a special part of Manhattan that has maintained over the years its unique charm and atmosphere. Several decades ago, this was the ultra-chic area for those New Yorkers who didn't want to live in the middle of Greenwich Village but wanted to be near enough to benefit from its night life. Today, the Gramercy Park section, in the upper teens and low 20's off Fifth Avenue eastward to Second Avenue, has charming shops and restaurants and undiscovered residential areas. The proximity of Gramercy Park on 20th and 21st Streets off Irving Place is the "key" to this area (you need a key to use this "private" park, and only residents of the area are entitled to a key—which costs $125 a year). Rents vary from the very expensive and hard-to-find townhouses and apartments to the "New York priced" highrise buildings on Second and Third Avenues. The nearby Waterside complex between 23rd and 28th Streets overlooking the East River is a lovely spot in which to live. It has a health club, indoor swimming pool, and beautiful views of the East River.

6. *Greenwich Village* is a fun place to live, especially the "West

Village" which includes the small, winding streets west of Seventh Avenue such as Barrow Street, Christopher Street, Charles Street, Perry Street, and Bank Street. But this area is not cheap, in spite of its bohemian façade. The brownstones and townhouses have all been redone in exceptional taste, and in New York City one usually has to pay dearly for tree-lined streets, old-fashioned gaslights, and charming historical buildings. Many artists and intellectuals enjoy this area because of its proximity to New York University and the New School, the unending choice of foreign films, lectures, and conferences, and the darkly lit jazz hangouts and European-style cafés.

7. *SoHo*, which means "south of Houston Street," developed when Greenwich Village became too commercial and far too expensive for its original inhabitants. Painters and sculptors needed more space and room to develop their expressions; renovated factories, old buildings, and forgotten warehouses seemed to be the right answer. Today, SoHo is characterized by large pre-war factories and warehouses that include on their upper floors some very imaginatively renovated lofts where artists can live and work, and on the ground floor some very interesting art galleries and cafés where they can meet and talk. When the tourists aren't there, SoHo is what Greenwich Village was thirty years ago but not as "inexpensive." (Tribeca — "Triangle Below Canal" near Canal Street, West Street, and East Broadway — in the past few years is still another creation of New York artists who have spread themselves in search of space and reasonable rents. SoHo is geographically adjacent to Tribeca.) SoHo's boundry on the east is Lafayette Street, on the north West Houston Street, on the west the Avenue of the Americas, and on the south Canal Street.

8. *Chelsea* extends its borders on the east to the Avenue of the Americas, on the north to West 32nd Street, on the west to the Hudson River, and on the south to West 14th Street. This is an area characterized by incongruous architecture and a group of heterogeneous residents. There are some charming tree-lined streets with superb brownstones, but they can be surrounded by dirty restaurants of fast foods and suspicious youths of fast habits. The Fashion Institute of Technology is located in this area, as are many businesses related to the fashion world. Rents vary from the very cheap to the very expensive as the caliber of residents varies from the very dangerous to the very chic.

9. The *Lincoln Center* area is perhaps the most quickly developing community in New York City. Extending from Central Park West to Broadway, from 59th Street to 86th Street, this area knows no curfew. In the evening, with its varied cafés on Broadway and its cosmopolitan restaurants on Columbus Avenue, one has the feeling that this

neighborhood is Lincoln Center's "encore"—the continuation of an exciting evening "on the town." The older section, which includes the stately co-operative buildings of Central Park West and the historical brownstones between Central Park West and Columbus Avenue, is an architect's delight for a rich man's taste. Many of these residents are the successful musicians and artists involved with Lincoln Center, or just those so enamored with the area's artistic life that they can't stand to live elsewhere. Many young singles have been attracted to this area for its comparatively reasonable rents on Amsterdam Avenue and Broadway. Most of the highrise apartment buildings near Lincoln Center area are expensive. But the Lincoln Towers complex at West End Avenue and 67th Street may have an available apartment at a reasonable rent. There are some excellent private schools, as well as recreational opportunities, in this community. Central Park is the city's recreational center, and it is this neighborhood's extended backyard for joggers, children, dog-walkers, and even romantics. Transportation is excellent in this area.

10. The *Upper West Side*, which includes the 80's and 90's from Central Park West to Riverside Drive, has perhaps the most beautifully styled apartment buildings and townhouses in New York City. The rents vary, depending on the specific street and building. Riverside Drive has superb views of the Hudson River and the George Washington Bridge. West End Avenue is the haven for young doctors, Ph.D.s, and intellectuals. To live "on the Avenue" has become a symbol of status for them. They enjoy the large apartments and the fair rents for large accommodations. Many of the older buildings of West End Avenue, Central Park West, and Riverside Drive have become co-operatives, and others will follow. However, there are rental apartments available on the side streets, in the smaller apartment houses, in the renovated walkups, and in the redone brownstones.

11. *Columbia University*, at 116th Street and Broadway, is a neighborhood of its own. Many students and professors live in this community, and one has the feeling that in this neighborhood books and learning are more important than fancy apartments. The rents are very reasonable; many apartment are owned or managed by Columbia University, and renting priority goes first to their students and faculty. Morningside Park on 110th Street, just above Central Park, offers beautiful views of gardens and hills. But in spite of the unique intellectual flavor of this area, one should be warned that Harlem fringes on its borders and that safety is not what it should be.

Some ethnic areas in New York City, which traditionally have attracted homogeneous groups of people since the beginning of the twentieth century, are worth mentioning. If you are of the same ethnic background, you may want to live in one of these communities. Common language, customs, and traditions will make you feel less like a stranger in New York City. In fact, the neighborhood will make you feel as if you never left home.

12. The *Yorkville* area, which is the German section of New York City, is centered mostly around 86th Street and Third Avenue, but it extends as far south as 75th Street and as far east as First Avenue. There is also a Hungarian section within this area, and that is located from 85th Street to 77th Street, York Avenue on the east, and Lexington Avenue on the western boundary. Czechoslovakians and Hungarians populate this area as well, mostly around 77th Street to 70th Street, between Third Avenue and First Avenue. In the shops and cafés, the employees speak German and Hungarian depending on the street in which you find yourself. After a few minutes of talking and shopping, you will forget that you're still in New York City.

13. The *Ukranians* have been living in a certain neighborhood since the 1870s. It is one of the most self-functioning neighborhoods in the City and maintains customs similar to those of a small village or town in the Ukraine. The Ukranian community is in the East Village, extending from 13th Street to 6th Street, from Broadway to Avenue A. There are many Ukranian restaurants, churches, and art galleries, as well as the St. George's Academy, a Ukranian school in the middle of New York City where children aged five to eighteen study Ukranian history, culture, and language.

14. The *Italian* section of New York, or *Little Italy*, very colorful and very well known, reminds us of a small community in Southern Italy. The Italian colony began in the 1880s around Mulberry Street, has spread itself to Houston Street, Broadway, the Bowery, and even as far south as Canal Street. Real estate is expensive, for there is very little available.

15. *Chinatown,* which dates as far back as the mid-1800s, was originally Mott Street and Pell Street, but has now extended its boundaries as far north as Canal Street and Little Italy. There are seven Chinese newspapers published in Chinatown with more than 90,000 readers. As in Little Italy, there is very little real estate available on these over-crowded, over-populated streets.

If you are not sure in which community you wish to live, it would be best to spend some time walking around in several of the neighborhoods we have described. This will help you get a "feeling" of each community. After you have an idea of where you would like to live, taking into consideration your needs, proximity to work, etc., you will then be better able to choose the ideal community for yourself. It is important to remember that each community in New York City is different and unique. It is not only the rents that vary. In any event, you will enjoy exploring the many neighborhoods of New York.

TEMPORARY QUARTERS

To find an apartment to rent in New York City can take some time. If you are lucky, and reasonable in your demands, you may be able to find an apartment within a few weeks. If you are more demanding, it could take longer. Until you find the apartment you want, and you can move in (most leases begin the first of the month), you may need temporary quarters. A hotel can become very costly, especially if you come to New York City with your family. The alternative is to consider renting a furnished apartment or a rented room for a month or two. This could be less expensive than a hotel. It would give you kitchen facilities so you won't have to eat in restaurants all the time. You can get a feeling of living in a residential neighborhood of New York City. Above all, you would not feel pressured to take the first apartment you see.

There are several reputable agencies in New York City that deal specifically with furnished apartments. The procedure is to call them and ask if they have the size of apartment you need for the requested period of time. Visit their office and fill out an application. Then go with an agent to see several apartments and decide if you want any of the apartments he has shown you. The important thing to keep in mind about apartment hunting in New York City—whether it is a rental apartment or a short-term furnished apartment—is that you must decide quickly. Perhaps the next day the same apartment will not be available.

If you decide on taking a furnished apartment for a short period of time, you will have to sign a lease. This is a standard lease which will specify the date you leave the apartment. You will be responsible for installing your own telephone and taking care of the furnishings as if they were your own. As for the other utilities, gas, water and electricity, you can arrange to pay the landlord directly. At the time of signing the lease, bring your checkbook (not cash or travelers' checks) and be prepared to write checks for the following:

1. The first month's rent.
2. One or two months' rent as a security deposit.
3. A commission to the agent for finding you the apartment.

Some reputable agencies that specialize in renting furnished apartments are:

Feathered Nest. 867–8500. 310 Madison Avenue (42nd Street). ½ month's rent commission for an apartment you rent for 1–2 month's; 1 month's commission for an apartment you rent for 3–6 months; 15% of the first year's rent for an apartment you rent for 9 or more months.

Senter Realty. 935–8730. 210 East 58th Street. 1 month's rent commission for an apartment you rent for 1–12 months; 15% of the first year's rent for an apartment you rent for 12 or more months. (They have co-operative apartments that they can sublet to you.)

Furnished Apartments Specialists. 307–6455. 250 West 57th Street (corner of Broadway). ½ month's rent commission for an apartment you need for 1–2 months; 1 month's commission for an apartment you rent for 3–6 months; 15% of the amount paid for an apartment you rent for 7–11 months.

Manhattan East Company. 744–5660. When you telephone, they will meet you at one of the eight hotels they own in New York City. Their procedure is unique. They own hotels which they renovated as apartments with kitchens and bathrooms. Maid service is included. (The rents may be slightly less expensive than in other hotels, and the advantage here is that you have kitchen facilities.) Some of their "corporate hotels" are:
The Surrey Hotel — 20 East 76th Street.
The Lyden House — 320 East 53rd Street.
Beekman Tower — First Avenue and 49th Street.
The Shelburne — Murray Hill at 37th Street and Lexington Avenue.

If you are interested in renting a "furnished room," there are several types of furnished rooms and several ways to do this. One way is the English system of "bed and breakfast." You rent a room with a private bath in the apartment of a reputable family or individual. They serve you a Continental breakfast as part of your daily rate. They get no fee or commission for their services. They will accommodate one to three people in the same room and charge you accordingly. For this option you can contact:

Urban Ventures. 594–5650. P.O. Box 426, N.Y. 10024. They have a file of 350 different types of accommodations.

The second option is to share an apartment with a roommate. This accommodation may be practical or impractical, depending upon your personality and your time schedule. Before you embark on this route, think about your other options and turn to this as a "last resort." If you're curious or interested, you can always contact:

The Roommate Finders. 489–6860. 250 West 57th Street. Their fee is $85 for registration.

You may also choose to stay at a hotel and hope that you will be lucky enough to find permanent quarters within a week or two. If you come to New York alone, without a family, this would be the most practical way to begin. There are several very reasonably priced hotels with cooking facilities available, such as:

The Wales Hotel. 876–6000. 1295 Madison Avenue (92nd Street).
The Excelsior Hotel. 362–9200. 45 West 81st Street.
The Essex House. 247–0300. 160 Central Park South (expensive but very elegant, with views of Central Park).

Now you are ready to search for an apartment. There is a recommended system for this madness. Taking into consideration that finding an apartment in New York City is not easy, we have broken down the steps into a "scientific" approach.

STEPS TO FOLLOW WHEN YOU LOOK TO RENT AN APARTMENT; NAMES OF RENTING AGENCIES

1. Walk in the neighborhood that is your first choice. It is important to walk in the area during the day as well as during the evening. At night, the atmosphere of each community changes. Be sure you feel secure and safe at all times.

When you actively go to each building in search of an apartment, take pencil and paper so you can write down the name and address of the building you enter as well as the name of the person to whom you spoke (doorman, superintendent, managing agent). Promise the "key" person a good tip if you receive help. Remember your notes, and follow up any possible hint. It is a good idea to speak directly to the superintendent, for the superintendent is the one who knows in advance if a tenant has not renewed the lease. (The tenants must give the superintendent and/or landlord at least one or two months' notice if they are not going to renew the lease, or they forfeit their security deposit.)

2. Call the managing agents of several large rental corporations. They manage their own buildings, and they know one month in advance which tenant has not renewed his lease. They do not charge a fee or commission for their service. They may have a waiting list, but it still may be worth calling them on a weekly basis. If they do have something, they will ask you to go and see the superintendent of that building.

Glenwood Management. 535-0500. York Avenue and 75th Street.
Charles Greenthal and Company. 754-9300. 18 East 48th Street.
Helmsley Spear, Inc. 687-6400. 60 East 42nd Street.
Rudin Management. 644-8500. 345 Park Avenue. They have a long waiting list.

3. You can contact a renting agency. A renting agent or broker is licensed and qualified in New York State, by nature of specific exams and courses, to work in a real estate agency and serve as a liaison between a client and a landlord. There are many qualified agents and brokers in New York City who are reputable and reliable. From the outset ask them what their fee is. Most agencies charge a commission of 10–15% of the first year's rent on a one-, two-, or three-year lease. (You pay them the commission only when they find you the apartment and you sign a lease.) It may be more efficient and practical to work with several agencies at the same time. They will be able to give you an idea of how long it will take you to find the apartment you want and at what price. You must be very persistent and aggressive in your hunt. There are many people out there looking for an apartment and just a limited number of rentals available. You will have to constantly call the agent, perhaps every day, and follow up every hint or suggestion. When you see something you like, fill out an application and put a deposit on it immediately. You can write on the back of the check "deposit refundable."

Some reputable renting agencies in New York City are:

Bellmarc Realty. 420-1790. 770 Broadway (9th Street). They specialize in the SoHo area.
Feathered Nest. 867-8500. 310 Madison Avenue (42nd Street).
Freda Green and Associates, Inc. 753-7950. 120 East 56th Street.
Gardner Realty. 860-2111. 1276 Lexington Avenue (86th Street).
J. Rodman Co. 741-1166 at 80 University Place (11th Street) and 935-7100 at 145 East 57th Street. The former address is for those who are interested in the Greenwich Village area.
P. Zaccaro Co., Inc. 226-1212. 218 Lafayette Street. They specialize in the lower Manhattan section.
Sopher Rental Agency. 486-7000. 425 East 61st Street.
Sotheby Parke Bernet International. 472-4760. 974 Madison Avenue.
Star Apartments Realty Co. 362-8777. 53 West 72nd Street.

4. Whichever method or combination of methods you choose, it is a good idea to get into the habit of reading the Sunday *New York Times* real estate section. There are many newspaper stands that will sell this section on Saturday afternoon. It may be a good idea to get an earlier start on Saturday before other apartment hunters. You must keep in mind that there are more people looking for apartments in New York City than there are apartments available.

The classified section can become confusing. For economical purposes, abbreviations are used instead of the formal word. Sometimes important information may be "eliminated" and at other times you have to read in between the lines. To help you decipher "real estate hierogly-phics," use the following codes:

"prin only" = principals only. Only a private individual, and not a broker, should respond to this ad.

"imm occ" = immediate occupancy.

"key money" = you may be asked to give a certain amount of money to be able to rent this apartment in addition to the agent's commission. This may happen when the apartment is very desirable and the previous tenant wants to make money. This may or may not be legal, but it is not an uncommon practice.

"pre war" = describes the type of building, which was built before 1940. Usually the rooms are very large, with high ceilings. Check to be sure that older buildings have appropriate lighting, bathrooms, kitchens, and laundry rooms.

"sub lease" = means that you can take over someone else's lease (depending on how much time is left on the lease). This is legal if the previous tenant has a sub-lease clause in the lease. Just check first with the landlord that you have the right to renew the lease once you move into the apartment and at what rent.

"E-I-K" = eat-in-kitchen.

"drmn" = 24-hour doorman building with maximum security.

Be careful when you read the classified section of the real estate ads. A lot of imagination and skill was used in writing them.

WHAT IS THE PROCEDURE ONCE YOU FIND THE APARTMENT YOU WANT?

1. If you find your apartment with the help of a renting agency, the broker who has been working with you will ask you to complete an application. The application will have such important questions as: "What is the family's total income?" Landlords believe that the amount

of the family's total income for one week should be enough to pay for one month's rent. Income can include salaries as well as interest from investments and other sources. You will also have to write on the application a list of business references, personal references, employers' references, bank and credit references.

2. A deposit, which will be used for the first month's rent, should accompany the signed application. If you are rejected, the landlord returns your check. Write on the back side of the check, "Deposit refundable for apartment ____."

3. The real estate agency submits your application to a credit company which, in turn, does a thorough search on your credit rating. If you are a foreigner, you can request your home bank to provide you with an international bank reference. If the bank will not provide you with this, then you can offer to give the landlord two to four months of rent as a security deposit. Once you have built up a strong American credit rating, then the landlord will return this deposit, plus the interest earned, which was put in a savings account for you.

4. The agency telephones the employer(s) of the future tenants and gets an oral recommendation.

5. The agency checks if the future tenants have any "litigation" or outstanding debts on their credit cards, charge cards, or credit.

6. You are asked to sign a lease. If you have the choice, it is better to take a longer lease than a shorter one. You can always terminate a lease without any penalty, but, if you want to stay on in your apartment when it expires, you will have to renegotiate another lease and pay a rent increase.

7. Review carefully the clauses of your lease and read all small print. Be sure you know what comes with the apartment, such as air conditioners, refrigerator, dishwasher, stove, light fixtures, etc. Before signing the lease, be sure that you are satisfied with their condition. If not, mention any problems, before signing, to the agent. Inquire about painting the apartment. The landlord is usually responsible for all expenses related to painting and cleaning your new quarters.

8. At the time of signing the lease, come prepared with a heavy checkbook. You will have to write a check for the first month's rent, another check equal to one month's rent as a security deposit, and another check for the broker's commission (inquire beforehand what this will be). If you are not satisfied with the terms of the lease, explain your feelings to the broker. It is in the broker's interest that you are satisfied and that you want the apartment. The broker will speak to the landlord and serve as a liaison between the two of you.

Try to negotiate all your terms before you sign the lease. After this "rite of passage," your next step is to contact the superintendent of your new building and prepare to move. The signing of the lease marks the end of a long ordeal; you are now initiated into the club of New York residents.

WHAT LEGAL RIGHTS DO YOU HAVE AS A TENANT?
LEASE; RENT-STABILIZATION

There are at least 52,000,000 Americans, or one out of every four residents of the United States, who rent their homes or apartments as opposed to owning them. Understandably, in America there has been a need to establish guidelines and rules to protect these tenants. These rights should be understood and exercised, for, as with anything, if you don't use them, they can be forgotten.

If at any time your tenant rights are ignored, or the landlord fails in his responsibilities, you can contact a real estate lawyer or call the Conciliation and Appeals Board of the New York City Rent Stabilization office at 903–9500 for assistance or advice.

What Exactly Are Your Rights?

Your landlord is responsible for providing you with the following:

1. A safe building, which includes security in hallways and elevator.

2. Adequate heat from October 1 through May 31 at a temperature of 68° between 6:00 A.M. and 10:00 P.M. and 55° between 10:00 P.M. and 6:00 A.M.

3. Well-maintained plumbing and electricity for the entire building, as well as your unit.

4. A strong, secure lock for your front door.

5. Smoke detectors, one per sleeping area. (Tenants are responsible for the repair and maintenance of the smoke alarms.)

What Is a Lease?

You, as the tenant, are also responsible for abiding by specific rules. There are usually regulations specified in the lease you sign at the time you agree to take possession of the apartment. A lease is an agreement between you and your landlord. The landlord is responsible for providing you with a safe, clean home. The tenant is responsible for paying the rent each month and for keeping the property in the same, original condition. The lease is a standard document except for the last pages, where there may be a list of "clauses," or additions. These clauses are added to the lease by the landlord's attorney. Therefore, it is very important that you read and understand every clause. They should be written in "plain English," an English that can be understood by everyone, as opposed to "legalese English," which is reserved for lawyers. If you sign the lease, which you will have to do in order to get your apartment or house, then you are responsible for adhering to all parts of the lease. If you do not understand or you do not agree with a specific clause or phrase, then you should discuss it with the agent or landlord or your attorney before you sign the lease. Once you sign, you are responsible for living up to the requirements of the lease.

Some clauses are clearly illegal, and it is a good idea to be familiar with them. They include:

• Prohibition against children or discrimination against who may live with you in your apartment.

• "Lockout." The landlord cannot lock you out of your own apartment. The landlord cannot change your lock or remove your belongings from your apartment.

• "Exculpatory clause." If you should have an accident on the property or in the building due to the landlord's lack of maintenance, the landlord is responsible. The "exculpatory" clause protects him from such responsibility—not you.

Some clauses are not illegal, but you may not like them included in your lease. For example:

• Prohibition to sublease or sublet your apartment.

• "Escalator clause"—by which the tenant agrees to pay a rent increase if there is an increase in the landlord's expenses. (If you agree to this clause, your rent can increase considerably if the building has a broken heating system or a defective elevator, etc.)

• No pets.

• A certain percentage of the apartment must be carpeted.

• "Defacing clause"—by which the tenant cannot alter the premises of his apartment such as removing walls, building partitions, or adding electrical outlets. (If you should do any unusual decorating, be sure to get written approval from the landlord.)

• "No illegal conduct." Ask the agent or landlord to define this for you. It should be amusing.

Rent-Stabilization Rules

The important question regarding leases is: what are your options once the lease expires? If you do not want to stay in the same apartment, contact your landlord two months in advance, so you will be able to get back your security deposit.

If you wish to renew your lease, contact the landlord and express this. The landlord will, in turn, tell you what monthly rent increase you will have to pay. Every time you or someone else signs a new lease, the landlord is entitled to a rent increase. However, the amount of increase is controlled by the government. Many apartments in New York City are either rent-controlled or rent-stabilized. The majority are rent-stabilized.

The rent-stabilization law of 1969 was created to protect the tenant. Under the rent-stabilization law, landlords are allowed to increase the monthly rent 4% to the same tenant, or a new tenant, if the tenant wants an extra one-year lease; 7% if it's a two-year lease; and 10% if it's a three-year lease. It is important, however, to be aware that every October 1 the percentage of increase is revised by the authorities and may change. For your purposes, though, it cannot change once you have a percentage and an amount written into your lease. But if you want to renew your lease or take out a new lease, then it is best to check what the most recent law states. You can call the Rent Conciliations and Appeals Board at 903–9500.

There are no guidelines or rules for those apartments that are not rent-stabilized. This includes furnished apartments and rented co-operatives and rented condominiums. The owners can determine their own rate of increase for leases.

It is important to remember that rent-stabilization laws can apply only to those people who keep New York City as their primary residence. A corporation, company, or bank, foreign or American, cannot be protected by rent-stabilization rules. A foreign national, who comes to New York City and intends to make New York City his primary residence, cannot qualify for rent-stabilization protection until he has all his legal papers intact. If a landlord encourages a foreign national who does not have New York City as his primary residence to sign more than a one year lease, the foreign national should be suspicious of that landlord. The landlord may want to encourage the newcomer to move into the apartment and then raise the rent indiscriminately.

A foreign national who rents an apartment in New York City should first seek the advice of an immigration lawyer. Think before you act. *And be sure to read your lease carefully before you sign it.*

It may be well placed to give one final warning about unscrupulous real estate businesses. A recent client of mine, the vice-president of a foreign bank, wanted to rent an apartment in Manhattan. He saw an ad in the *New York Times* advertising a three-bedroom apartment on the Upper East Side for $1,300 per month. The banker quickly called the telephone number and an agent answered, saying, "Yes, the apartment is still available, but I have two other families interested. However, if you want an apartment similar to this one, I can give you a list of apartments to see and I can guarantee to find you an apartment within sixty days." The banker, relieved that someone would guarantee him an apartment in two months, went to the agent's office. But before the agent would give the client the list, the agent asked for $100 "money up front" and even agreed to sign a paper saying that he would find the client an apartment within the agreed sixty days. Yes, the agent could probably *find* an apartment for the client, but would it necessarily be an apartment that the client would want to *rent?*

This is a sample of unscrupulous business in the real estate field. Unfortunately, there are some agents who practice this way, but you should not be the type of client who allows this to happen. Never pay "up front." Only pay the commission when the agreed services are rendered. If you have questions about false advertising, illegal sublets, or unscrupulous activities, it is best to seek a lawyer's advice or to call one of the following offices:

Bureau of Consumer Affairs: 732–8400.
Department of Housing and Preservation's Central Complaint Bureau: 960–4800.
Lower Manhattan Loft Tenants Association. 619–0889.
New York City Rent Conciliations and Appeals Board. 903–9500.
New York State Division of Real Estate Licensing. 587–5747.
Rent Stabilization Association. 903–9500.

Steps To Follow Once the Apartment Is Yours

1. After you decide on a date when you can move into the apartment, decide on how you want to move your possessions. Arrange a date and time with the superintendent. Sundays may not be a good day for the building, but ask. Find out what time you can use the "service elevator," if there is one. Remember to call the superintendent a week before your moving date to remind him that you need the service elevator on a specific day, and ask if there is anything else you should know or do beforehand.

2. There are many professional movers you can use. Ask your friends whom they have used in the past and if they were happy with that mover. Ask the superintendent of your new building for a recommendation. You

can also call the *Better Business Bureau* at 533-6200, or check the yellow pages of the telephone book. It is a good idea to call a few companies. They will make an appointment with you and send over a representative to give you a formal, written estimate. They are usually accurate. If your belongings are not available to show, then you may have to make other arrangements with the company. If your belongings are in storage, you can arrange directly with the storage company to move your belongings. But get a written estimate from them beforehand. Even though such an estimate is not binding, it's a good guideline to have. The estimate will depend upon such factors as: how much furniture you have; if you need china cartons, book cartons, mirror cartons, or picture cartons, and how many; if you want the movers to help you pack and/or unpack; if there is a service elevator in the new and old residences; if all your big pieces of furniture, such as a piano or sofa, can fit into the elevator or will they have to be hoisted in the air; how many men will be needed for the job; how many hours will it take; and what size van will be needed. They will also charge you for traveling time, even if they do not need the full one-hour minimum. The representative of the moving company will give you a price based on all of the above details and discuss how payment should be made (they usually don't accept personal checks). Be sure to take out insurance; one can never be sure about damages. Ask them what happens if it rains or snows and always expect a few extra hours for a very long day. It is necessary to plan your moving date with the movers as soon as you sign your lease. Often the first and last weeks of the month are busy ones for the movers. Try to remember to call them a week before your scheduled moving date to make sure everything is confirmed.

It is a good idea to have an inventory or "moving list" of all your belongings. If you have very valuable pieces and antiques, it would be wise to have them appraised. You may also want to take Polaroid photographs of them to show the condition they are in before the move. This will protect you in case there is any damage at the time of moving.

As you pack your belongings in the many cartons you will have, label each carton according to the room they will be going into, such as "KITCHEN DISHES," "BOY'S TOYS," "MASTER BEDROOM."

Plan to be with the movers the entire day of your move. Watch them as they put the cartons in the van, and watch them as they remove the cartons from the van. You can direct the movers to place the cartons according to which room for which the carton was marked. This will make it easier for you the next day. Look at all the furniture to see if there has been any damage. If there is damage, ask the man in charge of the moving crew for a receipt stating that a particular piece of furniture arrived in that condition. They should have the necessary forms available for you to fill out, so that you can later collect from their insurance company. Don't return the form right away. Mail the form to the moving company after you make a Xerox copy of it. Keep track of your claim. If you don't hear anything after a few weeks, call the moving company or the insurance company.

Even though you will be watching the crew carefully, try to stay out of their way as much as possible. Don't delay them, especially if they charge you by the hour. And try to stay calm—even if it is sometimes difficult.

You may want to tip the crew when the move is completed. It is not obligatory; it depends on the work, both in quality and quantity.

3. The next important preparation step is to decide on your telephone set-up. How many telephones do you want, where, what style, what color, what optional services and system? Call up the business office of the New York Telephone Company and set up a day and time for installation. You may want to plan this before the painters paint your apartment, so they can touch up any damage later on. Or you may want to arrange it for the day after you move in, so you can choose the locations for the telephones depending upon where your furniture is placed.

You may want to stop first at one of the telephone company's Phone Center Stores to see what type of telephone system you can have and to check the prices accordingly. If you want to keep your previous telephone number, ask them if this can be done. If you want the telephone listed in another name, tell them. If you want the telephone number unlisted, tell them that, too. If you want extra wiring or a different type of connection, mention all of this before they install your telephone. (One-time installation fee can cost about $80.00, billed to you the first month.)

You may want to consider buying your own telephone sets. You may not realize that you "rent" each telephone from the telephone company, and each set can cost many dollars extra per month. You can buy the sets from the telephone company or from a private dealer, depending on style, decor, and system. It may be more economical for a long period of time to buy your own sets.

4. If you are changing addresses, notify your present postman of the change and when it will be effective. You may also have to fill out a form which will, in turn, be sent directly to the Post Office, notifying them of your new address. If you receive magazines and journals, it would also be best to send each company a note about the change of address. They need four to six weeks to make the change effective. If this is your first residence in the United States, then you will not have to do the above. But the first day you are in your apartment, ask the superintendent what the procedure is for receiving your mail. If it is at all possible, try to

arrange to introduce yourself to your new postman. The superintendent will know how you can arrange this.

5. Notify the electric company and the gas company about the change of your address. (You may first want to ask your new superintendent if this is necessary. Perhaps the superintendent can do it for you.) Normally, fees for gas and electricity are not included in the monthly rent. Both the electricity and gas may come from the same utility company, Consolidated Edison, but the bills will be listed separately. In most cities, especially in New York City, there is no charge for water. Each utility company may require a security deposit before they give you credit. Ask what their policy is. Customer Service for Consolidated Edison is 614–2300. When you open up a new account, bring your lease or contract to the Con Edison office nearest you.

6. Cable television may be hooked up to your apartment building. Again, ask the superintendent which company is in your building. New York City, very diplomatically, has been divided into two territories served by two companies. Manhattan Cable TV operates below 79th Street on the West Side and below 86th Street on the East Side (674–9100). Group W Cable provides service above 79th Street on the West Side and above 86th Street on the East Side (942–7200). Call them and ask them about their rates and options. Monthly rates vary from $11.75 to $41.75, depending upon options. The one-time installation fee can cost from $43.00 to $54.00. You may want to make an appointment with them. If you are very particular about your decorating scheme, you may want the television people to wire your apartment the day before the painters come. You can arrange this with the superintendent and the cable TV company.

7. When you sign a lease and take over an apartment, the building usually pays a painter to paint your entire apartment. Decide on a date with the superintendent. If you can, try to arrange for the painting to be done at least one or two days before you plan to move in. You can choose the colors you want, but usually you can't demand too much *décor*. It is not necessary to tip the painter because the building pays him well, but it is a good idea to "visit" him while he is working in your apartment. In this way, you can supervise and politely check that he is using the colors you originally agreed upon. Nothing can be more upsetting than to find out too late that the painter confused the colors for the designated rooms.

8. Double-check that your name is listed with the doorman or on the directory in the lobby. It would be very embarrassing for your guests to visit you and not know which apartment is yours.

Moving is a difficult procedure. It takes a lot of time and energy and can produce much aggravation. It helps to have a sense of humor. But once you have finished your planning and work, you can sit back with pride and observe your new surroundings. It is at this moment that you can really enjoy your new city and your new home.

CHAPTER 2

How To Buy an Apartment in New York City

Buying a Co-operative Apartment in New York City
  Definition of a Co-operative
  Advantages and Disadvantages
  Criteria To Consider When Buying a Co-operative Apartment
  Real Estate Agencies
  What Is the Legal and Financial Procedure To Buy a Co-op?
  List of Some Co-operative Buildings in New York City
Buying a Condominium Apartment in New York City
  What Is the Difference Between a Co-operative and a Condominium?
  What Are the Advantages of a Condominium for a Foreigner?
  Which Buildings Are Condominiums in New York City
  Housing Price Ranges for Eighty-Two Communities (see Appendix A)
  Public High Schools in the Five Boroughs (see Appendix D)
  Private High Schools in New York City (see Appendix E)

BUYING A CO-OPERATIVE APARTMENT IN NEW YORK CITY

CO-OPERATIVE LIVING is indeed not a new concept. It has existed since long before the hectic New York City "co-operative market" of the 1970s and the New York "rental conversions" of the '80s. The Romans and Greeks, the Fabians and Utopians knew about this concept long before we did, as did the Europeans and the South Americans. It is only rather recently that New Yorkers have realized that the advantages of owning and living in a co-op may outweigh those of living in a rental apartment, providing they can afford it. In the past twenty years, several billion dollars have been invested in constructing co-operative apartments and converting rental buildings into co-ops, and several million New Yorkers own such dwellings; yet the concept of a co-operative still seems to be rather vague. What exactly is a "co-operative" apartment? What does it mean?

25

Definition of a Co-operative. A co-operative building is owned by an apartment corporation. Individual tenants do not actually "own" their apartments as they would own their own houses. They own "shares" in the corporation entitling them to a long-term "proprietary lease" which is valid if they pay their monthly maintenance and comply with the regulations of the corporation. The corporation pays the total amount of the building's mortgage, real estate tax, employee salaries, and other expenses for the upkeep of the building. The tenant-owner, in turn, pays a share of these expenses as determined by the number of shares the tenant owns in the corporation. The size of the apartment determines the number of shares owned. A managing agent is hired by the corporation to run the building. A staff of employees is also hired by the corporation to protect and secure the safety of the building and apartments, and a Board of Directors is elected by all the tenant-owners to supervise and control the management of the corporation. A building is legally set up to be a "corporation" because it does not derive a profit from its operation.

Advantages and Disadvantages. The over-all advantages of a co-operative apartment in comparison to a rental apartment is that, space for space, apartment for apartment, the co-operative apartment allows for a better maintained living accommodation in contrast with a rental apartment of the same size and price. The specific *advantages* are:

1. The tenant-shareholders can stay in their apartments as long as they wish.

2. They can make improvements to their homes that would not ordinarily be allowed in a rental building.

3. The co-operative is a non-profit corporation, and, therefore, there is no landlord's profit included in the rent. The rent (called a monthly maintenance charge) increases only when there is an increase in operating costs, taxes, and improvements to the building.

4. The tenant-owners have the right to "approve" or "disapprove" of any potential owner. The Board of Directors, which is elected by all the tenant-owners of the co-op, meets regularly. They interview all prospective owners. If the prospective owner does not meet the standards of the Board, the Board has the right to disapprove and veto that sale. The explanation for this procedure is that the Board is responsible for investigating the reputations of all future tenant-owners. Precautions are taken to ensure the high quality of the building's "co-operative" living.

5. The quality of maintenance and security of the apartment building is kept at a maximum.

6. For the tenant-owner, a significant portion of the monthly

maintenance is tax deductible. Each building has a different tax structure, but all co-operatives offer a tax advantage to their shareholders. The tenant-shareholder can deduct his portion of the building's real estate tax and the interest on the building's mortgage.

7. Taking into consideration inflation and the lack of availability of high-quality apartments in New York City, most likely, the owner of a co-operative can sell his apartment when he wants to, at a profit.

Unfortunately, however, as with everything, there are also disadvantages. The general disadvantage of a co-operative apartment is that it is expensive, and, if you buy a co-op, you may have to put more cash money down than if you bought a house. Each corporation has different rulings (1) *vis-à-vis* the amount of cash you must put down (this can vary from 33% to 100% of the total purchasing price) and (2) the amount of money you are allowed to borrow from the bank (not all banks will give a personal loan or a co-op loan; if they do, there is a maximum amount that you can borrow, and the rate of interest is usually high). More specifically, the *disadvantages* of buying a co-operative apartment are:

1. Subleasing a co-operative may be difficult. Even though the tenant owns the apartment, the tenant still needs the approval of the Board of Directors to sublease it. Boards usually don't like to allow this. If the tenant-owner is leaving the country for a period of time, or if the apartment cannot be sold, the tenant-owner will have to secure approval from the Board to sublease.

2. The owner must pay for all the expenses related to the maintenance of his individual apartment. This includes all electrical and plumbing work, painting, appliances, walls, floors, etc. In a rental apartment, these expenses and maintenance charges are usually included in the monthly rent.

3. The owner cannot use the apartment for commercial purposes. The freelance writer or actor or teacher or physician cannot see clients in the "residence" and derive an income.

4. The tenant-shareholder must pay the amount of maintenance that is asked, based on the number of shares owned. This can amount to a yearly increase of 5–15%, depending upon the building's expenses and costs of operation. Unexpected expenses, such as the installation of a new heating system or elevator, are passed on to all the shareholders as "special assessments". No matter what the increase is, the shareholders are obliged to pay it. They have no control over the amount of monthly maintenance. However, the increase can only occur once during the year.

5. If a tenant-shareholder cannot pay the rent, the corporation has the right to sell the apartment because of non-payment. When the apartment

is sold, the tenant-shareholder pays what is owed to the corporation for back rent and expenses (including legal expenses). But until the apartment is sold, all tenants must pay part of the overdue monthly expenses.

6. The Managing Agent of the building must approve all plans for construction, alteration, rewiring, window installation, electrical work, plumbing, etc. If approval is denied, the tenant-owner cannot begin construction. Workers are only allowed to work within certain hours and usually not on weekends.

7. Since the corporation owns the building and apartments, and the tenant-shareholder only owns shares in the corporation, the final decision as to who will buy the apartment depends upon the approval of the Board of Directors. The tenant-shareholder cannot sell the apartment to just any individual who can afford the price. Many Boards have been known to refuse celebrities and politicians because of the possible additional security needed and the increased amount of unwarranted publicity. Boards have also been known to refuse diplomats and foreign nationals, corporations, banks, and companies from buying apartments. They claim that the tenant-shareholder should live in the apartment the major part of the year, so as to ensure the maintenance of the apartment. The Board resents having a lot of different faces inhabiting an apartment or a continual flow of "house guests." Some Boards do not allow companies or banks or corporations to buy an apartment, for the Boards feel that they cannot keep a close control over who will be the new tenants. Boards have been known to reject singles, or homosexuals, or people with suspicious financial statements. There are no laws that oblige the Board to make public their criteria for approval or rejection.

Criteria To Consider When Buying a Co-Operative Apartment. Clearly, there are a certain number of disadvantages, as well as advantages, to the concept of buying a co-op. Before you begin to look into buying a co-op, you should keep in mind the above pros and cons to this living arrangement. If you should decide that the advantages outweigh the disadvantages, then there are other criteria which you should consider in addition to the actual apartment you wish to buy.

When you buy a co-op, you also "buy" the building and the neighborhood of that apartment. You are making an investment, and, by nature of putting down an amount of cash money, you must consider that one day, if you sell the apartment, you will wish to make a profit. Therefore, you must consider the safety, security, and hypothetical future of the neighborhood. Each neighborhood has a different real estate value. Co-ops located on Fifth Avenue are more expensive than those on East End Avenue, Central Park West, or Riverside Drive. Other neighborhoods, on the other hand, such as the Lincoln Center area and lower Manhattan, have a favorable future.

In addition, there are other criteria to consider when you contemplate buying a specific apartment. Ask the real estate agent who is showing you the apartment to inquire about the following information. This information will help you and your legal advisor determine the viability of the building and the security of your investment:

1. The amount of taxes assessed against the building.

2. The financial terms for purchasing the apartment (how much cash down; how much tax deduction on your yearly maintenance).

3. What is the monthly maintenance? What has been the maintenance for the past three years?

4. Are there any special assessments or extra expenses expected on the building for the next three years? Will the building need a new heating system, or automatic elevator, or new mortgage?

5. What is the mortgage on the property and building?

6. Does the building receive an income from commercial rent, or from a physician, or a store on the ground floor? If yes, what is done with this extra source of income?

7. Ask for a copy of the corporation's last financial statement. This will give you a specific breakdown of the corporation's expenses, expenditures, debits, and profits.

Real Estate Agencies. Looking for a co-op in New York City is no simple matter. Even though you may have a certain amount of money to spend, and it may even be a large amount, to find the exact apartment you want is not an easy task. It is a good idea to work with several co-op managing agencies and real estate brokers. They will give you an education as well as offer you exposure to a wide gamut of choices. Each agency may have exclusive rights to sell a specific apartment. Therefore, by working with several agencies at one time, you increase your chances to find what you are looking for. The following agencies are very reputable and would be able to help you accordingly. (Remember, it is the "seller" who pays the commission to the broker. This is usually 6% of the agreed selling price.) When you call the agency, ask them to recommend a broker from their agency who specializes in the area in which you are interested.

Albert B. Ashforth. 935–8100. 477 Madison Avenue.
Brown, Harris and Stevens. 697–8800. 14 East 47th Street.
Cross & Brown. 840–3200. 522 5th Avenue.

Douglas-Elliman. 832–4100. 575 Madison Avenue.
Freda Green. 753–7950. 120 East 56th Street.
L.B. Kaye. 888–1400. 655 Madison Avenue.
William B. May. 688–8700. 3 West 57th Street.

What Is the Legal and Financial Procedure To Buy a Co-op? When you find the co-operative apartment that you wish to buy, there is a complicated procedure to follow before that apartment becomes yours. Buying an apartment in New York City is like going to the horse races. You're not sure you're going to win until the final second. Most likely, these are the steps you will follow:

1. You will make an "offer" on the apartment. That price will be accepted or rejected. The seller may make a "counter proposal," and then you will negotiate.

2. Once the offer is accepted, you make out a check which will be a deposit on the apartment. This is usually 10% of the agreed purchase price. This deposit is called a "binder." It binds the seller to the purchaser until the purchaser can get the necessary finances and the Board's approval. On the back of the check the purchaser writes, "This is a binder for Apartment ____, at ____ address for x number of dollars."

3. If financing is needed, go to several banks and inquire about how much money you can borrow on a "co-op loan" or a "personal loan," and at what rate of interest. If you are a foreign national, and you have most of your money in a bank in your home country, you can either transfer a portion of your money to an American bank or get an "international banking reference."

4. You will need a strong "credit rating" for the bank as well as for the corporation. The bank will be hesitant to lend you money until they check your rating. The Board of Directors of the co-operative will not approve you until they check your financial statement and your credit rating. (Your accountant will be able to draw up a financial statement.)

5. Contact a real estate lawyer to represent you. He will check several things for you in order to be sure that the building and apartment are good investments. He will check what special assessments are expected in the next two or three years; if there are any mortgages coming due in the next two or three years; the financial statement of the corporation; the nature of the employees' contracts; and the condition of the building.

6. The lawyer will draw up a contract that will be signed by the seller and the purchaser. The contract will include all the details about what is to remain in the apartment, such as furniture, appliances, chandeliers, carpet, etc. There will be a contingency for financing if it is necessary. This means that your deposit is refundable if you cannot get the financing you need from a bank or other source. The contract will also

state that, if you are not approved by the Board of Directors, your deposit check is to be returned.

7. Make an appointment with the Chairman of the Board of Directors for an interview. Try to find out beforehand from your broker and lawyer what the Board wants to hear or likes to see. Perhaps you can find out who were the last people to be interviewed by the Board and speak to them. Don't take the interview lightly! It is not automatic that you are approved, even if you can afford the price of the apartment.

8. After you have all your finances together and you have been interviewed and approved by the Board of Directors, the apartment is finally, theoretically, yours. However, there is one more step left, and that is the "closing."

9. The "closing" occurs when you finalize all negotiations. At the time of the closing, you have a meeting at the office either of the seller's or the purchaser's lawyer. You will need to receive the "proprietary lease" from the seller. The proprietary lease is the document that gives you, the tenant-owner, the rights to use the portion of the building that is allocable to the shares of your apartment. Read the proprietary lease carefully, for it states the rules and regulations of the corporation. The seller will also turn over to you the shares of stock in the corporation that are allocable to your apartment. At the closing, you will need a bank's check, or checks, to pay the seller for the apartment. You will need to pay the first month's maintenance. You may need a check, also, to pay your lawyer for his fees. You may have some other expenses, as well, so come with a few extra checks.

After you have passed through (or agonized through) the above steps, the apartment is yours. The closing marks the end of a difficult ordeal and the beginning of another ordeal—getting your home set up. At this point, you may want to decorate the apartment or make a few changes. Before you start, the word is caution. Find out from the Managing Agent the corporation's rulings regarding what changes you can make; approval of any structural changes; who can work in your apartment; the need for licenses; what hours they can work. Try to find out all this information before you embark on a lot of time and expenses. You don't want to be embarassed as soon as you move into your apartment.

LIST OF SOME CO-OPERATIVE BUILDINGS IN NEW YORK CITY

1 Fifth Avenue	834 Fifth Avenue	900 Fifth Avenue
40 Fifth Avenue	860 Fifth Avenue	907 Fifth Avenue
641 Fifth Avenue	870 Fifth Avenue	910 Fifth Avenue
785 Fifth Avenue	875 Fifth Avenue	920 Fifth Avenue
820 Fifth Avenue	880 Fifth Avenue	930 Fifth Avenue

955 Fifth Avenue	975 Park Avenue	112 East 19th Street
956 Fifth Avenue	993 Park Avenue	147 East 19th Street
969 Fifth Avenue	1020 Park Avenue	30 East 42nd Street
1010 Fifth Avenue	1040 Park Avenue	430 East 47th Street
1016 Fifth Avenue	1050 Park Avenue	230 East 50th Street
1025 Fifth Avenue	1065 Park Avenue	345 East 50th Street
1030 Fifth Avenue	1070 Park Avenue	251 East 51st Street
1035 Fifth Avenue	1088 Park Avenue	420 East 51st Street
1040 Fifth Avenue	1120 Park Avenue	315 East 52nd Street
1045 Fifth Avenue	1125 Park Avenue	345 East 52nd Street
1056 Fifth Avenue	1133 Park Avenue	435 East 52nd Street
1060 Fifth Avenue	1155 Park Avenue	444 East 52nd Street
1067 Fifth Avenue	1160 Park Avenue	450 East 52nd Street
1133 Fifth Avenue	1172 Park Avenue	233–235 East 54th Street
1158 Fifth Avenue	1185 Park Avenue	450 East 52nd Street
1215 Fifth Avenue	30 Sutton Place So.	333East 55th Street
23 Park Avenue	1 Sutton Place So.	111East 56th Street
55 Park Avenue	2 Sutton Place So.	110 East 57th Street
425 Park Avenue	14 Sutton Place So.	117 East 57th Street
465 Park Avenue	20 Sutton Place So.	200 East 57th Street
470 Park Avenue	25 Sutton Place So.	303East 57th Street
475 Park Avenue	36 Sutton Place So.	325 East 57th Street
480 Park Avenue	45 Sutton Place So.	345 East 57th Street
510 Park Avenue	50 Sutton Place So.	350 East 57th Street
535 Park Avenue	60 Sutton Place So.	410 East 57th Street
570 Park Avenue	30 Beekman Place	411 East 57th Street
575 Park Avenue	860 U.N. Plaza	430 East 57th Street
620 Park Avenue	870 U.N. Plaza	444 East 57th Street
625 Park Avenue	34 Gramercy Park	425 East 58th Street
655 Park Avenue	39 Gramercy Park	118 East 60th Street
700 Park Avenue	44 Gramercy Park	30 East 62nd Street
720 Park Avenue	45 Gramercy Park	175 East 62nd Street
730 Park Avenue	1 Lexington Avenue	116 East 63rd Street
733 Park Avenue	955 Lexington Avenue	125 East 63rd Street
760 Park Avenue	1349 Lexington Avenue	139 East 63rd Street
765 Park Avenue	1261 Madison Avenue	205 East 63rd Street
784 Park Avenue	1 East End Avenue	31 East 64th Street
785 Park Avenue	2 East End Avenue	32 East 64th Street
791 Park Avenue	55 East End Avenue	30 East 65th Street
800 Park Avenue	60 East End Avenue	1 East 66th Street
829 Park Avenue	75 East End Avenue	53 East 66th Street
830 Park Avenue	91 East End Avenue	116 East 66th Street
840 Park Avenue	120 East End Avenue	131 East 66th Street
860 Park Avenue	130 East End Avenue	115 East 67th Street
876 Park Avenue	180 East End Avenue	167 East 67th Street
885 Park Avenue	1 Gracie Square	6 East 68th Street
888 Park Avenue	7 Gracie Square	12 East 68th Street
898 Park Avenue	10 Gracie Square	38 East 68th Street
911 Park Avenue	1 Gracie Terrace	11 East 68th Street
929 Park Avenue	30 East 10th Street	210 East 68th Street
930 Park Avenue	49 East 12th Street	150 East 69th Street
935 Park Avenue	7–11 East 13th Street	333East 69th Street
940 Park Avenue	12 East 14th Street	10 East 70th Street
950 Park Avenue	142 East 16th Street	33 East 70th Street
969 Park Avenue	230 East 18th Street	179 East 70th Street

30 East 71st Street
135 East 71st Street
176 East 71st Street
213 East 71st Street
36 East 72nd Street
45 East 72nd Street
114 East 72nd Street
125 East 72nd Street
132 East 72nd Street
140 East 72nd Street
141 East 72nd Street
160 East 72nd Street
165 East 72nd Street
360 East 72nd Street
530 East 72nd Street
11 East 73rd Street
19 East 73rd Street
150 East 73rd Street
175 East 73rd Street
20 East 74th Street
112 East 74th Street
174 East 74th Street
175 East 74th Street
39 East 75th Street
57 East 75th Street
103 East 75th Street
120 East 75th Street
65 East 76th Street
165 East 76th Street
3 East 77th Street
50 East 77th Street
70 East 77th Street
169 East 78th Street
31 East 79th Street
50 East 79th Street
63 East 79th Street
119 East 79th Street
120 East 79th Street
139 East 79th Street
156 East 79th Street
161 East 79th Street
175 East 79th Street
180 East 79th Street
201 East 79th Street
501 East 79th Street
105 East 80th Street
162 East 80th Street
222 East 80th Street
18 East 81st Street
120 East 81st Street
140 East 81st Street
108 East 82nd Street
8 East 83rd Street
40 East 83rd Street
3 East 84th Street

234 East 84th Street
421 East 84th Street
3 East 85th Street
111 East 85th Street
11 East 86th Street
25 East 86th Street
49 East 86th Street
520 East 86th Street
525 East 86th Street
535 East 86th Street
22 East 88th Street
40 East 88th Street
47 East 88th Street
50 East 89th Street
161 East 90th Street
15 East 91st Street
125 East 92nd Street
4 East 94th Street
4 East 95th Street
17 East 95th Street
19 East 95th Street
27 East 95th Street
49 East 96th Street
60 East 96th Street
150 Central Park South
50 Central Park West
55 Central Park West
88 Central Park West
91 Central Park West
101 Central Park West
115 Central Park West
145 Central Park West
211 Central Park West
257 Central Park West
262 Central Park West
271 Central Park West
285 Central Park West
320 Central Park West
336 Central Park West
262 West End Avenue
270 West End Avenue
290 West End Avenue
325 West End Avenue
333 West End Avenue
470 West End Avenue
522 West End Avenue
600 West End Avenue
610 West End Avenue
5 Riverside Drive
37 Riverside Drive
70 Riverside Drive
118 Riverside Drive
160 Riverside Drive
175 Riverside Drive
522 Riverside Drive

111 Fourth Avenue
77 Seventh Avenue
491 Broadway
393 West Broadway
200 Mercer Street
100 Hudson Street
571 Hudson Street
116–118 Perry Street
131 Perry Street
725–731 Greenwich St.
17 West 10th Street
45 West 10th Street
64 West 10th Street
62 West 11th Street
37 West 12th Street
40 West 12th Street
101 West 12th Street
60 West 13th Street
139 West 13th Street
25 West 15th Street
4 West 16th Street
201 West 16th Street
133 West 17th Street
356 West 30th Street
28–30 West 38th Street
25 West 54th Street
415 West 55th Street
100 West 57th Street
205 West 57th Street
2 West 67th Street
15 West 67th Street
39 West 67th Street
50 West 70th Street
315 West 70th Street
20 West 71st Street
59 West 71st Street
1 West 72nd Street
15 West 72nd Street
146 West 74th Street
159 West 74th Street
171 West 76th Street
6 West 77th Street
40 West 77th Street
44 West 77th Street
164 West 79th Street
11 West 81st Street
51 West 81st Street
54 West 82nd Street
119 West 82nd Street
139 West 82nd Street
306 West 90th Street
250 West 94th Street
7 West 96th Street
12 West 96th Street
24 Central Park South

Buying a Condominium Apartment in New York City

If you want to buy an apartment in New York City, but the concept of a co-operative does not please you, there is another type of apartment building which you can investigate, and that is the "condominium." In recent years, there have been an increasing number of condominiums being built to satisfy the needs of New York's growing foreign population and corporate investment. But first, a brief description.

What Is the Difference Between a Co-operative and a Condominium?
1. When you buy a condominium, you buy a piece of real property. You buy tangible, concrete property. You get a deed for buying your property as if you were buying a house.

2. You also have a separate tax lot. That means you pay your own real estate taxes on your own property.

3. You pay your own mortgage to the bank. When you borrow money from the bank, you take out a "mortgage," not a personal loan or a co-op loan. The seller can take back a second mortgage if the purchaser doesn't have enough cash to buy the apartment.

4. You have monthly maintenance fees which are constituted by the common elements of the building. The maintenance of a condominium will be less than that of a co-operative, but the monthly expenses will probably be similar. (In a co-operative apartment your maintenance includes real estate taxes, the building's mortgage, and interest. In a condominium you pay this too, but separately and independently from your monthly maintenance charges.)

5. A condominium is run by a Board of Managers that traditionally is more lenient and flexible than the Board of Directors of a co-operative building.

What Are the Advantages of a Condominium for a Foreigner? Clearly, there are certain advantages to a foreigner's owning a condominium rather than a co-operative apartment. The condominium offers the foreigner more flexibility and a greater ability to use the property as the individual sees fit. More precisely:

1. In a condominium, you get actual ownership of a tangible piece of property. In the future, you can use this as collateral if you want to invest in the United States or begin a business here.

2. You don't have to be approved by the shareholders.

3. You don't have to show a financial statement for the approval of the Board.

4. You don't have to concern yourself if another tenant does not pay his monthly maintenance.

5. You have more flexibility in sub-leasing your apartment. You don't have to ask permission from the Board or have the sub-tenant approved by them.

6. You are not bound to rules regulating the length of time visitors can stay with you.

7. The condominium apartment can be used as a *pied-à-terre*. You are not obliged to spend a minimum amount of time per year in your apartment.

Condominiums tend to be more expensive to buy than co-operative apartments in New York City. But it is a route to consider. A condominium may be especially advantageous for a company or bank or corporation that may want to own its own apartment and do with it as it pleases. The condominium offers more flexibility. However, even though the concept of buying a condominium is a good one, you must remember that there are many more co-operatives available in New York City than condominiums.

When you are ready to buy a condominium, the procedure is very similar to that of buying a co-operative. Just the prices may differ. When you buy a condominium, it is important, at the closing, that your lawyer requests a "title search" — to make sure that the people who are selling you the property have proper title to it. All the other steps are very similar to those followed when you buy a co-operative.

Whichever concept you decide to choose — buying either a co-operative apartment or a condominium — you will have to give yourself a good deal of time and lots of flexibility. It's not true that "New York is a nice place to visit, but not to live." Many people want to live in New York City, at least for a period of time, and there are just so many buildings, just so much space, and paradoxically not so much sky space left.

The same brokers and agents who deal with co-operative apartments also represent condominiums. Refer to that list for the names and addresses of reputable agencies.

The following addresses represent some condominium buildings in New York City.

WHICH BUILDINGS ARE CONDOMINIUMS IN NEW YORK CITY

29 East 10th Street	137–141 East 55th Street	21–25 East 79th Street
330 East 30th Street	150 East 55th Street	523–527 East 80th Street
343 East 30th Street	117 East 57th Street	520–528 East 81st Street
300 East 33rd Street	152 East 63rd Street	501 East 82nd Street
35 East 38th Street	340 East 64th Street	16 East 84th Street

419 East 84th Street	30 West 61st Street	817 Fifth Avenue
55 East 93rd Street	100–106 West 70th St.	988 Fifth Avenue
59 West 9th Street	14 West 71st Street	42 Hudson Street
60 West 13th Street	311–315 West 83rd St.	77 Park Avenue
207–217 West 25th St.	155 West 93rd Street	900–906 Park Avenue
231 West 26th Street	149 West 94th Street	45 Second Avenue
438–448 West 37th St.	59 Bank Street	47 Second Avenue
535–547 West 45th St.	160 Central Park South	34–40 Sutton Place
62–72 West 47th Street	2–8 Cornelia Street	260 West Broadway
73–77 West 55th Street	641 Fifth Avenue	12 White Street
348–356 West 58th St.	816 Fifth Avenue	

This list may not be complete. Each day new listings are presented to the New York City Real Estate Board.

CHAPTER 3

Alternate Apartment Living Within Thirty Minutes of New York City

Map of Residential Neighborhoods in the Five Boroughs
Descriptions of Safe, Desirable Communities in the Five Boroughs
   Queens
      1. Roosevelt Island
      2. Long Island City, Astoria and Sunnyside
      3. Flushing
      4. Rego Park, Forest Hills and Kew Gardens
      5. Bayside, Little Neck and Whitestone
         Recommended Renting Agencies
   Bronx
      6. Riverdale
      7. North-east
      8. Pelham
      9. Tremont Avenue
         Recommended Renting Agencies
   Brooklyn
      10. Brooklyn Heights
      11. Carroll Gardens and Cobble Hill
      12. Prospect Park and Park Slope
         Recommended Renting Agencies
   Staten Island
      13. St. George
         Recommended Renting Agencies
Advantages and Disadvantages of Living Outside Manhattan
Housing Price Ranges for Eighty-Two Communities (see Appendix A)
Commuting Options for Forty-Five Suburban Communities Outside
      New York (see Appendix B)
Public High Schools in the Five Boroughs (see Appendix D)

37

ALTERNATE APARTMENT LIVING WITHIN THIRTY MINUTES FROM NEW YORK CITY

Key

Queens
1. Roosevelt Island
2. Long Island City, Astoria and Sunnyside
3. Flushing
4. Rego Park, Forest Hills and Kew Gardens
5. Bayside, Little Neck and Whitestone

Bronx
6. Riverdale
7. North-east
8. Pelham
9. Tremont Avenue

Brooklyn
10. Brooklyn Heights
11. Carroll Gardens and Cobble Hill
12. Prospect Park and Park Slope

Staten Island
13. St. George

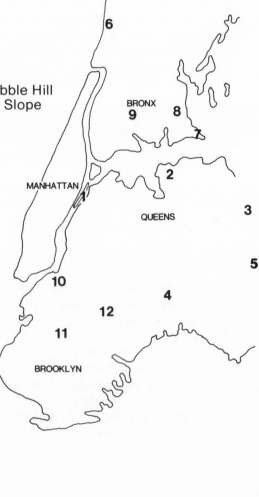

DESCRIPTIONS OF SAFE, DESIRABLE COMMUNITIES
IN THE FIVE BOROUGHS

To live in New York City in the past few years has become extremely expensive. The rentals are very costly, the apartments can be small, and privacy is at a premium. If you have small children and you do not want them to attend the public schools in New York City, the private schools are very expensive and very competitive. (It may be more difficult to get your children into the leading New York City private schools than into the American "Ivy League" universities.) Living in New York City, with all its excitement, stimulation, choice, and variation, has become very costly. If a couple or family is not already settled in appropriate housing in New York City, it is extremely difficult to achieve this now unless they have a great deal of money or a very generous expense account. But for the majority, who are middle-class, working people, New York City has become just too much of a luxury.

One of the most practical options is to move elsewhere, near Manhattan, where housing is less expensive, community living is very pleasant, and one can use public transportation very easily. Such areas are in the other boroughs of New York—Queens, Bronx, Brooklyn, and Staten Island.

For those who want apartment living outside Manhattan, there are several beautiful, safe, and friendly communities bordering on Manhattan. The public schools are good. The commute is relatively easy and inexpensive, and the cost of living is cheaper than living in New York City. The following are some recommended areas in the other boroughs of New York that are only a thirty-minute commute from mid-town Manhattan.

Queens

1. *Roosevelt Island,* politically part of Manhattan, geographically mid-way between Manhattan and Queens, and strategically accessible via air from Manhattan or via bridge from Manhattan or Queens, is still considered, for commuting purposes, outside Manhattan. From 60th Street and Second Avenue, the commuter can take the "aerial tramway" which for a subway token offers a three-minute, panoramic ride across the East River, or the commuter can choose to take a bus or car and travel across the Queensboro Bridge. Because automobile and bus traffic are restricted on the island, all cars are required to be parked in a garage at the gates of the island and travel by the (free) minibus which regularly circulates the island. Roosevelt Island is a cosmopolitan, ethnically

diverse, community where rentals are certainly less expensive than in Manhattan but perhaps more costly than in Queens. There are a nursery and elementary school on the island as well as stores and supermarkets. Parks, playgrounds, fishing areas, and majestic views of the East River and the East Side of Manhattan make this area an aesthetically pleasing community in which to live.

2. *Long Island City, Astoria and Sunnyside.* The residents of these three neighboring sections come from all over the world. Eastern Europeans, Irish, Italians, Russians, Hispanics, Indians, Koreans, and Filipinos all live together in harmony and friendship. There is a strong community feeling in each one of these neighborhoods. The community located nearest to Manhattan is Long Island City. Once an area of factories and warehouses, and a cheap storage area for neighboring Manhattan companies, Long Island City is now changing. In the next few years, it will claim the attention of many ambitious real estate developers who will be constructing expensive highrise apartment buildings on the banks of the East River. Sunnyside, the adjacent community, has not yet been built up. Most of the housing in Sunnyside is comprised of two-family homes, garden apartments, and modest apartment buildings. "Sunnyside Gardens," near Queens Boulevard and Greenpoint Avenue at 46th Street, is especially nice. The community is safe, and the atmosphere is very pleasant. There is excellent shopping and international stores, and a variety of aromas fill the streets. Another excellent community in which to live is Astoria. It is a cosmopolitan neighborhood, friendly, safe, and community-oriented. Many of the residents were born in other countries and have brought with them their tastes and customs from the "Old World." A stroll down Astoria Boulevard, the main thoroughfare, would cause you to forget that you are in New York. Housing is reasonably priced, and you get excellent value for your money.

3. *Flushing* has an old and honorable past. As early as 1643, the Dutch founded a small settlement in what is now Flushing. Today, more than three hundred years later, it is by far not a small settlement, but there are still many sections of parks and natural areas. There is the beautiful Flushing Meadow Park, a 1,275-acre park which was twice the site for New York's World Fairs. There are also the scenic Meadow Lake, the Hall of Science, and the Unisphere, a stainless steel sphere representing the continents—all vestiges of the 1964–65 World's Fair. To the north of Flushing Meadow Park is Shea Stadium. In the surrounding residential area of Flushing are private homes, garden apartments, and apartment buildings which blend together in a country-like setting. Rents are reasonably priced; schools are good; and transportation to mid-town Manhattan by bus, subway, or car takes less than thirty minutes. For the

Japanese residents, there is the Japanese School, located at 196-25 Peck Avenue (454-4200). Co-ed elementary and junior high school full-time classes, as well as Saturday programs, are available to Japanese students who plan to return home and prepare for college entry exams.

4. *Rego Park, Forest Hills and Kew Gardens.* These three communities are adjacent to one another. Kew Gardens is positioned the farthest from Manhattan, but it is the quietest. Its parks and gardens are reminiscent of a small village in Europe. The winding cobblestone streets and quaint shops of the village resemble a Swiss town from a Christmas calendar. Kew Gardens, bordered by Queens Boulevard on one side and Forest Park on the other, has the advantage of being a small, charming community within a large, bustling area. There is a wide variety of housing from which to choose. Private homes near Forest Park are majestic but expensive. Apartment buildings off Queens Boulevard are spacious and comfortable and more reasonably priced. The garden apartments and two-family houses located near Queens Boulevard are set on tree-lined streets with front and rear gardens. They, too, are reasonably priced. Transportation is good, but it is better from Rego Park and Forest Hills. Forest Hills has a large choice of schools, private and public (Forest Hills High Schools serves the three communities), shopping, cinemas, and restaurants. The private homes in Forest Hills Gardens are very expensive, but the highrise apartment buildings on the southern side of Queen Boulevard are moderately priced. Forest Hills has many buildings of various architectural styles and different monthly rents. Rego Park's apartment buildings and two-family houses are the most reasonably priced of the three neighborhoods. Fair prices and good value can be found in Rego Park.

5. *Bayside, Little Neck and Whitestone.* The northeast Queens area, consisting of Bayside, Whitestone, Douglaston, and Little Neck, has and will remain a prime residential location. Several factors have contributed to this: (a) transportation convenience; (b) zoning; (c) private schools; (d) real estate taxes.

(a) There are several choices for commuting to mid-town and downtown Manhattan. There is the MTA subway system (the IRT–Flushing line); the Long Island Railroad (Port Washington line); and the express buses. By car, without traffic, and not in rush hour, one can be in midtown in less than half an hour.

(b) The zoning is designed in such a way as to encourage more one-family homes. This accounts for the residential atmosphere of the communities.

(c) The public school districts, 25 and 26, have continuously ranked in the top 5% of the city school districts. Their students' test results in reading and mathematics have been consistently outstanding.

(d) Geographically, these communities are located mid-way between Manhattan and the expensive North Shore suburbs of Long Island. But their tax base is considerably lower because officially they are part of New York City; the borough of Queens is part of New York City. This part of Queens is very special, for it has the same atmosphere and residential quality of Long Island, but it is considerably closer to Manhattan and has lower real estate taxes. Homes have increased at an average of 10–15% per annum with a 100% increase since the mid-1970s.

Recommended Renting Agencies:

Roosevelt Island:
    J. I. Sopher and Co.
    425 East 61st Street
    New York City
    (212) 486-7000

Long Island City:
    Sunnyside Realty
    41-06 Greenpoint Avenue
    Sunnyside
    (212) 392-7494

Flushing:
    Koester Agency Inc.
    161-15 29th Avenue
    Flushing
    (212) 746-3817

Rego Park, Forest Hills and Kew Gardens:
    Novak Realty
    81-63 Lefferts Boulevard
    Kew Gardens
    (212) 441-8500

Bayside, Little Neck and Whitestone:
    Abatelli Realty
    24-55 Francis Lewis Boulevard
    Flushing
    (212) 352-9000

Bronx

6. *Riverdale* has many faces. In Fieldston, which is a small enclave east of the Henry Hudson Parkway, there are opulent mansions, castle-like towers, and sprawling gardens. West of the Henry Hudson highway, there are tall modern apartment buildings with breathtaking views of the Hudson River, the George Washington Bridge, and the Jersey Cliffs. Down by the foot of the river is yet another area of Riverdale. These are private houses with expensive façades and country roads, hilly land, and

the feeling of the river nearby. In yet another section, adjacent to town, there are small garden apartments and modest accommodations. These houses are located in walking distance to town and the stores. Whichever area you choose, Riverdale, only thirty minutes from Manhattan, emits a feeling of country living. Its population is cosmopolitan. There's the choice of Japanese and Korean markets, kosher pizza restaurants, and the best appetizers and delicatessens outside of Manhattan. Riverdale boasts of the best private schools in the New York area: Horace Mann–Barnard School, the Riverdale Country School, and the Fieldston School. There is also the Japanese Saturday school and several private yeshivas. To get to Riverdale from Manhattan you can take the Express Bus or the subway; commuting time is less than half an hour.

7. *North-east*. On the other side of the Bronx, the northeastern section, is another very beautiful residential area. Again there are highrise apartment buildings with beautiful views of the water and private homes with gardens. Rents are very reasonable. Parts of Queens, the Bronx, and Manhattan, by bus or subway, are all within half an hour away. For those who enjoy sailing and fishing, the colorful City Island is a bus-ride away. Co-Op City is a pleasant community in this area.

8. *Pelham* is situated in the northeastern section of the Bronx. Its proximity to Long Island Sound and to City Island is a great advantage for those who like to fish and boat. Located nearby is the Pelham Bay Park, which is a beautiful, luxurious park. The main road of Pelham Parkway continues from this park and offers a wide avenue lined with tall trees and green grass. There are some stately apartment buildings and private homes located directly on this main road. In the adjacent area is a group of apartment buildings called "Co-Op City," which offer to their residents lovely views of the Long Island Sound for modest rents.

9. *Tremont Avenue* is one of the older sections of the Bronx. The lovely New York Botanical Garden and the New York Zoological Park (the Bronx Zoo) are located nearby. In this neighborhood, the feeling of park and country mixes with the city scenery. There are apartment buildings, two-family houses, and modestly priced private houses. Neighboring communities are Parkchester, Morris Park, and Pelham Gardens.

Recommended Renting Agencies:

Riverdale:
Kahan and Kahan
3723 Riverdale Avenue
Riverdale
(212) 796–2222

North-east:

Mills Real Estate
1004 East Gun Hill Road
Bronx
(212) 881-7700

Morea Realty
2964 Middletown Road
Bronx
(212) 824-9698

Pelham:

City Island Realtors
626 City Island Avenue
City Island
(212) 885-1166

Locascio Realty Co.
2139 Williamsbridge Road
Bronx
(212) 931-9400

Tremont Avenue:

Better Homes Realty
Morgan Services
40-27 East Tremont Avenue
Bronx
(212) 931-5600

Brooklyn

10. *Brooklyn Heights* is famous for its historic brownstones, intellectual residents, safe streets, and strong community ties. A stroll on the wide Esplanade or a trek across the walkway of the Brooklyn Bridge will convince you that Brooklyn Heights is a very special place to live. The row of brownstone houses and red brick buildings have maintained their architectural styles of the 1820s Federal period and the 1890s Victorian period. Liberal and open-minded residents live together, disinterested in differences of race, religion, and creed. This area is well located for those working in Brooklyn and downtown Manhattan. Rentals are reasonable and transportation practical. Over the past years, many cafés, Lebanese restaurants, and picturesque shops have opened in the neighboring communities. The BAM—Brooklyn Academy of Music—is nearby, and their productions in music, theater, and dance are so excellent that you may not feel the need to go to Broadway.

11. *Carroll Gardens and Cobble Hill* are two other lovely communities in Brooklyn, just south of Brooklyn Heights. Carroll Gardens lies to the southeast of Cobble Hill and is bordered by DeGraw Street, Hamilton Avenue, the Brooklyn-Queens Expressway, and the

Gowanus Canal. Carroll Gardens is more ethnic and blue collar than Cobble Hill and is characterized by many Italian residents. On a warm summer night, the *paisanos* sit outside and speak their local Italian dialects, and many longshoreman play *bocci* in the open streets. Carroll Gardens is less "discovered" than its neighboring Brooklyn Heights, and real estate is consequently less expensive. Cobble Hill has been considered a historic district since 1970 and extends within a 22-block area from Atlantic Street to De Graw Street and Hicks Street to Court Street. The Cobble Hill area is comprised of many restored brownstones, but they are less stately than those in Brooklyn Heights. Both the Cobble Hill and Carroll Gardens sections are attracting more young professionals who are just beginning their careers and can afford the more reasonably priced rents compared with those of Brooklyn Heights.

12. *Prospect Park and Park Slope* are very elegant parts of Brooklyn. Prospect Park, which is a 526-acre park located mid-center between the Park Slope area and the Flatbush community, was designed by Frederick Law Olmsted and Calvert Vaux, the same architects of Central Park. At that time, in the 1880s, the elegant Park Slope area also began to grow. Large Victorian mansions were built in Prospect Park West to take advantage of the beautiful park views. Today, these houses are still impeccably maintained and remind us of the elegance and grace of that era. The apartment buildings in this section are equally well designed. As one walks in the area, one has the feeling of returning to the nineteenth century. At the north point of the park is the Grand Army Plaza, which has excellent shopping and spacious apartment buildings. In Prospect Park are located the Brooklyn Botanic Gardens, Zoo, Conservatories, lake, tennis house, carousel, the Brooklyn Public Library, and the Brooklyn Museum. The cultural climate is inspiring, and the artistic life is rich. Transportation is good to Manhattan and to other parts of Brooklyn. Housing is modestly priced, especially the apartments.

Recommended Renting Agencies:

> Brooklyn Heights:
>> Cranford–Heights, Inc.
>> 144 Montague Street
>> Brooklyn
>> (212) 624–7000

>> Townhouse International
>> 111 Montague Street
>> Brooklyn
>> (212) 875–1761

Carroll Gardens and Cobble Hill:

Carroll Gardens Realty
262 Smith Street
Brooklyn
(212) 625-9635

Prospect Park and Park Slope:

Prospect Park Realty, Inc.
71 6th Avenue
Brooklyn
(212) 638-6831

Park Slope Realty
895 4th Avenue
Brooklyn
(212) 788-5000

Staten Island

13. *St. George,* often compared to the small communities of California's Marin County, is located within walking distance of the Staten Island Ferry. It is an area of big Victorian houses interspersed with very modest apartment houses. Its quiet, hilly streets overlook the waters of New York's Upper Bay toward Manhattan, and the breathtaking views of the city are very special. St. George has excellent public schools, a strong friendly community feeling, and a quiet safe neighborhood. From Manhattan you take the No. 1 subway train and RR train to the Staten Island Ferry. The ferry ride, most beautiful and romantic on a white winter night or a balmy summer morning, takes twenty-five minutes and costs 25¢. You can put a car on the ferry for an extra $2.00 charge and 25¢ per passenger. When you look out at the Statue of Liberty and Ellis Island, you are reminded how special New York City is and how lucky we are to be here. Staten Island is being rediscovered because it's a beautiful place to live. Not so long ago, at the beginning of the twentieth century, St. George was an elegant resort area for wealthy New Yorkers. Today, it has maintained its splendor as well as its close community feeling for all New Yorkers.

Recommended Renting Agencies:

St. George

Daniel Master
3130 Amboy Road
Oakwood
(212) 987-3000

Russi and De Simone Realty
402 Manor Road
St. George
(212) 447-3000

ADVANTAGES AND DISADVANTAGES OF LIVING OUTSIDE MANHATTAN

The following advantages and disadvantages are enjoyed or tolerated by apartment dwellers as well as homeowners. The pros and cons are directed toward the total concept of "living outside Manhattan."

The advantages of living in a small, friendly community directly outside the Manhattan boundary, but still within "New York limits," are numerous. As a resident of one of New York's boroughs, you have access to public transportation. You can use the bus system and the subways if you do not wish to drive your car to work. It is certainly less expensive to commute with public transportation than with your own car. You don't have to worry about car maintenance, garage, gasoline, tolls, and traffic jams. In the winter, during some of New York City's snowstorms and icy nights, it can be impractical and even dangerous to drive your own car. If you can depend upon city transportation, your commuting may be easier.

As soon as you leave Manhattan proper, you get another feeling about living in New York. Each community is an independent entity, characterized by a certain atmosphere, often influenced by the many nationalities who inhabit that area. There are many neighborhoods in Queens and Brooklyn that would remind you of small towns in Europe, where shopkeepers and customers speak the same dialect and everyone knows the family.

The public schools outside Manhattan are usually of a higher academic level, especially in the elementary schools (Kindergarten to Sixth Grade), than those in Manhattan. The parents are actively involved in the Parent Teachers Association (PTA), and they offer their time, energy, and talents to keep the school at the academic level they want. They are involved in revising curriculums and maintaining high academic standards.

In the small communities outside Manhattan, neighbors are more ready to help one another and group together if need be. There is a stronger community feeling. For a newcomer to New York, this could be a very reassuring and comforting situation. The atmosphere is certainly more "homey" than in the "Big City" and perhaps less threatening.

Apartment living, in particular, has its advantages because you do not have to worry about gardening, maintenance, roofs, pipes, heating, garbage, snow, etc. Each apartment building has a superintendent who alone, or with a staff, is responsible for the maintenance of the building and the property on which the building is located. If you have a problem with your individual apartment, you can always arrange with the superintendent or handyman to take care of your needs. This is always easier than having to worry about doing it yourself. For a newcomer, apartment living has its advantages, also, for it is easier to make friends. You see your neighbors in the elevator, mail room, or lobby. It is easy to start a conversation about where to shop or find what you need. Some buildings have a "tenants' committee," and they arrange social events or meetings. Perhaps there is a "car pool" into Manhattan for those commuters or students who travel to the same area each day. Children can make friends with the other children in the building, and young mothers can find friendship and support from one another.

Let us not forget the financial advantages. To rent an apartment in New York City, you have to pay dearly. For the same amount of space, outside Manhattan, your rent could be one-third or one-fourth of what you would have to pay in Manhattan. With the money you save, you can have a larger apartment with more privacy and more amenities. Above all, you can use your money for other things.

And yet, to be fair, we must look at the disadvantages, for no situation, anywhere in the world, is perfect. When you live outside Manhattan, you may not take advantage of the rich cultural life New York City offers. If you live outside the City, it takes a planned effort to stay in town for the evening. During the week, you may work so hard that in the evening you may be happy to return to your quiet neighborhood and not choose to stay in town for a concert or show, movie or dinner. It is easy to get lazy after you have worked so hard during the day. But then again, many New Yorkers would answer that their reward for a "hard day's work" is a "fun evening out."

The problem of traffic must also be considered, for this is perhaps the greatest disadvantage of all. If you commute by bus or subway, rush hour can be very unpleasant, especially in the summer on those 90° days, or in the winter when everyone seems to grow with three layers of clothing. On the subway or bus, it is hard to get a seat; sometimes it is even hard to get space or air. Certainly, it is not always the best way to begin or end the day. For those who take their cars into Manhattan, traffic can be at a standstill if there is an accident or breakdown on the road. There is no way to go, no possibility to move elsewhere. You are stuck! When it rains, or hails, or the wind gales, driving can also be dangerous. New York roads are known for their "potholes," detours, and endless repair work that somehow does not seem to improve the overall commute. To resolve this problem, you may want to travel when the roads are not so crowded—before 7:00 in the morning and after 6:00 in the evening.

Yet two million people commute to New York each day, and they seem to survive. They may share the driving or take public transportation. They may alternate their schedules to work earlier one day or later the next day. Imagination does help the situation.

All in all, commuting to and from New York City is no more or less difficult than for those who commute in Paris, London, Tokyo, or any other major city. And New York certainly has many attractions to keep you busy on the weekends, when traveling is never a problem.

CHAPTER 4

How To Find a House in the Suburbs

Map of Recommended Suburban Communities
Thirty-Two Suburban Communities That Have Highly Recommended
Public School Systems
Thirteen Suburban Areas Which Are Moderately Priced
Rental vs. Purchase
Useful Telephone Numbers for Commuters
Housing Price Ranges for Eighty-Two Communities (see Appendix A)
Commuting Options for Forty-Five Suburban Communities Outside
New York (see Appendix B)
Public High Schools in the Suburbs (see Appendix C)

MANY visitors and newly arrived residents to New York City wish intentionally not to live in the city. They are not accustomed to apartment living, the lack of privacy, the absence of nature, the abundance of dirt, and the overwhelming presence of noise. They feel that the rents in New York City are outrageously expensive and the private schools too costly. Therefore, when they come to work in New York for a few years and their families accompany them, they feel that it's better to live in the suburb's, commute to work, and take advantage of the city's cultural life on special occasions. This is a practical decision, and New York offers a wide variety of very comfortable and desirable living areas in the other boroughs as well as in the suburbs. Some areas offer very good public schools, which are free and available to all residents of that community. Other areas offer an easy accessibility to Manhattan via the train or bus. And other areas offer a scenic, country-like atmosphere which will remind foreign visitors of home. Some areas are more expensive than others. In the suburbs, property value varies greatly according to community, proximity to the water, real estate taxes, public school system, community services, reputation of the town, and availability of homes.

In most suburban areas, it is possible to rent houses, even to rent furnished houses, or to rent apartments, co-ops, and condominiums. For those who do not wish to invest a large amount of capital and do not wish to worry about inflated mortgage rates, the option of renting a home or apartment in the suburbs may carry a great advantage. This is a choice to keep in mind and to discuss with your real estate broker.

Perhaps the first and most important question you must ask yourself is: where do you wish to live? Which community? Which state? If you know people from work or from your home country, the most reasonable approach would be to consider living near them. In the past years, the French have congregated around Larchmont in Westchester County, where they find many of their compatriots living. There is a French school for young children (Nursery to Fourth Grade), and for the older children who wish to attend the French Lycée in New York City there is a bus which will take them early in the morning from Larchmont to the Lycée and then back home again in the late afternoon.

Many Germans are happy living in White Plains or neighboring areas of Westchester in order to profit from the new Deutsche Schüle that has recently opened its doors in White Plains. They have many excellent Saturday programs in which German children can take courses in the German language, literature, and arts.

Following the schools of their country, the Japanese have traditionally lived near Riverdale, where they, too, have a Saturday program for their children at the Japanese School. Within the past few years, many of the leading Japanese executives and businessmen have gravitated more into Westchester to areas such as Scarsdale, Hartsdale, Bronxville, and Tuckahoe, where the public schools are excellent, commuting by railroad is easy, and their wives and families have cultural and linguistic ties with their compatriots. Westchester is not too far from Riverdale's Saturday Japanese School (fifteen minutes). Japanese nationals have also gravitated to communities in Queens, where there is a full-time Japanese school.

Israelis, who also like to live near schools for their children, have traditionally chosen parts of Queens (Forest Hills), Brooklyn (Flatbush) and the Bronx (Riverdale). Manhattan also offers them the appropriate Hebrew schools such as Ramaz, which is one of New York's best private yeshivas. In addition, every community in New York and New Jersey has a synagogue which offers religious education.

Relocated Americans, coming from other parts of the United States, enjoy living in communities in New Jersey, where they find housing and community affairs very much like the towns in which they grew up. Yet commuting to and from New Jersey may be a little more complicated than commuting to parts of Westchester or Connecticut. Most of the commuters from New Jersey often depend on their own cars or car pools or buses. But the time it takes to traverse the Lincoln Tunnel, the Holland Tunnel, or the George Washington Bridge seems to be considerably longer and out of proportion to its short geographical distance. (Bergen County and Essex County in New Jersey are very reasonably priced, and there are some lovely undiscovered areas in these sections of New Jersey.)

Other relocated American executives, especially those who work on Wall Street, tend to gravitate traditionally to the "golden coast" of Connecticut. It is so named because the towns, such as Greenwich, Darien, Cos Cob, and Stamford, are located on the shores of the Long Island Sound. This sumptuous part of Connecticut has always been popular with the "country club" set; Westport and Norwalk more recently so. Fairfield County of Connecticut is a very expensive area, and one pays dearly for its beauty and privacy. The public schools are excellent. They rate the highest in the state. For those who work in New York City, the best way to commute is by railroad (Metro-North's New Haven Line to Grand Central Terminal at 42nd Street and Lexington Avenue). The trains are so civilized that you can enjoy a cocktail and the *New York Times* before you arrive home for dinner. (Traveling by car, on the other hand, is tedious and difficult. The roads are always crowded during rush hour.)

Long Island gets a lot of transplanted New Yorkers who can no longer tolerate Manhattan's problems. They find on the North Shore and the South Shore of Long Island many other relocated New Yorkers, excellent public schools, and many opportunities for sports and pleasures.

If you choose to live in the "suburbs," there are many areas in which to live within one hour's commuting distance from Manhattan. To the north is Westchester County and Rockland County; on the west is New Jersey; to the northeast is Connecticut; and on the southeast is Long Island. Whichever direction you choose, you will find that property values vary, even within the same community. Prices can range from $40,000 to $1,000,000+, from a modest two-bedroom house to a seaside mansion. Prices vary according to several factors. The closer you are to the water (Long Island Sound, Atlantic Ocean, bay, lake, or river), the more expensive will be your property. If you choose a community with a very fine public school, your property value will also increase. The price increases when you have more land and extras like swimming pool, garage, and gardens. You also pay according to the size of your house (measured in square footage) and the architectural style. Some types, such as a very stylishly designed home or a stone house or a renovated barn or a historic farmhouse, can bring higher prices. Being near the train or village or school also carries an advantage, and will consequently increase the value of the real estate.

In this chapter, we are listing precise information on more than forty desirable suburban communities located within one hour from New York City. The information has been divided into two sections: (1) areas which have highly recommended public school systems and (2) areas which are moderately priced. The communities have been divided into: Connecticut (Fairfield County); New York (Westchester County, Rockland County, Long Island – North Shore and South Shore); and New Jersey (Bergen County and Essex County).

The "suburbs" of New York City are very beautiful. Many people enjoy being in the middle of nature and still near enough to New York City. If you work in New York City and you have a large family, "living in the suburbs" is an option to consider.

THIRTY-TWO SUBURBAN COMMUNITIES THAT HAVE HIGHLY RECOMMENDED PUBLIC SCHOOL SYSTEMS

Connecticut

1. *Darien* (Fairfield County, Connecticut; 30 miles from New York City). This beautiful area is part of Connecticut's "golden coast" because it's located on the shores of the Long Island Sound. Many of the residents work in Manhattan and commute daily on Metro-North's New Haven Line to Grand Central Terminal (42nd Street and Lexington Avenue) in forty minutes. The commute is well worth being able to live in such a beautiful area. Homes, however, are very expensive, especially near the shore. All seasons are charming; the community offers a lot of recreational activities. For a nominal fee, during the summer the residents can enjoy the town beaches and docks. The public school system is excellent, traditional, and conservative in philosophy. Darien spends more money on each of its students than any other school district in Connecticut. It is not surprising that 90% of their high school graduates continue on to college.

2. *Greenwich* (Fairfield County, Connecticut; 25–26 miles from New York City). Greenwich is considered one of the most affluent communities in Connecticut. A favorite address with many of the old American families and with famous politicians and celebrities, this town has many different sections, and each one has its distinct characteristics. There is the estate section, the "old Greenwich" section, the country club area, the waterfront section, and the new modern part. There is

HOW TO FIND A HOUSE IN THE SUBURBS

Key

NEW YORK STATE
Westchester County:
6. Chappaqua
7. Edgemont
8. Rye
9. Scarsdale
20. Harrison and Port Chester
21. Hastings-on-the-Hudson
22. Katonah, Pound Ridge and North Salem
23., 37. Pelham
24. Pleasantville
34. Bronxville
35. Hartsdale
36. New Rochelle
38. Tuckahoe
39. White Plains

Long Island:
11. Great Neck
12. Roslyn
13. Woodmere
26., 41. Manhasset
27., 42. New Hyde Park
28. Syosset
43. Port Washington

Rockland County:
10. South Orangetown
25. Orangeburg, Tappan, Palisades and Sparkill
40. Nyack

NEW JERSEY:
14. Franklin Lakes
15. Ridgewood
16. Tenafly
17. Montclair
18. Millburn
29., 44. Fort Lee
30. Summit
31. Upper Saddle River
32. Westfield
45. Teaneck

CONNECTICUT
1., 19. Darien
2. Greenwich
3. New Canaan
4. Norwalk
5. Westport
33. Stamford

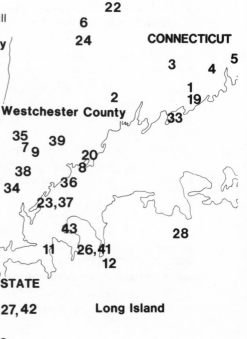

something for all tastes. But due to its location as the nearest community to the New York State border, the residents pay dearly for being close to Manhattan and yet being in Connecticut. The public schools in Greenwich are excellent. Wealthy residents have made generous donations to the many schools, their libraries, and their laboratories. There are also a good number of private day schools which feed the "Ivy League" colleges with students. Greenwich is known to be a very "social" community; belonging to the "right" club and knowing the "right" people are very important to many of the residents. Nearby towns such as Riverside and Cos Cob are equally as beautiful and probably less "snobbish" than Greenwich. Trains of Metro-North's New Haven Line travel regularly into Grand Central Terminal. The thirty-five minute ride is very pleasant.

3. *New Canaan* (Fairfield County, Connecticut; 34–35 miles from New York City). New Canaan, very rural and relaxed, is surrounded by picturesque reservoirs, horse ranches, and rambling New England barns. This is New England scenery at its most natural. Real estate values vary, depending on the amount of land, the size of the house, and the amenities that accompany it. However, nothing is cheap in this well-established, old-family community. Those who travel to New York City do so by car or drive their cars to the train station at Norwalk or Stamford. From there they take the train, and within forty minutes they arrive at Grand Central Terminal. The schools are known for their physical beauty, athletic facilities, and traditional curriculums. Neighboring towns of Long Ridge and Silvermine are also desirable suburbs of New Canaan.

4. *Norwalk* (Fairfield County, Connecticut; 32–33 miles from New York City). Norwalk has been evaluated by the *Places Rated Almanac,* 1981 edition, to have the highest student-teacher ratio in the United States (8.49 students per teacher) and the number one rank for best metropolitan area for educational quality and opportunities in the United States. Norwalk is an affluent, homogenous community of upward mobility. It is well located between New York City and New Haven. Houses are not cheap, but they are still more reasonably priced than in Greenwich or Westport. Neighboring Rowayton, on the Sound, is a beautiful spot in which to live for those who love the sea and maritime ambiance. Rowayton is expensive, and houses may have very little land or privacy. Commuters to New York City from Norwalk take Metro-North's New Haven Line and arrive in the City within forty-five minutes.

5. *Westport* (Norwalk County, Connecticut; 41–42 miles from New York City). Westport, the community on the Sound and its inland, rural

brother Weston, are two special communities. In the summer, the population increases, and the public parks, beaches, and clubs bustle with cars, noises, and laughter. The schools are so good, the community facilities so superb, and the style of living so pleasant that this area has doubled and tripled its real estate values in the past five years. This is fine for those who already live there, but for newcomers, it makes moving into the area expensive. There is a community bus that travels from street to street and takes the residents of Weston and Westport to the train station, allowing the New York bound commuters the luxury of not needing a car. The train ride to Grand Central Station takes about forty-five minutes. Green Farms on the Long Island Sound and Southport are very beautiful neighboring communities of Westport, but equally expensive. As you move inland toward Weston and Wilton, real estate values lower slightly. Americans pay dearly for "water views" and "water rights."

In the past few years, all Fairfield County has grown and developed very rapidly. Companies and corporations that were once located in New York City have moved their buildings and employees in search of lower taxes and more modern facilities. Fairfield County was an excellent choice—possessing rural setting as well as proximity to Manhattan. Consequently, more people have moved into this area, and real estate values have increased. Supply and demand have always been contributing factors in the fluctuation of the real estate market, especially in the tri-state area of Connecticut, New York, and New Jersey.

New York State — Westchester County

6. *Chappaqua* (Westchester County, New York; 27-28 miles from New York City). Many ex-Manhattanites have moved to this area for its beautiful nature and superb public schools. School taxes and property taxes are high, but the schools are considered, along with Scarsdale's and Edgemont's, as the three best public school systems in Westchester County. The homes are varied, some more expensive than others, and it is not impossible to find a nice house at a reasonable price. This is a community popular with executives from I.B.M., as well as other corporations and companies that have their headquarters in Westchester. Chappaqua has a cosmopolitan and diversified population. Its residents come from all over the world and live together harmoniously. They all share the common interest of maintaining the charm and high standard of their community. The commute to Manhattan, however, is not easy. If you drive your car, you must consider 60 to 90 minutes each way. The

commute on the train via the Harlem Line to Grand Central Terminal may take less.

7. *Edgemont* (Westchester County, New York; 24 miles from New York City). Edgemont, in spite of its superb school system and beautiful location, is not as well known as some of the other towns in Westchester, perhaps because it has always lived in the shadow of its famous neighbor, Scarsdale. Even the public schools in Edgemont have a Scarsdale address. But today, Edgemont need not take a back seat to any community. It can stand very solidly and securely on its own. Edgemont is an ideal community in which to live. The schools are located in rural settings and resemble universities more than high schools. In 1982, 19% of the high school graduates won Regents Scholarships, the highest percentage in the United States. Many of the high school students finish their courses in 3 or 3½ years and have time to travel or work before they resume their studies. To accommodate the increasing number of foreigners who are moving into this area, the Edgemont Public School System has developed a superb, free, English as a Second Language program. During the day, students aged 5–18 can receive private tutoring, and, during the evening, parents can attend their own ESL programs. For the working commuters to New York City, the Harlem Line goes to 42nd Street and Grand Central Terminal and takes forty minutes.

8. *Rye* (Westchester County, New York; 25 miles from New York City). Unlike the other towns of Westchester County, Rye is homogeneous. There is less racial and social interchange in this community. The population is mostly comprised of upper-middle-class citizens of financial means. Rye is the most residential town in Westchester, with only a small number of small businesses and companies in the village. Rye is blessed with hilly inland areas as well as winding brooks and a protected harbor on Long Island Sound. The school system is very good and boasts of high national testing results. The elementary schools have a flexible program—encouraging quick learners as well as giving special care to those who need more help. Many of the residents spend most of their time in Manhattan, either to work or to enjoy themselves. Metro-North's New Haven Line to Grand Central Terminal offers them a comfortable, forty-minute ride.

9. *Scarsdale* (Westchester County, New York; 21–22 miles from New York City). Scarsdale is famous throughout the United States for its public schools. They are well equipped, well staffed, and very well maintained. The schools are well endowed, and the latest computers, science labs, and artistic equipment can be found there. But school taxes are very high. Homes are very expensive, and real estate taxes are high.

The residents of Scarsdale pay to maintain their schools. However, if a family wants to live in Scarsdale and take advantage of the free public schools, but cannot afford to but a house, there are apartments to consider. There are apartments in some sections of Scarsdale for rent or sale, and there is a choice of co-ops and condominiums one can buy for less money than one would spend for a house. The commute into Manhattan is easy on the Harlem Line train to Grand Central Terminal. The trip takes a little more than thirty minutes. Scarsdale is a beautiful town. Recently, it has become a favorite community among the Japanese, Koreans, and Brazilians because of its many golf courses and its superb English as a Second Language program in the public schools. (At the Junior High School and Senior High School, foreign-speaking students form small tutorial groups and receive special English instruction for 45 minutes each day.)

Rockland County

10. *South Orangetown* (Rockland County, New York; 20–22 miles from New York City). Rockland County is a suburban area of New York City which has been discovered by New Yorkers in the last decade. And yet the towns of the South Orangetown School District (Orangeburg, Tappan, Palisades, Piermont, and Sparkill) have been well established communities for many decades. The public schools are among the best in the country, and high pupil achievement is good proof. The pride of South Orangetown is its individualized learning program that provides each student the right to advance at an individual pace. Property values are fair here, and it is possible to find good value for land and house. Most of the commuters who work in New York City use their cars, for the bus ride tends to be long and tedious (it must be mentioned that the commute by car is also long and tedious). The most popular route into the City is via the Palisades Parkway and over the George Washington Bridge. During rush hour these roads are always crowded.

Long Island

11. *Great Neck* (North Shore, Long Island, New York; 23–24 miles from New York City). Great Neck is a beautiful suburban area which has some very expensive real estate located inland as well as on the Long Island Sound at Kings Point and Sands Point. Great Neck Estates, which is partly inland and partly on the coast, is also an expensive section. In the 1920s, the American author F. Scott Fitzgerald and his wife Zelda lived in Great Neck and helped create the image of this community as a residential area for the "social set." Since then, many celebrities and prominent people have enjoyed this elegant and manicured suburban

community. The schools are excellent, especially the Great Neck High School, which has many modern athletic and academic facilities. School taxes are high, but the schools prosper from their healthy budgets. Homes are not cheap, and many of the residents are very wealthy. There is the Long Island Rail Road that goes to Penn Station at Eighth Avenue and 34th Street very frequently. The ride is only thirty minutes. When the weather is warm and the sun shines, this community is reminiscent of an affluent coastal town in Southern France.

12. *Roslyn* (North Shore, Long Island, New York; 26–27 miles from New York City). Known for its coastal pleasures and suburban country clubs, Roslyn is an affluent suburban community. The public schools are very good, and no student is deprived of sports, computers, or laboratories. Houses are not cheap, however, especially on the coast, in Roslyn Heights, in the Brookville area, or near the Engineers' Country Club. For those who work in New York City, there is the Long Island Rail Road, which goes to Penn Station. The commute is relatively pleasant, but, for those who drive a car into the City, the daily traveling is very difficult. Driving to and from Manhattan each day on the Long Island Expressway is a very tedious pilgrimage. If one can, it is better to take the railroad.

13. *Woodmere* (South Shore, Long Island, New York; 22–23 miles from New York City). This section of the South Shore has proven for many years to be a consistently desirable community. The public school system, comprised of Woodmere and Hewlett, is very good. There is also a fine private school, the Woodmere Academy, for boys and girls aged five to eighteen. Woodmere tends to be more reasonably priced than the neighboring township of Hewlett. Woodmere is one of the "Five Towns"; the other four being Hewlett, Cedarhurst, Lawrence, and Inwood. Each town has its own ambiance. The expensive section of Woodmere is Woodsburgh, boasting of some very prestigious estates. The adjacent town of Hewlett has its expensive areas also, and they are Hewlett Bay Park, Hewlett Harbor, and Hewlett Bay. Shopping in these communities is very easy. The residents have a large choice. Many of the stores and boutiques are similar to those in New York City. Summertime is especially pleasant in this community because of the proximity to the Atlantic Ocean. One can be in Atlantic Beach in twenty minutes.

New Jersey

14. *Franklin Lakes* (Bergen County, New Jersey; 19–21 miles from New York City). Franklin Lakes is located in Northwest Bergen County. It is one of New Jersey's most affluent small towns. It is very rural in atmosphere, and yet it is conveniently located near a good-sized city,

Paramus. Paramus is Bergen County's shopping center. Real estate values are very high in Franklin Lakes, especially on or near Franklin Lake, and values have increased considerably. One of the reasons for this town's secure property values is its school system. The schools have the finest equipment and are located in the most scenic spots of the community. The school program is neither traditional nor progressive. Emphasis is placed on individualized instruction. High school students attend the Ramapo–Indian Hills High School or one of the country's many fine private boarding schools.

15. *Ridgewood* (Bergen County, New Jersey; 17–19 miles from New York City). This community can be described as a "manicured town," where all the residents take pride in maintaining their beautiful lawns and gardens. The streets are wide, with many trees, and one has the feeling of opulence. The residents are as proud of their properties as they are of their schools. The educational program is diversified, and the faculty very well trained. Real estate taxes are high in this community in order to pay for the expensive public school system. Many of the residents work in New York City, especially near Wall Street, and commuting is a way of life. The term "bedroom community" is a phrase that emerged to describe suburban towns such as Ridgewood, Greenwich, Scarsdale, Great Neck, and many others. A good percentage of the male residents use their communities as "bedrooms." They work all day in New York City and use their homes during the week as a "place to sleep." This tends to be characteristic of many suburban areas in the United States, yet the term carries no pejorative connotation. It has merely become a style of life. Ridgewood has the reputation of having the best public school system in New Jersey. There are a number a rental homes available also.

16. *Tenafly* (Bergen County, New Jersey; 10–12 miles from New York City). Tenafly has been considered by many professionals, especially physicians and attorneys, as the ideal community in New Jersey if you work in Manhattan. Excellent public schools, proximity to the George Washington Bridge, and good suburban living have made Tenafly very popular—even more so than its changing neighbor, Englewood. In Tenafly, real estate has remained steady and secure over the years. Tenafly is a family-oriented community; public facilities are excellent and private ones even better. Many people commute to work by car, since Tenafly is located near the George Washington Bridge. But if you want to get into Manhattan without using your car, there is a bus service between Tenafly and the Port Authority at 41st Street. Call the New Jersey Transit Company at 1–201–762–5100 to reconfirm the schedule. Bus #166 from Platform 62 at the Port Authority Building leaves every half hour for Tenafly and vice-versa. Neighboring areas that use the

Tenafly High School and have their own excellent elementary school systems are Cresskill, Howarth, Demerest, and Closter (these four communities may have homes for sale that are less expensive than those in Tenafly, and the communities are equally beautiful).

17. *Montclair* (Essex County, New Jersey; 12-18 miles from New York City). Montclair is known for its cosmopolitan community and its pleasant surroundings. On a clear day (clair) you can stand on one of the elevated areas of Montclair (mont) such as Lloyd Road and see New York. Theodore Dreiser, in his semi-autobiographical novel *The Genius,* spoke of this beautiful view. In Montclair the public schools are characterized by high parent participation. The value of the houses varies considerably, from very expensive older estates to newer split-level ranches. Commuting by car may be tedious, as it can be from all parts of New Jersey, but there is a bus that goes to and from New York City. You can call the DeCamp Bus Line at 1-201-783-7500 for the schedule. When leaving Manhattan, you go to the Port Authority Building at 41st Street and Seventh Avenue, to Platform 237, and take Bus #66. The bus from New York City to Montclair leaves every hour on the half hour (4:30, 5:30, 6:30, etc.) and vice-versa. The trip can take thirty minutes, depending on traffic.

18. *Millburn* (Essex County, New Jersey; 18 miles from New York City). Millburn is an affluent town, comprised of residents who are highly educated and very well placed socially. The Short Hills section is especially affluent, and the homes in this northern part of town are extremely costly. This community is very rural, but it has excellent shopping. The school system is superb. 70% of the faculty have at least master's degrees. A good number of the high school graduates win national merit scholarships. The school system is high-pressured, which is encouraged by over-achieving parents who carefully scrutinize the schools' policies.

Other Suburban Communities That Have Recommended Public Schools

Connecticut:
   19. Darien

Westchester:
   20. Harrison and Port Chester
   21. Hastings-on-Hudson
   22. Katonah, Pound Ridge, and North Salem
   23. Pelham
   24. Pleasantville

Rockland County:
25. Orangeburg, Tappan, Palisades, and Sparkill of the South Orangetown Public School District

Long Island:
26. Manhasset
27. New Hyde Park of the Herricks School System
28. Syosset

New Jersey:
29. Fort Lee
30. Summit
31. Upper Saddle River
32. Westfield

THIRTEEN SUBURBAN AREAS WHICH ARE MODERATELY PRICED

Connecticut

33. *Stamford* (Fairfield County, Connecticut; 30–31 miles from New York City). Stamford enjoys its location on the "golden coast" of Connecticut, as well as its status as a city. The hospitals and schools and public facilities are very well equipped. Shopping is as good as it would be in any considerably sized city with its department stores and varied boutiques. Real estate inland, near North Stamford and Glenbrook, is considerably less expensive than in the coastal communities of Stamford Harbor, Shippan Point, and Westcott Cove. New Haven Line trains make regular stops in Stamford, and commuting is easy – forty minutes. Executives, Wall Street stockbrokers, and New York businessmen make their regular commute with their *New York Times* and coffee in the morning and their *New York Post* and cocktails in the evening. Weekends and warm months are reminiscent of any affluent coastal resort in the world. In the past few years, Stamford has known a great increase in its population. Many corporations that were once located in Manhattan have moved to Fairfield County, especially near the Stamford area. Taxes and expenses were too costly in New York City; consequently, a fair number of prestigious companies crossed the border into Stamford. Many more residents have, therefore, moved into the area. Real estate prices have increased considerably because of this, but so has the quality of such community facilities as schools and hospitals. The Stamford area is considered to be the fastest growing community in the tri-state area.

New York — Westchester County:

34. *Bronxville* (Westchester County, New York; 21 miles from New York City). Bronxville is known for its cosmopolitan population, including members from the United Nations and foreign companies. Property values vary. There are some very expensive estates and luxurious condominiums, as well as modest apartments, for rent. By living in the more reasonably priced areas you still have the benefits of the community's affluent population and excellent facilities, including very fine public schools, and an extensive bus system. The train is accessible for commuting. You take the Harlem Line to Grand Central at 42nd Street. You can be at your destination in thirty minutes.

35. *Hartsdale* (Westchester County, New York; 23 miles from New York City). In the past ten years, beautiful apartment buildings and co-ops have been built in this private Westchester community. This allows many families to take advantage of the facilities and schools of the community without having to purchase a house. Hartsdale has become particularly popular with Japanese and Korean executives who came from their homeland to work in New York City for several years. There are Oriental groceries, and the public schools offer excellent English as a Second Language programs. Real estate is less expensive than in the neighboring towns of Scarsdale and Edgemont. Commuting by train allows you to leave the car at home. The Harlem Line into Grand Central is only a thirty-five-minute ride.

36. *New Rochelle* (Westchester County, New York; 18–19 miles from New York City). New Rochelle, extending its borders from the coast of Long Island Sound to the inland fields of Westchester, has a very heterogenous and varied population. This adds to the interesting mixture of residents, contrasting to the more homogeneous neighboring towns of Scarsdale and Rye. In New Rochelle, one can find "good buys" in real estate, especially inland and near town. For those who like sailing, New Rochelle has the largest number of marinas and yacht clubs within close proximity to New York City. The bays and harbors are well protected, and many races up the Long Island Sound begin in the waters of New Rochelle. There are the private colleges of New Rochelle and Iona for those of all ages who wish to attend college or take courses in the Adult Education programs. The public schools in New Rochelle are fair; students have diversified backgrounds. The train, New Haven Line, to Grand Central Terminal can take you into the city within thirty-five minutes and gives you the option of leaving your car at home.

37. *Pelham* (Westchester County, New York; 15–16 miles from New York City). Pelham, which is the first town of Westchester County from New York City, enjoys the position of being in the suburbs as well as

near Manhattan (it is adjacent to the Bronx and City Island). There are many beautiful homes in Pelham, in traditional Italian styles. There are also beautiful country clubs and marinas. The public beaches are crowded, but the private clubs are beautifully kept. Golf, horseback riding, sailing, and fishing are all available in this coastal community. The adult residents work in New York City and commute by car. There are also the city buses from nearby City Island and the Bronx to make commuting less fatiguing. The New Haven Line to Grand Central is another option for commuters. Pelham is a quiet, family-oriented town which has not been "discovered." For many years, it has been overshadowed by its larger neighbors, New Rochelle to the north and Mt. Vernon to the west. But Pelham's public school system is better than those of New Rochelle or Mt. Vernon. Pelham Manor and the areas near North Shore Road are particularly beautiful and desirable residential communities.

38. *Tuckahoe* (Westchester County, New York; 23 miles from New York City). Tuckahoe, in conjunction with its neighboring town of Hartsdale, has become a favorite with Japanese and Korean businessmen and executives. They like the good public schools, reasonable real estate values, apartment living, and proximity to Manhattan. These new residents have helped to make this area cosmopolitan and diversified. The opportunity to commute by train via the Harlem Line is a great advantage. Within forty minutes you can be in the city and not have to worry about driving a car.

39. *White Plains* (Westchester County, New York; 22 miles from New York City). White Plains is the major city of Westchester County. It is the seat of Westchester's government agencies, courts, county offices, and business corporations. Nestlé's, I.B.M., and other leading companies have moved their headquarters out of Manhattan to these more pleasant and reasonably priced surroundings. The train goes regularly to New York City's Grand Central Terminal, and in less than thirty minutes you can change your environment from country to city. The public schools of White Plains are fair. The Deutsche Schüle has a Saturday program for German children. There are several universities located in White Plains, as well as Pace University's Law School. The Westchester Council for the Arts is very active in White Plains and has done a lot to develop the cultural and artistic life of Westchester County. White Plains is a very heterogeneous community with a wide availability of living quarters and prices. Apartments, garden apartments, co-ops, condominiums, two-family houses, and estates are all available in White Plains. Shopping is excellent. Neiman-Marcus, Bloomingdale's, and

Altman's have beautiful stores in the shopping malls, as well as the new shopping center, "La Galleria."

Rockland County

40. *Nyack* (Rockland County, New York; 26 miles from New York City). Nyack, known for its cliffs and beautiful views of the Hudson River, is a charming area in which to live. For those who are interested in scenic views, abundant parks, and all-year-round sport facilities, this northerly area is lovely. Real estate values are fair and stable. Perhaps this is due to the fact that commuters must rely on their cars and do not have the luxury of a wide choice of travel. For those who enjoy winter sports, Nyack is a stepping stone to many of New York's ski slopes. The Hudson River is not used for swimming, but one can use it for power boating. Sailing, however, is difficult in this area because of the inconsistent winds coming from the surrounding cliffs and rocks.

Long Island

41. *Manhasset* (North Shore, Long Island, New York; 22–23 miles from New York City). Manhasset, nestled between the expensive towns of Great Neck and Port Washington, is fairly priced and equally beautiful, especially Manhasset's Plandome Heights and Plandome Manor. Those sections located on the water are costly, but probably less so than equal acreage in Great Neck and Port Washington. During the summer months, fishing, sailing, and swimming are favorite activities of the residents in this area. In July and August, the flavor of the town changes from one of a commuting appendix of New York City to a seaside resort. Manhasset Bay is exceptionally beautiful, and its protected harbors attract many sailors and racing enthusiasts. Public facilities such as the railroad are also good. Commuters can take the Long Island Rail Road into New York's Penn Station. Manhasset's school system is excellent. Low school taxes and high spending per student gives Manhasset the best of both worlds. Real estate taxes from the successful shopping district, "Miracle Mile," bring in a good deal of commercial tax money and relieves the residents of a large tax burden. The school budgets benefit from the commercial revenue.

42. *New Hyde Park* (Long Island, New York). This is a conservative community of small homes in which daily living is very pleasant. You don't have to be a millionaire to live like one in this area. Real estate taxes are low; property values are reasonable; and one can find a nice home for a fair price. The school system is very good, mostly traditional in philosophy. Emphasis is on the reading program. Based on national tests, the students from New Hyde Park score very well.

43. *Port Washington* (North Shore, Long Island, New York; 25 miles from New York City). Port Washington is a long-time favorite of the maritime crowd. At one time, many years ago, Port Washington shared with Kings Point and Sands Point the reputation of being the "chic" summer residences for many affluent New Yorkers. But today it is more known as a year-round community and a very desirable section in which to live. Commuting on the Long Island Rail Road is comfortable. The public schools are good, and the people are very community-oriented. It is not an over-priced community, especially inland, and good real estate value can still be found.

New Jersey

44. *Fort Lee* (Bergen County, New Jersey; 10 miles from New York City). Fifty years ago, there was a poor, sleepy little town at the foot of the George Washington Bridge on the New Jersey side. This town was called Fort Lee. It resembled in no way the Fort Lee of the 1980s, however. Today, it is sometimes called the "sixth borough" of New York, for many ex-New Yorkers live in and commute from Fort Lee. They have left New York City in search of less expensive rents, more comfortable living, and more beautiful scenery. Opposite to Riverside Drive, they have found many lovely apartment buildings with panoramic views of the George Washington Bridge and the Hudson River. Fort Lee is also a community of expensive co-ops and condominiums, fancy yachts, and luxurious waterside homes. Inland, near town, one can still find reasonable prices for buying or renting either private houses, two-family houses, or apartments. The residents enjoy the easy commute by bus to New York City and the scenic beauty of the New Jersey cliffs. To get to Fort Lee from New York City, you can either take your car for a short drive across the George Washington Bridge or take a bus. The #9 bus of the New Jersey Transit Company leaves very frequently from the Port Authority Bus Terminal near Penn Station at 34th Street and Eighth Avenue. Depending upon the amount of traffic, either by car or bus, your commute can take from twenty to forty-five minutes.

45. *Teaneck* (Bergen County, New Jersey; 15–18 miles from New York City). Teaneck, a bustling community, always has some activity going on. This is an area for all tastes and all pocketbooks. The public schools are fair. Many of their outstanding alumni attend the country's leading colleges, and the residents are very active in the school system as well as in community affairs. This is an area for those who like to have a "voice" in their neighborhoods. Commuting to New York City is fairly simple, and many of the residents work in Manhattan. From the Port

Authority Bus Terminal, you take Bus #167 from Platform 60. The bus leaves every half-hour to and from Teaneck.

RENTAL VS. PURCHASE

In all the previously mentioned forty suburban communities, located within one hour from New York City, there is always the possibility of renting a house instead of buying one. If you do not have a large amount of available cash, or you are not sure how long you will be remaining in the New York area, or you just do not want to buy a house, perhaps renting may be a practical way to proceed. You may even consider renting a house in a particular neighborhood for a few months in order to give yourself time to find what you want. Your agent will have a list of homes that are for rent, for how long you can rent them, and if they are furnished or not. Often the house you can afford to rent is more luxurious than the house you can afford to buy. Renting, instead of buying, gives you a certain amount of freedom to invest your money in another way rather than tying up a large amount in residential real estate. On the other hand, if you are interested in living in a certain community and you know that the real estate values for that area have shown a constant rise, then it may be to your advantage to buy a house. This is especially true if you can purchase the house at a fair price and if you are handy or willing to make some "home improvements" such as adding solar energy, a swimming pool, gardens, landscaping, additional rooms, etc. Then, when you sell the house, you can make a profit on your expenditures.

There are advantages and disadvantages to both renting and buying a house. It is difficult to say when one should rent or purchase. However, you should always inquire what is available for rent and investigate that option. When a family looks for a home, every lead and suggestion should be pursued. It is hard work to find the proper home and right community for your family—be it an apartment, a co-op, an estate, or a beach house. And it takes time, patience, and perseverance to find the "exact" home for your family. So give yourself some time and never take the first thing you see.

USEFUL TELEPHONE NUMBERS FOR COMMUTERS

Amtrak 736–4545
DeCamp Bus Line (New Jersey bus line) 1–201–783–7500
Greyhound Bus 635–0800
Metro-North Commuter Railroad (Harlem, Hudson, New Haven,
    Port Jervis, and Pascack Valley lines) 532–4900
Long Island Rail Road 739–4200
New Jersey Transit 1–201–762–5100

PART II

Setting Up: How To Arrange Your Household

CHAPTER 5

Personal Services

Banking: How To Get a Checking Account; Savings Account; Safe Deposit Vault
Credit Cards
Traveler's Checks and Currency Exchange
How To Get a Driver's License
How To Get Domestic Help: Babysitter; Help for the Elderly; Governess; Housekeeper; Chauffeur; Dog Walker
Postal Services and Telephone Services
Telephone Answering Service
How To Have Your Utilities Installed: Telephone; Television; Gas; Electricity; Water; Air Conditioner
Voltage Equivalence
Insurance Policies: Health; Homeowner's; Life Insurance; Disability; Automobile; Comprehensive Liability
How To Move "By Yourself"
Shopping: Discount Clothing Stores for the Family; Speciality Stores for Setting Up Your Home; Specialty Sections and Districts of New York City
Size and Measurement Equivalence

BANKING

UNDERSTANDING the banking system of the United States could take anyone, American or newcomer, a good deal of time. However, there are some basic facts that we can relate to you in these pages. There are two types of general banking accounts: a checking account and a

71

savings account. To "open up" either type of account, you can go to any bank. Your choice of bank can depend upon the bank's location, reputation, rates of interest, and possibility of borrowing money. It is advisable to have both accounts in the same bank. A "savings" bank in opposition to a "commercial" bank offers a greater rate of interest for your money. Therefore, it would be to your advantage to shop around and see which savings bank offers you the greatest amount of interest quarterly (every three months), semi-annually, or annually for each type of account.

To open up either a checking account or a savings account, you will have to go to the bank and fill out some forms with a representative of the bank. You will need a permanent address and a Social Security number (for information on how to get a Social Security number refer to Chapter 18). You will be able to use your accounts immediately.

Checking Account. America, especially New York, is becoming a "cashless society." People are using checks instead of cash for security reasons. It is not uncommon to see Americans writing checks for many different purposes. A good checking account is important. There are many plans from which you can choose. A regular account requires a specific balance in the bank at all times. A special account does not require as large a balance, but there is a charge for each check and sometimes a monthly fee as well. There are combination checking and savings accounts. There are business accounts that pay interest on the amount of money in the checking account.

When you go to the bank to open up a checking account, it is a good idea to give yourself a few minutes to ask the representative some of the following questions: Do you need to keep a minimum amount of money in the checking account? Do you need to write a minimum number of checks per month? What are the bank's charges for a checking account? Can you borrow money from the bank if you have only a checking account and not a savings account? Can you earn interest on the month's total balance? If you overdraw on the checking account (write a total amount of money for your checks that exceeds the total balance you have in your account), can the bank automatically transfer money from your savings account to cover the deficit you have in your checking account?

Before you go to the bank to open up a checking account, it is a good idea to have thought about some of the above questions. Then you will be able to intelligently compare the different options from different banks.

Savings Account. As with checking accounts, there are also many different types of savings accounts. The criteria which can influence what type of savings account you choose are the following: What is the maximum amount of money you need to have in your account? Do you need to keep a certain amount of money in your account for a certain period of time? What rate of interest are you earning on your money? Is this interest paid to you once every four months, once every six months, or once every twelve months? Is your money insured by the federal government (FDIC) if the bank should go bankrupt or be robbed? Savings banks offer greater rates of interest than commercial banks. Brokerage houses such as "Merrill Lynch" may offer more interest, but Merrill Lynch does not insure your money, while most savings and commercial banks will insure up to $100,000 of each account with the FDIC. There are also savings accounts that offer "tax-free" interest rates. For those who have a lot of money in savings accounts, this may be an advantageous tax arrangement, so you will pay fewer taxes on the interest you earn from your savings.

There are "custodial savings accounts" such as the "Clifford Trust Fund" which parents set up for their children. They give their children gifts each year, not to exceed $10,000 from each parent, and the parents are in turn the custodians or managers of these moneys until the children reach a certain age. This is a good way for parents to save for their children's costly college education.

C.D.s, or Certificates of Deposit, represent another system of saving money. With this option, you have to put in an account a certain amount of money for at least six or twelve months. But the rate of interest you earn is usually higher than what you would ordinarily earn at a savings bank. The only thing is that you need a certain amount of money, usually a lot, which you are not using immediately.

There are some banks that offer "prizes" or "gifts" when you open a savings account. It is always nice to receive presents, but be sure how much these presents are indirectly costing you. Ask yourself, as well as a representative at the bank, what you are doing to deserve these presents. Are you to keep a minimum amount of money in the bank, for how long, and at what rate of interest? It may be cheaper to buy your own present and put your money in another bank.

Safe Deposit Vaults. If you have valuable jewelry, stock certificates, bonds, leases, wills, or other documents, you may find that it is safer to leave them in a vault at your bank than at home. Vaults can be rented by the year for a certain amount of money ($10.00 and higher) depending on size. Only you and one other person that you specify to the bank (spouse or relative) has the right to use this vault. You are given two keys. Every time you go to the bank to put something in the vault, or take something out, you have to sign your name on a card so that they can check your signature, and present your key. Your key and the master key from the bank are both needed in order to open your vault. But you must remember that you can go to the vault only when the bank is opened. You can't go to the vault Saturday night before you dress for a fashionable party. You must plan your visits to the bank according to your needs. There are, however, some vaults in New York City that are now open seven days a week, twenty-four hours a day. But one pays for this privilege, and they are not located within a bank.

One must be aware that banks or private companies are not insured for the contents of your individual vault. Granted, only you can open the vault because you have the necessary key. But if there is a robbery, your vault could be opened and its contents removed. You may be insured personally for your jewelry, but it is difficult to insure documents and papers.

It is also unwise to put cash money in vaults. Banks would prefer that you circulate your cash or deposit it in a checking or savings account. Cash in your vault is unredeemable in case of theft.

CREDIT CARDS

The major credit cards in the United States are Visa, American Express, Diners Club, and MasterCard. If you can obtain one of these credit cards in your home country before you come to the United States, getting your first American credit card or subsequent credit cards will be easier.

In any event, if you will be living in the United States for a period of time and you wish to apply for a credit card, the procedure is the same for everyone. Each company does a "credit check" on each applicant. After you have filled out the necessary application, a credit company will check to see if you earn at least $15,000 per year, that you have been employed for at least two or three years with the same company, and that you do not owe anyone money. If all goes well and your credit rating is considered good, in two to four weeks you will receive your requested credit card. Those who have recently arrived in the United States, and don't have a permanent job or a fixed income, may still want to have one of the above credit cards. They may want to apply to the "International Department" of the credit company and have their credit checked in their home country and home bank. It is best, however, to call the credit company directly if you have any questions:

American Express: 212-323-2000
Diners Club: 1-800-525-7376

MasterCard: 212-974-5700
Visa: 212-291-9700

Each company has its own system of making money from giving you credit. American Express charges you an annual membership fee of $35.00 for each card. Visa bills you a minimum of $5.00 per month. Diners Club charges a $45.00 membership fee per year. It is best to inquire what your membership fees are before you apply for several cards.

The advantages of using a credit card are rather obvious. No one likes to carry a lot of cash in his pockets. One card may suffice for paying all your bills at restaurants, hotels, stores, etc., and that may be all you need to carry with you. At the end of the month, you receive a copy of all your receipts. It is an easy way to save and categorize your expenses for tax time.

The disadvantage is that, if you lose your card, or if someone steals it, you are liable for all purchases and cash advances made on your card unless you are personally insured for such an occurrence or you report immediately the loss of the card. In order for you not to be liable for the lapse of time between your loss and your claim of that loss, the company may have a policy about verifying signatures. Write the company a letter after you have reported your lost card and give them all the necessary information again. It is always a good precaution to keep your credit cards separate from your wallet. Most thieves are attracted to wallets.

The procedure for obtaining a credit card for one of the major department stores in New York City is very much the same. Some of the department stores may accept the Visa or the American Express card. But if you want a specific credit card for a specific department store, you will have to fill out an application and mail it back to the store's credit office. Upon receiving your application, they will do a routine credit rating. This will entail checking your position at your place of business, checking your home bank and your New York bank for your credit status, and checking all past and present credit cards you have. This will include all international and domestic credit cards. The entire procedure should take two to four weeks. If you wish to call or visit the major New York department stores, they include:

Bergdorf Goodman. 753-7300. Fifth Avenue and 58th Street.
Bloomingdale's. 355-5900. Third Avenue and 59th Street.
Lord and Taylor. 391-3344. Fifth Avenue and 38th Street.
Gimbel's East. 348-2300. Lexington Avenue and 86th Street.
Saks Fifth Avenue. 940-5555. Fifth Avenue and 50th Street.

Obtaining credit cards for gasoline companies entails the same procedure. If you wish to charge your gasoline at the same gas station, you may find it easier to have a credit card from that oil company. Call the company directly and ask them to send you an application: Mobil at 1-914-328-6000, Exxon at 212-398-3000. They will do a credit check similar to that which the department stores do. This check will also take into account any past or present credit cards, bank rating, and position at your place of business.

TRAVELERS' CHECKS AND CURRENCY EXCHANGE

In spite of all the foreigners who travel and live here, individual stores in New York are not equipped for nor accustomed to handling foreign currency. It is unwise to walk into a New York restaurant or store and assume that they will accept your foreign currency. They will, however, most likely accept American Express travelers' checks or Barclay's travelers' checks. It would be wise, therefore, for you to purchase some of these in your home country or when you arrive in New York. The disadvantage of using travelers' checks is that a bank in New York City, unlike in Europe, will not cash them for you, even if you have an account in the bank. They will allow you to deposit them in your account, but they will not cash them. Barclay's will cash their traveler's checks, but you will have to go to a Barclay's bank. Call 406-4200 for the Barclay's bank nearest you. The same restriction applies to American Express travelers' checks. Banks will sell them to you, but they won't cash them. Call American Express at 323-2000 for the company's location nearest you.

In New York there are several foreign exchange companies which sell and buy foreign currencies. You will get the best rate of exchange from one of the following. If you are looking specifically to buy foreign currency, it is best to call them first and see if they have the amount you need.

Bank Leumi Trust Company of New York. All branches are open Monday through Friday, 8:45 A.M. to 3:00 P.M., unless otherwise noted. Call 382-4193 for the location nearest you.

Barclay's Bank of New York. All branches are open 8:30 A.M. to 3:00 P.M. Call 644-0850. If you wish to purchase foreign currency, they don't always have all the currencies available. It's a good idea to call first.

Perera or Deak-Perera. Hours vary according to location. Call 757-0100 for exact information.

HOW TO GET A DRIVER'S LICENSE

The New York State *Driver's Manual* begins by stating, "In New York State, no person may operate a motor vehicle or motorcycle on public highways unless he has a valid license. . . . To drive in this State, a new resident who already holds a valid driver's license from another jurisdiction must obtain a license within 30 days."

The first thing to do is take your foreign driver's license to your Consulate to be translated on official stationary. Then inquire at the Department of Motor Vehicles in your state about reserving a date for a written test, a road sign test, and a vision test. The written test is given in English as well as in many foreign languages — Spanish, French, German, Italian, Chinese, Hebrew, Korean, Vietnamese, etc. It is best to ask them first to send you a free copy of the *Driver's Manual* in English or in a foreign language. Then you will have some time to study the manual before you take the written test.

If your driver's license is from a foreign country which is part of the United Nations Convention on Road Traffic, you may not need to take a new road test.

For a license application and *Driver's Manual,* call the Department of Motor Vehicles. In New York City, the telephone number is 587-4620. No appointment for the written test can be made by telephone. Write to the Preliminary Test Office of the Department of Motor Vehicles in whichever borough you live (in New York City the address is 155 Worth Street, New York City 10013). The written test is given Monday through Friday, 7:30 A.M. to 3:00 P.M. The written tests are graded immediately. If you pass, you can pick up your driver's license after you take the test. Complete the application form and show proof of identification and a current driver's license. You will have to pay a fee for the written test and to validate your new license.

If you are a tourist in the United States and you have a tourist visa, your valid driver's license from your home country is valid in the United States for one year, providing that you have the license translated officially by your Consulate in New York. An international driver's license is also valid in the United States.

The minimum age in New York State for a driver's license is eighteen years. For a learner's permit or junior license, the minimum age is seventeen years. A minor must have signed consent from his/her parent or guardian approving such a license.

All residents of New York now have to renew their driver's licenses in a new way because each license is now issued with a photograph on it. Drivers will have to pay more and can expect longer lines since they will not be able to renew by mail. As his license expires, the motorist will have to go to the Motor Vehicles Department office to have his photo taken and receive a temporary license. One proof of date of birth and two proofs of current address and signature are required.

How To Get Domestic Help

Babysitter. Finding a reliable babysitter in New York City can be as frustrating and complicated as finding an apartment or a private school. But one should not despair. There are several practical ways to proceed.

There are a number of nursing schools affiliated with the major university hospitals. Inquire which one is nearest your home. Ask if you can put a card on their bulletin board.

Cornell Nursing School Babysitting Service. 420 East 70th Street. 472–5454.
St. Vincent's Hospital School of Nursing. 27 Christopher Street. 790–8484.

Some agencies, for an agency fee, can help you find a reliable babysitter. Inquire what the hourly fee is. Is there a minimum number of hours? Do you have to pay for traveling?

The Babysitter's Guild. 60 East 42nd Street. 682–0227.
Avalon Nurses Registry. 30 East 60th Street. 371–7222.

There are also some very important competent nonprofit services that may be able to help you for less money:

Barnard College Babysitting Service. 606 West 120th Street. 280–2035. There is the opportunity to have one of the students live in at your home.
Parents League. 115 East 82nd Street. 737–7385. They have a list of high school students who are interested in babysitting. Maybe one of them lives nearby.

Help for the Elderly. Help for the elderly has become a very important issue. Some young people may not wish to talk about it, and others may not want to think about it. But parents do inevitably grow older and unfortunately do grow less independent. Many years ago, daughters and daughters-in-law were expected to stay at home. Now, many of these daughters and daughters-in-law are working. The problem of taking care of older parents has not diminished, but the problem of where to get the help has increased. The following telephone numbers can serve as a beginning:

Catholic Charities of the Archdiocese of New York. 1011 First Avenue. 371–1000, ext. 2029.
Friends and Relatives of Institutionalized Aged. 425 East 25th Street. 481–4422.
Gericare. 130 West 72nd Street. 873–1887.
Help Line. 532–2400.
Jewish Association for Services for the Aged. 40 West 68th Street. 724–3200.
New York Association for the Blind. 111 East 59th Street. 355–2200.
New York City Department for the Aging. 577–0800.
New York Service Program for Older People. 188 West 88th Street. 787–7120.
New York State Department of Labor. 1515 Broadway. 488–7207.
New York State Office of Mental Health. 496–7760.

Search and Care. 316 East 88th Street. 860–4145.
Selfhelp Community Services. 300 Park Avenue South. 533–7100.
Social Security Administration. 432–3232.
Service Program for the Aging. 340 East 24th Street. 679–0100.
Visiting Nurse Service of New York. 104 East 71st Street. 535–7404.
West Side Ecumenical Ministry to the Elderly. 165 West 86th Street. 362–6772.

Governess. If you have a newborn infant or a child who needs a lot of care and professional attention, you may want to call an employment agency which specializes in child care. (Remember to ask the agency what their fee is.) When you interview the prospective helper, ask for two or three references from families for whom she previously worked. It is very important that you call these references and take a few minutes to speak to them about the person you have interviewed. This will certainly not be time wasted.

Avalon Nurses' Registry. 30 East 60th Street. 371–7222.
London Employment Agency. 767 Lexington Avenue. 755–5064.
Park Avenue Home Employment Agency. 118 East 59th Street. 753–5950.

Housekeeper. It is always best to hire a housekeeper who has been personally recommended. "Word of mouth" is always most reliable. If you live in an apartment building, you can put a notice on the bulletin board or in the mailroom asking if a housekeeper who already works in the building has some free time. If you live in a private house, ask your neighbors and friends. They may know someone who knows someone. If these means do not work, you can always call an agency, specifying what type of person you want.

Maids Unlimited. 767 Lexington Avenue. 838–6282.
Taylor Maid Service. 767 Lexington Avenue. 838–7171.

Chauffeur. If you are interested in hiring a chauffeur, you can hire a uniformed chauffeur with limousine, or you can hire just the chauffeur to drive your own car. The following agencies have hourly as well as daily and monthly rates (gratuities are usually not included).

Fleetwood Chauffeur Agency, Inc. 1 World Trade Center. 524–0440.
Gotham Chauffeurs. 328 East 85th Street. 772–1610.
Regency Chauffeurs. 1980 East Tremont Avenue, Bronx. 751–3200.

Dog Walkers. Dog walkers can be very much in demand, especially if you work and there is no one home to take care of your dog. There is not yet a formal agency that specializes in dog walkers, but you can use your imagination to resolve the problem. If you live in an apartment building, put an announcement in the mailroom or ask the doorman or superintendent. Ask other dog owners if they know someone. If you see a dog walker near your home, ask if that person can take another dog (ask for references and call them). Ask your veterinarian if the office has a list of dog walkers.

POSTAL SERVICES AND TELEPHONE SERVICES

There are several ways to mail your goods in New York, depending on size and urgency. The most traditional way is to drop your letter into one of the mail boxes you will find on every other corner of New York City. Schedules for pick-up are posted directly under the chute. If you need stamps or to register a letter or to certify an envelope or to mail a package, you may need to go to the post office. The main post office for New York City is located in a massive and impressive building at Eighth Avenue and 33rd Street. It is open Monday through Friday, 7:30 A.M. to 5:00 P.M., and has self-service machines which operate 24 hours a day. There are many other branches located throughout New York, and each one may have a different schedule. Those in residential areas may be open Saturday mornings. For further information regarding which post office is located near your home or office, call 971–7731.

If you want to mail a letter in the U.S. which will arrive 24 hours later, you can mail an "Express Letter." Not all branches have this service, however, so call 971–7379 to find out which post office near you can accommodate your needs. United Parcel Service (U.P.S.) can also accommodate special delivery requirements. Call 695–7500 for specific details. There is also an "International Express Mail" service that will deliver a letter or package within two or three days to nineteen foreign destinations.

If you need some time before you get a permanent address in New York and you wish your mail to be delivered directly to the post office, you can rent a mailbox. The boxes come in several sizes, are government-approved, and have locks. You have to go in person to the post office to complete an application, show two forms of identification, and give the names of two personal references. If the post office has no boxes available, you can try a private company, such as:

> Citipostal. 949 Broadway (23rd Street). 460–9550.
> ComCenter. 70 Greenwich Avenue. 807–6077.

Messenger Services. If you want to have a letter or package delivered within the city or neighboring areas, you can dispatch it via a messenger service. They will send a messenger to pick up your parcel and deliver it. They will have the person to whom it is addressed sign for it. Some reputable messenger services in New York City are:

> Air Couriers International: 1–800–528–6070
> Hotline Delivery Service, Inc.: 408–8100

For mailing large packages long distances, you may want to use air cargo, a service provided by all the major airlines and many private companies. They will pick up the package free of charge. Some request payment in cash or by credit card, or, if you have an account, you can charge the fees.

Air Couriers International: 1–800–528–6070.
Hotline Delivery Service: 408–8100.

Telephone Services. There are many public telephones located throughout New York City. One phone call (as of 1984) costs 25¢ to Manhattan and the Bronx – all numbers within the 212 calling area. Some public pay phones are "dial tone first" phones. This means that you hear the dial tone before you insert the coin. Alongside each pay phone there is a complete listing of how to reach an operator (O) and emergency numbers (911), and how to place a long distance, credit card, or collect call. For your first twenty-five cents, you have three minutes in which you can speak. Then the operator will interrupt you and request that you deposit more change for additional talking time.

To call Long Island, you dial 1–516 before the seven-digit telephone number. To call Westchester County and Upstate New York, you dial 1–914 before the number. For New Jersey you use 1–201 before the telephone number, and for Connecticut use 1–203. To call Brooklyn, Queens, and Staten Island, dial 1–718 before the telephone number.

When you make a long distance call, it is possible to "reverse charges" or place a "collect" call. This means that the party you are calling will pay for the telephone call. But they must first approve verbally to the operator. It is also possible to charge the phone call to your home number, if that telephone number is listed in your name, or to your business number.

For telephone information, you dial 411 for a Manhattan telephone number when you are in Manhattan. For the Bronx, also dial 411. For Brooklyn, Queens, and Staten Island, dial 1–718–555–1212. For out-of-town information, dial 1 + area code + 555–1212. For Operator assistance, when in doubt of anything, dial O.

You can send telegrams or cablegrams by telephone and charge the fee to your telephone number. For a telegram, call Western Union (1–800–257–2241) and for a Cablegram call ITT Communications (797–3300) and/or RCA Global Communications.

For calling foreign countries, you can ask the Operator (O) to assist you, or, if you know the particular country's code, you can dial it directly (dial 011, then the country code, then the complete telephone number). For international information, you call 1–800–874–4000. Bell Telephone advertises a special overseas telephone rate. You can call Europe at special prices between 6:00 P.M. and 7:00 A.M. New York time. One minute during this time will cost $1.42, and each additional minute 80¢. You dial the call directly and do without an Operator's assistance to be eligible for the special price.

TELEPHONE ANSWERING SERVICE

Telephone answering services are used frequently in New York City. Answering services either answer your own phone or assign you a number. If they answer your own telephone, they charge you an initial one-time fee to have the telephone company connect your service to their equipment. If you use their telephone number, this is not necessary. Each answering service has several options from which you can choose, and each one offers different types of services. Call the following to compare prices and services:

Allen Business Service: 564–5850
Executive Answering Service: 246–7677
Tel-Anser-Phone: 787–5600

Telephone answering services cost at least $50.00 per month. If you do not want to pay this amount each month, but you still want to receive messages when you are not at home or at the office, the alternative is to buy an answering tape machine. It is not difficult to install it yourself, and, after your initial purchase of the machine, you have no more monthly fees to pay.

How To Have Your Utilities Installed

Telephone. As soon as you know which day you are moving, or which day you will have possession of your new residence, you may want to call the business office of the telephone company and arrange a date for them to install your telephone. You must be at home to show them where you want the telephone(s) and to verify what special options you want. If the painters will be painting your residence before you move in, you may want to arrange the telephone installation then, so that "touch-ups" can be done after the installation. Or you may want to wait a day ot two after you move in, so you'll have a better idea of where your furniture will be.

When you have the telephone put in, you will be charged an installation fee on your first bill. They will also charge you for your "extras." Such extra options can be long distance cords, additional telephones in other rooms with the same telephone number, second or third telephone numbers, color telephones, fancy shapes, extra buttons, technical options, etc. These extras will also appear on each consecutive bill. Ask the specific prices for everything. You may feel it will be cheaper to buy your own telephone equipment and not pay a monthly rental fee to the telephone company. Department stores, appliance stores, and the New York Telephone consumer offices have a wide assortment of telephones for you to buy. Many of them are the same units you would rent from the telephone company.

If you want your telephone number unlisted, or if you want it listed a certain way, specify your wants at the time you make arrangements with the business office and fix a date for installation. They will ask you some questions, even before they put in the phone, to make sure your credit rating is good.

If you want a telephone credit card, inquire about this also at the time of making your appointment for installation. This "calling card" is free and allows you to make telephone calls or send telegrams and cables from any other telephone—public or private—and to have the call charged to your home account or business account. It could be very useful, especially if you use public telephones frequently, and you never have enough coins.

Don't forget to ask at the time of installation for the Yellow Pages classified telephone directory and the regular alphabetical directory. Take a few minutes to become familiar with them. They are invaluable.

Each month you will receive an itemized bill from the telephone company which includes the equipment rental, the basic rate for a fixed number of local calls during the day, and night calls. The bill will also list all of your long distance calls, information requests, lengthy conversations, telegrams, and cables.

Television. In New York City, you most likely do not need a private antenna for your television. All large buildings in New York City have a master antenna on the roof, and its power should be sufficient for all the tenants. Reception in New York is not optimum from these master antennas, however. If you want to improve your reception, you have the choice of installing your own antenna (if the building allows it) or connecting your television to one of the two cable companies described on p. 23. The superintendent of your building will be able to tell you which company to call. The cable services offer you an increased choice of movies, sports programs, and live closed-circuit performances. They charge you an installation fee and a monthly charge according to your options. If you're interested in this, call them and inquire over the telephone about their programs and fees.

Outside New York City, where there is less interference from the skyscrapers, you may get better reception. Yet you may still need to install your own antenna. Cable television may be available in your community. The best person to ask about this is the television repairman in your community whom you will want to contact in any event to help install your television set; that is, if you need an antenna or if your reception is not good.

In the past few years, several video tape machines such as Betamax, VHS, etc. have appeared on the market. These systems allow you to tape television programs, movies, and other video tapes. You connect the video machine to your television set, and you view the video tape on your own television screen. You can most likely connect the video set yourself, or ask the television repairman to do it.

Gas. In New York City, most of the stoves and ovens use gas. If you live in a modern apartment, you may never have to worry about the gas, except to keep your stove burners clean. Gas is not an expensive commodity, and it may or may not be included in your monthly rent. Ask your superintendent what the building's policy is. If you do receive a bill, it will usually come from the electric company, and each utility—gas and electricity—will be listed separately.

Outside of New York City and in residential suburban areas, your gas stove may be fueled by bottled gas which is stored in a tank. For this type of gas you are billed separately by the gas company. To have your gas turned on and off, and to have the account put in your name, find out from the previous tenants, superintendent, or manager of your residence which company you should call.

Some cooking stoves and ovens in suburban homes may be electric. In that case, you will have to call the electric company to make sure your supply continues and that the account has been transferred into your name.

If you live in an apartment in New York City, heating your home is not difficult. Heating is usually "central heating," and when the building heat is turned on during the fall and winter months, you will feel it come through your radiator. The radiator will have a gauge indicating low, medium, and high, and you will be able to regulate it as you wish. Legally, all buildings in Manhattan must provide heat to their tenants from October 1 through May 31 at a temperature of 68° between 6:00 A.M. and 10:00 P.M. and 55° between 10:00 P.M. and 6:00 A.M. Most Manhattan apartment buildings are heated by gas.

In a house, you are on your own. You can leave the thermostat at whatever temperature you please. But be sure that you know what type of heating unit you have (gas, oil, or electric), how to use it, and which company is responsible for your supply and maintenance. Again, call them during the very first days to set up your new account and to ask them for an emergency telephone number and what you should do if the heat goes out on a very cold winter Sunday night.

Electricity. All appliances such as refrigerators, freezers, dish washers, washing machines, dryers, air conditioners, televisions, stereos, and radios, as well as lights and most other modern devices, are run by electricity. Electricity is not cheap, especially for the homeowner who has a lot of appliances. In New York, Consolidated Edison is the electric company. Notify them of your address and of the opening or closing of an account. You will have to go yourself with your lease or contract to begin a new account. Call for the location nearest you (460-4600). Every resident, either in an apartment or private house, has an electric meter for his specific dwelling. In apartment buildings, they are usually located in the basement.

Water. Most Americans drink "tap" water. The water is safe but may taste unpleasant to some people, especially if a particular town's supply has a lot of purifying chemicals which have been added. If this is the case, bottled spring water or mineral water can be bought in supermarkets.

In the city, there is no charge for the use of tap water. In the suburbs there may be a charge, and you may have a water meter near your other utility meters. If this is the case, the water company will bill you directly. Water rates, however, are not expensive.

As anywhere in the world, the water from rivers, lakes, and streams is not for drinking. It is difficult to be sure if these waters are polluted. It is safer not to drink them.

Air Conditioner. In New York City, many of the modern buildings have central air conditioning. That means the building controls the strength of the cool air, and the cool air comes out of the radiator unit. You can turn it on and off, however, as you wish.

In older buildings, or in private homes, there may not be central air conditioning systems. In that case, you may want to install window units. These have to be bought individually by you in appliance or department stores. They are not difficult to install if they fit directly into your window. Be sure of the measurements of your window and of the size of the room or area you want to cool, and relate all this information to the dealer when you buy the units. At that point you can ask him if you can install it yourself or if the store can take care of it. If you plan to take the individual units overseas, double check about voltage and converters.

Air conditioners, be they central or window-set air conditioners, run by electricity. In some New York buildings, you don't pay for this type of electricity; in others you do. You will certainly pay for the electricity if you live in a private house. During the summer, your increased electric bill will give you an idea of how hot the New York area can get.

VOLTAGE EQUIVALENCE

Foreign electricity, rated at 220/240 volts, is different from standard American power, which is 110/120 volts. If you want to take your American-bought appliances to another country, you must use a converter to reduce the foreign electricity and to avoid damaging the appliance. All you need do is plug the appliance into the converter, plug the converter into the wall outlet, and use your appliance.

The wall outlets in some places, such as Great Britain, Germany, Austria, Switzerland, Africa, Hong Kong, South America, and the Caribbean, require a special adapter plug in addition to the converter. You can buy adapter plug sets in hardware stores. They have several plug sizes and shapes, depending on what you need.

Converters come in different sizes, also, depending on the size of the appliance and whether it has a motor (inquire if the speed of the motor will be changed or distorted when you use a converter). For a television you need yet another type of converter, for the converter will have to adapt to another country's television frequencies, which are different from America's.

There are some appliances that already have a built-in converter, and they are marked "dual voltage." When you buy appliances in the United States and plan to take them overseas, it would be advantageous to buy those with dual voltage. Then you won't have to worry about converters or adapter plugs. There are some stores in New York City which deal in special appliances having this dual voltage. Avis Appliances at 239 East 53rd Street (888–7775) and BBS Electronic International at 21 West 38th Street (869–8204). They have an excellent choice of appliances that can be used both in the United States and overseas. Franzus is a company that manufactures converters and adapter plugs. You can contact them for information at 352 Park Avenue South (889–5850).

INSURANCE POLICIES

Insurance is important to have, especially in New York City. If you work for a company or bank, inquire immediately about the types of insurance policies they offer you and your family. If you need supplementary coverage, it is always cheaper to become part of a "group" and to take out "group insurance." Some associations and organizations may offer group policies to their members. The types of insurances which it would be wise to have for your own protection are:

1. *Health insurance.* Inquire if this policy provides coverage for hospital stay, private doctors, dental care, maternity, and your entire family. Children over eighteen years of age may not be included in a family policy. You may have to take out separate policies for them. This may also be the case for a relative who lives with you.

2. *Homeowner's insurance.* It doesn't matter if you live in a rental, co-op, condo, or private house—you should be insured for fire and theft. If you have valuable furniture, jewelry, furs, camera equipment, stereo equipment, televisions, etc., you can ask for a "floater policy." This will insure your personal properties even if they are stolen outside the home, be it in your car or hotel or on the street or somewhere else.

3. *Life insurance.* The two types of policies are "term" and "full life." The insurance broker will be able to explain the differences and recommend which would be best for you. Your company may offer you a policy, but inquire about details. You may want to supplement that coverage or take another policy for the other type of insurance.

4. *Disability insurance.* If you have an accident and you cannot work, this type of insurance will guarantee you and your family a certain level of income per month for a fixed amount of years. It is expensive coverage, but many people believe it is very important, especially if the head of the family depends upon his work for his income.

5. *Automobile insurance.* If you drive a car, you will need automobile insurance. If you rent a car, or if the company rents a car for you, be sure that the coverage is adequate.

6. *Comprehensive liability.* If someone falls or hurts himself at your home, or if your child hurts someone, the victim may sue you and demand you pay damages. This can be expensive if the person takes you to court and wins. Liability insurance will protect you by paying that person for damages. In selecting your various coverages, be sure to inquire about several points.

(a) Do you have enough coverage? With inflation your needs may change.

(b) Do you have a reliable broker? Was he highly recommended? Did you ask your colleagues what type of coverage they have?

(c) Did you ask a lawyer or competent person to review your policies and check to see that your coverage is good?

(d) No insurance company will reimburse you completely for lost or stolen valuables. You will need receipts for the purchase value or appraised value of the valuables you insure.

How To Move "By Yourself"

In Chapter 1, we talked about how to arrange moving from one residence to another. It's always a good idea to plan this at least six weeks in advance, so as to make sure you get the dates you want. Speak to a few moving companies and compare prices. When you tally the hourly rate, consider how many men they will have working and what size truck they use and if they charge you a minimum "travel time."

If you are not going a long distance, or you do not have many belongings, you may want to move "by yourself." This is a very American concept—to do things "by yourself." You can rent a van for the day, or, if you have a car and a small number of belongings, you may just need a trailer. The company will attach the trailer to your car. There are many different sizes of vans and trailers, depending upon your needs. You don't even have to return the van or trailer to the exact same place from which you rented it. Tell them your place of origin and designation. They may have a "drop-off" spot near the town you are moving to. The most reputable companies are the following. Ask them for the location nearest you and reserve what you need a few weeks in advance. In this way you will be sure to have everything arranged beforehand.

U-Haul. 562 West 23rd Street. 562–3800.
Ryder. 624 West 30th Street. 924–9330.
Jartran. 622 West 57th Street. 582–4924.

Shopping

New York City is certainly a shopper's paradise. You can find not only choice and variety, sizes and colors, but the highest quality at the most reasonable prices. New York City can satisfy all tastes. There are the chic boutiques reminiscent of Paris and Rome; the *marchés aux puces* in imitation of the European capitals; and there are the large department stores where you can shop for days, spend all your money, and find everything you need. But what makes New York City really unique are the large number of discount shops which carry high-quality merchandise at very reasonable prices. Often they provide designer clothes, name-brand goods, and one-of-a-kind merchandise. This is the type of store that we will concentrate on here. We will list goods according to their categories and list those shops where you can get the best prices.

New York City is also unique because there are geographical sections of the city where you can buy certain goods. If you are looking for jewelry or antiques, plants or lamps, there are specific streets in New York where you will be able to find groups of stores selling specific merchandise. You will find that information also listed in this chapter.

All stores in New York City will accept travelers' checks. Most stores will accept credit cards—American Express, Diners Club, MasterCard, Visa, Carte Blanche. Many stores will only accept a personal check if your bank is located in New York City and you can show two forms of identification.

All market prices do not include the 8¼% New York sales tax. If you have diplomatic status, however, you are exempt from this tax.

Not all stores will send packages home for you. The large department stores generally do, however. When the store does take care of the delivery, you will be asked to pay additional shipping charges. Their prices are accurate. To take care of your own shipping, you can go to the post office nearest you or call the Post Office Mail Classification Division at 971-7533.

Discount Stores

Women's Discount Clothing

Bolton's. 1180 Madison Avenue at East 86th Street (722-4419). 225 East 57th Street (755-2527). 27 West 57th Street (935-4431).

Damages. 768 Madison Avenue. 535-9030.

European Liquidators. 1404 Second Avenue at East 73rd Street. 879-9140.

First Class. 117 Orchard Street near Delancy Street. 475-8147. Closed Saturday, open Sunday.

Fishkin. 314 Grand Street at Allen Street. 226-6538. Closed Saturday, open Sunday.

Gucci on Seven. 2 East 54th Street. 826-2675.

Loehmann's. 9 West Fordham Road at Jerome Avenue in the Bronx. 295-4100. This store is worth the trip.

S & W. 291 Seventh Avenue. 924-6656.

Women's Discount Shoes
Anbars. 93 Reade Street near Church Street. 227–0253.
Jerri's Shoe and Bag Outlet. 538 Second Avenue at East 30th Street. 889–6491.
Lace-Up Shoe Store. 110 Orchard Street at Delancy Street. 475–8040. Closed
   Saturday, open Sunday.
Shoe Steal. 116 Duane Street at Church Street. 964–4017.

Men's Discount Clothing
BFO. 149 Fifth Avenue at 21st Street. 254–0059.
Barney's. Seventh Avenue and West 17th Street. 929–9000.
Eisenberg & Eisenberg. 149 Fifth Avenue at 21st Street. 674–0300.
Moe Ginsburg. 162 Fifth Avenue at 21st Street. 242–3482.
Lordae Formal Wear. This is for renting tuxedos and smoking jackets. They
   have many branches in Manhattan. Call 597–5100 for the store nearest you.

Men's Discount Shoes
Lord John Bootery. 428 Third Avenue at East 30th Street. 532–2579.
McCreedy and Schreiber. 37 and 55 West 46th Street (719–1552). 213 East 59th
   Street (759–9241).

Children's Discount Clothing
A & G Children's Wear. 261 Broome Street (corner of Orchard and Allen
   Streets). 966–3775. Closed Saturday, open Sunday.
Kleins of Monticello. 105 Orchard Street. 966–1453. Closed Saturday, open
   Sunday.
Little Rascals. 101 Orchard Street. 226–1680. Closed Saturday, open Sunday.
Rice and Breskin. 323 Grand Street at Orchard Street. 925–5515. Closed
   Saturday, open Sunday.

Children's Discount Shoes
Richie's Shoes. 183 Avenue B near 11th Street. 228–5442.

Speciality Stores

Appetizing Stores. New Yorkers love delicatessen foods and smoked fish,
especially for large parties.
Russ and Daughters. 179 East Houston Street near Orchard Street. 475–4880.
   Closed Tuesday.
Barney Greengrass. 541 Amsterdam Avenue at West 86th Street. 724–4707.
   They serve an excellent Sunday brunch.
Schacht. 99 Second Avenue near 6th Street. 475–1232.

Appliances – televisions, dish washers, refrigerators, washing machines, etc.
   Benny's Impex. 51 Canal Street near Orchard Street. 925–7535.
   Eichter Brothers. 70 Canal Street near Allen Street. 925–5750. Closed
      Saturday, open Sunday.
   Kaufman Electric. 365 Grand Street near Essex Street. 475–8313.
   L & J Audio. 3 Hanover Square near William Street. 425–2530.

Bicycles
   Bicycles Plus. 204 East 85th Street. 794–2201.
   14th Street Bicycles. 351 East 14th Street. 228–4344.

Carpets
   ABC Carpet Company. 881 Broadway at East 19th Street. 677–6970.
   Einstein Moomjy. 150 East 58th Street. 758–0900.
   Kaufman Carpet. 26 West 40th Street. 921–5353.

Fabric
   S. Bechenstein, Inc. For women: at 130 Orchard Street near Delancy Street.
      For men: at 125 Orchard Street (475–4525). Closed Saturday, open Sunday.
   Conran's. 160 East 54th Street. 371–2225. Modern fabrics for the home.
   Fabric Warehouse. 406 Broadway near Canal Street. 431–9510. All types of
      fabrics for all purposes.
   Fabrications. 146 East 56th Street. 371–3370. Fabrics for children's rooms.
   Fabric World. 283 Grand Street. 925–0412. They will convert your fabric into
      wallpaper.
   Silk Surplus. 843 Lexington Avenue at East 64th Street. 794–9373. They have
      many locations. Known for their designer quality fabrics such as silks, velvets,
      and tapestries.

Furniture—Contemporary
   A.F.R. The Furniture Rental People. 986 Third Avenue at East 59th Street.
      751–1530. If you want to rent quality furniture.
   Conran's. 160 East 54th Street. 371–2225.
   Decorator's Warehouse. 665 Eleventh Avenue at West 49th Street. 489–7575.
   Foremost Arthur. 8 West 30th Street. 242–3354.
   Mondrian Custom Cabinetry. 1021 Second Avenue at East 53rd Street.
      355–7373.
   The Workbench. 2091 Broadway at 72nd Street (724–3670). 470 Park Avenue
      South at 32nd Street (481–5454). 1320 Third Avenue at 75th Street
      (753–1173).

Photographic Equipment
   A good source for prices is the Arts and Leisure Section of the *New York Times*
Sunday edition. This is the "camera" section, where many of the leading photo
stores advertise their weekly specials. After you get an idea of price and
equipment, the following stores will give you equally fair prices:
   Alket Camera Shop. 866 Third Avenue at 52nd Street. 832–2101.
   Camera Discount Center. 89A Worth Street near Broadway. 226–1014.

Forty-Seventh Street Photo. 67 West 47th Street. 260–4410.
Hirsch Photo. 699 Third Avenue at 44th Street. 557–1150.
Willoughby's. 110 West 32nd Street. 564–1600.

Records and Tapes
Dynamite. 1165 Broadway at 27th Street. 689–8908.
Record Hunter. 507 Fifth Avenue at 42nd Street. 697–8970.
Sam Goody. Many stores at different locations. One of New York's largest
selections is at 1290 Avenue of the Americas at West 51st Street (246–8730).
Tower Records. 692 Broadway. 505–1500; 1965 Broadway. 799–2500.

Sports Equipmnt — general
Herman's. Several stores in New York City: 135 West 42nd Street (730–7400).
845 Third Avenue at East 51st Street (688–4603).
Paragon Sporting Goods. 867 Broadway at East 18th Street. 255–8036.

Stereo Equipment
Crazy Eddie's. Several locations, but the one at 212 East 57th Street has the best
selection. 980–5130; 165 East 86th Street. 427–8800.
Radio Shack. 330 Fifth Avenue at 32nd Street. 244–0444. Many other locations
throughout the city. Call for the one near you.
Tech Hi-Fi. 12 West 45th Street. 869–3950.

Speciality Sections of New York City
Antiques. New York is an antique lover's haven. The antique shopper
can spend days roaming in and out of mysterious stores, looking for the
oddest and oldest trinkets. But if you want to browse in geographical
areas, you will find specific antique "streets" with many shops located on
University Place and Broadway from East 9th Street to East 13th Street
and on Hudson Street from Christopher Street to Arlington Street.

Flowers. This is not London or Nice, but the flowers are indeed
beautiful and fresh. You can find quality and quantity at reduced prices
if you walk on the Avenue of the Americas and West 28th Street.

Hardware. For those who need special hardware, the area to stroll
through is Canal Street from Lafayette Street to West Broadway. In this
multitude of shops you will find what you need. If you get hungry,
Chinatown is to the east of Canal Street. A good lunch or dinner is not
difficult to find. If you get thirsty, Little Italy is to the west of Canal
Street. Some *vino* or *espresso* will make you feel you are in Italy.

Housewares. This category includes all the tools and utensiles you will
need for your kitchen and cooking. Most of the department stores have
excellent quality goods, but, if you are looking for quantity and/or price,
the Bowery area is the place to shop. This is the Bowery and Grand
Street. Many restauranteurs and professional cooks come to this area.

Jewelry. It doesn't matter if you are looking for diamonds or silver, gold or precious stones, antique or modern, watches or rings — West 47th Street from Fifth Avenue to the Avenue of the Americas is the place you should look first. There are hundreds of stalls and shops. You will get different ideas, different prices, and different conversation as you stroll in and out of the well-stocked stalls. Bargaining may be possible. Comparison shopping is a must.

Lamps and Lighting. Department stores have a limited and expensive selection, but, if you are looking for price as well as choice, there is a section in New York just for lighting. The Bowery, from Delancy Street to Grand Street, is the district. You will find all styles for all decors and for all purposes.

Linens. The department stores have linen sales ("white sales") in January and August, and their prices on pillows and bedding goods are excellent. But if you can't wait for these sales, there is a section on the Lower East Side for linens. Grand Street, from Allen Street to Forsyth Streets, offers first quality and designer sheets and goods. They also will make to order bed covers, curtains, and whatever you want for the bedroom, bathroom, and kitchen. Just bring your measurements and a good deal of patience. (Most of the stores in this area are closed on Saturday but open on Sunday.)

Musical Instruments. West 48th Street between Seventh Avenue and the Avenue of the Americas is the street for music lovers.

Notions — which would include buttons, ribbons, lace, ropes, trimmings, etc. — can be found on West 38th Street between Fifth Avenue and the Avenue of the Americas. All you need is imagination, and you will find everything you need for your own creations.

Office Furnishings. If you need desks, file cabinets, and office supplies, it would be worthwhile to visit West 23rd Street between Ninth and Tenth Avenues. All sizes, colors, and qualities of office furniture can be found there.

Plants. It is always surprising to see beautiful trees and green plants in New York City apartments. Perhaps it's because New York gets excellent quality plants from all over the world. You will see beautiful foliage and tree-like plants of the best quality and price on the Avenue of the Americas from West 25th Street to West 30th Street. A stroll on the Avenue will remind you that New York is not devoid of greens.

Markets

Fish. Chinatown is the best area for quality fish of all types. The main streets are Mott Street and Canal Street.

Meat. "Store 48 for Steak," 48 Ninth Avenue at West 14th Street

(924-3043), for the best quality beef, lamb, and pork. Closed Sunday and Monday.

Vegetables. Apart from the excellent quality of the Korean fruit and vegetable stores all over Manhattan, there is a section of New York for vegetables — "Paddy's Market" on Ninth Avenue from West 37th Street to West 42nd Street.

SIZE AND MEASUREMENT EQUIVALENCE

Newcomers to any country are like children when they have to shop. After years of automatically asking for the same shoe size, they have to stop and think and do all types of mental calculations to figure out their "new" shoe size. They find the same problem when they go to the market or butcher and request freshly weighed or sliced food. "How much do you want?" is a good question, but first you have to change from one system to another. It becomes difficult even to take someone's temperature and report to the doctor how sick that person really is. Perhaps the following tables and measurement equivalences can help.

Americans are nearly the last of all people in the world to adopt the metric system. We are in the process of changing over, but, until we do, this table will help you.

Weight

1 ounce (oz.) = 28 grams (g.)
1 pound (lb.) = 16 oz. = 454 g. = 0.45 kg.

| Grams (g.) | 10 | 15 | 20 | 100 | 500 |
| Ounces (oz.) | .36 | .54 | .71 | 3.6 | 18 |

| Ounces (oz.) | ½ | 1 | 8 | 16 |
| Grams (g.) | 14 | 28 | 227 | 454 |

| Pounds (lb.) | 1 | 5 | 10 | 20 | 100 |
| Kilograms (kg.) | .45 | 2.25 | 4.50 | 9 | 45 |

| Kilograms (kg.) | 1 | 5 | 10 | 20 | 100 |
| Pounds (lb.) | 2.20 | 11 | 22 | 44 | 220 |

Temperature

1. To convert Fahrenheit to Celsius (centigrade), subtract 32 from Fahrenheit and divide by 1.8.

2. To convert Celsius (centigrade) to Fahrenheit, multiply Celsius by 1.8 and add 32.

Freezing point = 0° Celsius; 32° Fahrenheit
Normal body temperature = 37° Celsius; 98.6° Fahrenheit
Boiling point = 100° Celsius; 212° Fahrenheit

Liquid Measure
1 liter = 1.06 American pint
1 American quart = .95 liter
1 American gallon = 4 quarts = 3.81 liters
1 liter = .26 gallon

Liquid Measure Abbreviations
t., ts., tsp. = 1 teaspoon (cuillere à café, una cucharilla, una cucharita)
T., tb., tbsp. = 1 tablespoon (cuillere à soupe, une cuchara grande, una cuchara de sopa)
oz. = 1 ounce (ounce, onza, piza)
c. = 1 cup (tasse, taza, copa)
pt. = 1 pint (equals 2 cups and ½ quart)
qt. = 1 quart (quarte, cuarta)
gal. = 1 gallon
fifth = ⅘ quart; this is a unit of liquor
stick = ¼ pound of butter or margarine

Lengths
in. = 1 inch = 2.54 centimeters
ft. = 1 foot = 12 inches = 30 centimeters
yd. = 1 yard = 3 feet = 91 centimeters
1 cm. = 0.39 inch
1 m. = 3.28 feet

Distance
1 mile = 1.609 kilometers
1 kilometer = .62 mile

Cooking Measure
1 teaspoon = 2 liquid grams
1 tablespoon = 6 liquid grams

Oven Settings
140°-250° = low or slow = 70°-121° Celsius
300°-400° = moderate = 150°-205° Celsius
400° and up = high or hot = 205° Celsius and more

Qualities of Food (the best grade on this list appears first)
1. Beef, veal, lamb: U.S. Prime; Choice; Good; Standard.
2. Poultry: U.S. Grades A and B. "Young" or "Broiler" or "Fryer" mean that the poultry is tender. "Mature" means it is tough and you must cook it a lot.
3. Eggs: Jumbo; U.S. Grade; Grade AA; Grade A; Grade B. The quality of the eggs is not related to the white or brown color.
4. Butter: U.S. Grades AA, A and B.

Clothing Sizes — Women
1. Dresses and coats — misses

U.S.A.	10	12	14	16	18	20
British	10	12	14	16	18	20
Continental	38	40	42	44	46	48

2. Dresses and coats — women's

U.S.A.	34	36	38	40	42	44
British	34	36	38	40	42	44
Continental	42	44	46	48	50	52

3. Dresses and Coats — juniors

| U.S.A. and British | 7 | 9 | 11 | 13 | 15 | 17 |
| Continental | 34 | 35 | 38 | 40 | 42 | 44 |

4. Stockings

| U.S.A. and British | 8 | $8\frac{1}{2}$ | 9 | 10 | $10\frac{1}{2}$ | 11 |
| Continental | 0 | 1 | 2 | 4 | 5 | 6 |

5. Blouses, sweaters, slips

| U.S.A. and British | 30 | 32 | 34 | 36 | 38 | 40 |
| Continental | 38 | 40 | 42 | 44 | 46 | 48 |

6. Shoes

U.S.A.	5	$5\frac{1}{2}$	6	7	8	$8\frac{1}{2}$	9
British	$3\frac{1}{2}$	4	$4\frac{1}{2}$	$5\frac{1}{2}$	$6\frac{1}{2}$	7	$7\frac{1}{2}$
Continental	35	35	36	38	$38\frac{1}{2}$	39	40

Clothing Sizes — Men

1. Coats, suits, sweaters, and pajamas

| U.S.A. | 34 | 36 | 38 | 40 | 42 | 44 | 46 |
| European | 44 | 46 | 48 | 50 | 54 | 56 | 59 |

2. Shirts

| U.S.A. | $14\frac{1}{2}$ | 15 | $15\frac{1}{2}$ | 16 | $16\frac{1}{2}$ |
| European | 37 | 38 | 39 | 40 | 41 |

3. Shoes and slippers

| U.S.A. | 8 | $8\frac{1}{2}$ | $9\frac{1}{2}$ | 10 | $10\frac{1}{2}$ |
| European | 41 | 42 | 43 | 44 | 45 |

4. Socks

| U.S.A. and British | $9\frac{1}{2}$ | 10 | $10\frac{1}{2}$ | 11 | $11\frac{1}{2}$ | 12 | $12\frac{1}{2}$ |
| European | 39 | 40 | 41 | 42 | 43 | 44 | 45 |

Americans sometimes use other means to mark and measure their clothing. For women, "petite" means in American terms smaller than size 10. "Small" means size 10 or 12. "Medium" means size 14 or 16. "Large" means sometimes 16 and usually 18. The Americans use half sizes. $14\frac{1}{2}$, $15\frac{1}{2}$, etc., to indicate a stocky, heavy figure. "King size" or "stout size" are men's wear terms used for heavy, tall men. For men such terms as small, medium, and large are also used. Small sizes are for men under size 36 American or 46 European. Medium is for 36–38 American or 46–48 European. Large is for size 40 American and 50 European. Anything larger than that is called "extra large."

Shopping in another country is always difficult at first, but certainly a lot of fun. In all the large department stores in New York City, there is an "international desk." You can always address yourself to the hostess or saleslady there, especially if you are not sure of your English vocabulary. In smaller boutiques or shops, the sales people are always polite and helpful and will be happy to answer any of your questions.

CHAPTER 6

Transportation In and Around New York City

Bus Information
Subway Information
Taxis
A Car in New York City: How To Rent a Car; Some Useful Hints When You Buy a Car; Insurance Coverage and Registration; What To Do When You Have an Accident; When Your Car Is Stolen; When Your Car Is Towed Away in Manhattan; Road Signs and Their Meanings; Parking a Car in New York City
Limousines
Railroads and Out-of-Town Transportation
Airports
New York by Foot
Commuting Options for Forty-Five Suburban Communities Outside New York (see Appendix B)

TRANSPORTATION

GETTING AROUND in the streets of New York City is very simple. Unlike Washington, D.C. with its confusing angled streets and hidden corners, or Boston with its unending streets named after American heroes, or the average American town with the same name for an avenue, a boulevard, or a lane, New York City's streets, for the most part, just have numbers. As you travel in the city, be it by foot, bus, or car, you will recognize several landmarks which will help you find your directions. If you are looking toward the easily recognizable "twin towers" of the World Trade Center, you are looking south. More northerly is Central Park, which separates the city into the East Side and the West Side. The Empire State Building is at 34th Street and Fifth

97

Avenue, the Chrysler Building at Lexington Avenue and 43rd Street, and the Citicorp Building at Lexington Avenue and 50th Street.

While strolling in New York City, you don't need to be an accomplished navigator. If you can identify north, south, east, and west in relationship to the island of Manhattan, you can continue with full sails.

You will soon realize that Manhattan is quite small (26 square miles; 13 miles long and 2 miles wide). No matter how you choose to travel within the city, it won't be difficult. On the contrary, if you have time to walk and look around, you will be perpetually viewing "life as a stage." Many newcomers to New York City prefer walking, if time and weather permit it, for they can leisurely study everything. Every day they can admire a different store, or a different structure, or a different group of people.

Manhattan is a city of "choice." It has been said that one of the good things about New York living is the variety of choices you have for everything. There is even a large choice to the ways in which you can travel within the city. This chapter will give you an idea of the various options.

Bus Information

Most bus stops in Manhattan are marked with red and white "BUS" signs, or rectangularly shaped shelters, or yellow painted areas on the street curbs. Next to the bus stops, there is usually a diagram of that bus's route and the bus number. While you are waiting for the bus, it is a good idea to become familiar with your route. When you recognize your bus approaching, double check the number and enter the bus from the front. You pay the exact fare in coins or subway tokens. Since 1984, the bus fare and the subway fare are 90¢. If you need to take another bus – that is, to transfer buses to go in a new direction – ask the bus driver for a "transfer" as you pay your fare. Transfers are free. There is a reduced fare of 45¢ for senior citizens and handicapped persons. Children under five years old travel free, and school children who travel back and forth to school by bus get a reduced rate. Smoking is not permitted on a bus, nor are bicycles. Collapsible strollers are allowed on buses, but you must have the infant out of the stroller and the stroller folded up before you get on the bus. Animals are not allowed, except seeing-eye dogs and small pets in carrying cases. When you want to get off the bus, you notify the driver to stop at a designated bus stop by pulling a cord above your head or ringing a bell. You can exit from the front or the rear of the bus.

By and large, riding the bus within New York City is more pleasant than riding the subway. Comparatively, the bus is safer, cleaner, and more efficient than the subway. But buses are much slower, especially in traffic and during rush hour. In the evening, they are certainly recommended instead of the subway, especially after rush hour.

For the other boroughs check with the Metropolitan Transit Authority (MTA) at 330–1234 for information regarding which bus or subway you should take from your home to your destination, the schedule, the route, and the fare. Most often the same 90¢ fare will be charged, but, if it is called an "EXPRESS" or "SPECIAL ROUTE," then the fare will be slightly higher. For example, the bus to and from Riverdale in the Bronx to Manhattan costs $2.50 one way, and Bayside, Queens to Manhattan costs $3.00 one way.

If you commute to parts of New Jersey and take the bus, you can call either the New Jersey Transit Company at 1–201–762–5100 or the DeCamp Bus Line at 1–201–783–7500 for information related to routes, schedules, fares, pick-ups, and destinations. For both companies, the destination in New York City is the Port Authority Building at 42nd Street and Eighth Avenue.

If you are interested in traveling out of the city to New Haven, Philadelphia, Boston, Washington, D.C., or other towns, the bus is a very pleasant way to travel and sightsee at the same time. The following companies can help you. Ask them for information regarding their rates, fares, schedules, pick-ups, and destinations.

Greyhound Bus: 635–0800
Port Authority Bus Terminal, Bus Information: 564–8484
Trailways Information: 730–7460

SUBWAY INFORMATION

New York City's subway system, in spite of its hundreds of stations and thousands of miles of railroad track, is not the most efficient nor the most agreeable means of transportation in the world. But it is fast, and during the day it is probably the most practical way to travel if you are going more than one mile. Rush hour in New York is 7:00 A.M. to 9:00 A.M. and 4:00 P.M. to 7:00 P.M. Monday through Friday, and that is when the subway system seems to be the least pleasant. Yet it is quick, for the only place in Manhattan where there is not much traffic during rush hour is underground. Trains run on regular schedules with usually not more than a ten-minute wait between trains.

The subway costs 90¢, the same as a city bus. You need a token to pass through the turnstile. You can purchase tokens at the toll booths in the subway station. It is always a good idea to buy several at one time, since the lines at the toll booths can be long and tiresome. This is especially true on Monday morning. You can also use the same tokens for the bus. In all the subways, there is a reduced fare of 45¢ for senior citizens and handicapped persons, except during rush hour. Children under five years old travel free, and students can get a special fare. Subway trains run every day, including Sundays and holidays, but perhaps not as frequently as during the work week.

There are six main tributaries to New York's subway system. Each one covers a different geographical section of the city and its boroughs. The "local" train makes more stops than the "express" and is slower.

1. *IRT—East Side Line.* This serves the East Side of Manhattan and is also called the Lexington Avenue Line. This is the subway you would use for East 86th Street, Gimbel's, 59th Street, Bloomingdale's, Alexander's, SoHo, Chinatown, Little Italy, Chambers Street, Wall Street, and the Stock Exchange.

2. *IRT—West Side Line.* This serves the West Side of Manhattan and is also called the Broadway Line or the Seventh Avenue Line. In the northerly direction, the local runs to northern Manhattan and the Bronx. In the southern direction, the train goes into Brooklyn.

3. *IND—Sixth Avenue Line.* These are also known as the D and F trains. The D train connects Manhattan with the Bronx, and the F train connects Manhattan and Queens.

4. *IND—Eighth Avenue Line.* These are also known as the A and E trains. The A train connects the West Side of Manhattan with Brooklyn. The E train connects the West Side and East Side of Manhattan with Queens.

5. *BMT Line.* Connects Brooklyn, the West Side of Manhattan, and Queens.

6. *IRT Flushing Line and 42nd Street Shuttle.* The 42nd Street Shuttle runs along 42nd Street from the West Side to the East Side. In this way you can transfer from one subway line to another without paying another token. The Flushing Line also serves as a tributary to Queens from one of the major Manhattan lines. You can get this connection at 42nd Street.

New York City's subway is efficient during rush hour because it is underground and it can get you to your destination quickly. However, it is certainly not the most elegant or secure means of traveling in New York City. Try not to use it after evening rush hour, and be wary of any suspicious characters loitering in the cars or on the platforms.

Another type of train system for New York City is the PATH (Port Authority Trans-Hudson Corporation) train which connects New York City to parts of New Jersey—Hoboken, Jersey City, Harrison, and Newark. This train runs 24 hours a day. During rush hour, the system is so efficient that there is another train every six minutes. For 75¢ each way, commuters can enter New York City at the downtown station in the World Trade Center or uptown at 33rd Street and Sixth Avenue. Commuting with the PATH train is very civilized, and the trip from New Jersey to New York varies from twenty minutes to twenty-five minutes. For more information regarding travel assistance, call 466–7649 or 1–201–963–2558.

TAXIS

New York taxi drivers are a rare breed. They may be playwrights, entertainers, businessmen, or students. They may come originally from the steppes of Russia or the waters of Hong Kong. You can never tell who will be your chauffeur and what life he leads when he is no longer behind that wheel. It is always interesting conversing with a New York taxi driver. They are eager to talk about New York City.

Most often, New Yorkers "hail" a cab when they want one. They raise a hand, wave frantically, and hope an empty cab will see them soon. If the "TAXI" light is on, that means the cab is available. "ON RADIO CALL" light on means that the cab is not available; it has been reserved by someone else. If you need a taxi at a specified time for a specified reason, e.g., to go to the airport at 6:00 A.M. Monday from SoHo, you would be wise to call a private company and reserve a taxi 24 hours in advance. There will be an extra charge, so ask them the price. When the "OFF DUTY" light is on, that means the driver is going home or returning to his garage. He would prefer not to take you in his cab. You may be lucky, however, or, if it's raining or snowing, he may take pity on you; so flag him anyway and see. In semi-unsafe areas, a taxi driver may travel with his "OFF DUTY" light on for security purposes. He may be very happy to pick you up. So again, flag him anyway.

Whenever you enter a taxi, have an idea of where you are going, how you should get there, and how long it should take. Always take a metered, yellow-colored taxi and not a "gypsy" taxi with a livery license plate (the metered taxis are medallion taxis, and they are licensed by the state). Make sure the taxi driver resets the meter as soon as you start your trip. If he "forgets" to reset it, remind him. There are too many stories of visitors, taking taxis from the airport or hotel, whose driver forgets to put the meter on or charges them an outrageous fee to enter the city by taxi. It's an upsetting way to begin your stay. Always take note of the driver's name and taxi number. You can find this information next to the meter on the glove compartment by his photograph.

There is a charge of 50¢ per suitcase, sometimes 50¢ extra after 8:00 P.M., and you reimburse the driver for all tolls. You tip the driver traditionally about 15% of the total fare. If you feel a driver has been unfair to you, take down his name and license number and call the New York Taxi Commission Complaint Bureau at 869-4237.

If you need to reserve a taxi by telephone, the following are a few reputable companies:

> Minute Men: 899-5600
> Love Taxi: 633-3333
> Scull's Angels: 457-7777

Ask them what the extra charge is and how much in advance you must reserve. During rush hour, it may be difficult to reserve a taxi, however, for the taxi companies offer priority to their corporate accounts. For companies and corporations, the taxi companies offer a charge account plan and send their taxis first to accommodate these customers. At the end of each month, the company is billed for the total monthly rides plus a service charge. It may become more expensive than if you just paid per ride, but you have the option of calling for the taxi when you need it, and the corporation can deduct the total monthly bill as an expense.

By and large, taxis are a great luxury in New York City, but, when it is raining or snowing or you are tired or you have walked too much in the city, there is no better feeling than to sit back and marvel at how interesting New York City is while someone else drives.

A CAR IN NEW YORK CITY

How To Rent a Car. Driving a car in New York City is no pleasure. The traffic is unbearable; the roads are full of pot holes; and garage rates are expensive. If you are spending most of your time in Manhattan, it is best to avoid driving a car and to depend on other means of transportation. However, if you commute to work or do business in other towns, having a car may be important. To rent a car may be better for your needs than to own one. This is especially true if your company rents it for you or if you have no time to take care of maintaining a car. (When you rent a car, the automobile leasing company takes care of all repairs and gives you a substitute car until all the repairs are completed. Some companies may even deliver and pick up the substitute car, saving you a great deal of aggravation and time.)

If you want to rent a car there is a certain procedure:

1. Call several auto rental agencies and price the car you want. There are different options. Be sure to note and compare each one. Inquire about their weekly, monthly, and yearly rates, extras for insurance, service, and maintenance.

2. After deciding on which agency you want, call them and ask them where their nearest location is to your home or place of business. In New York City, you have to pick up the car yourself and deliver it also. The agency's location may influence your decision.

3. Reserve the car you want and specify which days, which model, and from which location you will pick up and return the car.

4. At the airport, you can pick up the car and return it more easily than in the city itself. The agencies at the airports are open 24 hours, while in the city they are open from 7:00 or 8:00 A.M. to 10:00 P.M. Don't forget to ask them their working hours.

5. When you pick up your car, you need to show a driver's license (an international driver's license or your valid home license will be sufficient). They prefer if you pay by credit card. If you don't have a credit card, you may have to leave a sizable cash deposit.

6. Check that you have a spare tire, and ask them if you must return the car with a full tank of gas and at what time of day.

The following are several reputable agencies that are good for short-term renting (less than one year):

> Avis: 1–800–331–1212.
> Budget Rent-a-Car. 225 East 43rd Street. 883–0832.
> Econo-Car. 234 East 85th Street. 737–2800.
> Hertz: 1–800–654–3131.
> National Car Rental: 1–800–328–4567.

If you wish to rent a car for more than one year, you can lease directly from the car dealer of your choice. Once you decide on which car you want, check the name and address of the dealers nearest your residence or work and visit them. You can find this information in the Yellow

Pages of the telephone directory under "Automobile Dealers." Price what their plans are for leasing the car you want. Inquire about insurance, extras, maintenance, option to buy, and how long it will take to receive the car.

Some Useful Hints When You Buy a Car

1. If you buy a car in New York or the United States and you have diplomatic status, you do not have to pay federal excise tax. However, in order to take advantage of this option, you must not buy the car from a dealer but directly from the international division of the car manufacturer (any dealer will be able to give you this information upon request).

2. Before you buy a new car, "shop around." Don't buy a car at the "list price." Always try to bargain. Prices may vary from one month to another. After the summer, many dealers are eager to get rid of the present year's cars so as to make room for the coming year's models.

3. If you want to finance a new car, you will probably get a better rate of interest from a savings bank than from the automobile dealer. You are not obliged to arrange the financing through the dealer.

4. If you consider buying a used car, take an auto mechanic with you to inspect it. It may be cheaper to pay him a consultation fee than to buy a bad car. Have the mechanic test-drive the car.

5. There are excellent listings in Sunday's *New York Times* for used cars. There are ads listed by private owners as well as used car dealers.

Insurance Coverage and Registration. Your car must be insured and registered before you are legally able to drive it in New York State.

Any insurance company will take care of automobile insurance. The optimum coverage will include theft, accident, collision, and liability. Your insurance coverage should comply to the rules of the state where you live and where you will be registering your car. Try to use the same insurance company that is taking care of your other forms of insurance. It is more practical to deal with one reputable and recommended company for all your insurance.

In order to register your car, you need to show several papers: proof of ownership; a bill of sale; a "title" if you bought a used car; a Form MV50, which is a receipt for New York sales tax if you bought the car in New York, or a "sales tax clearance"; valid automobile insurance; a driver's license; and your passport if you are not an American resident. You take all these papers to the Motor Vehicles Department. You will have to pay a registration fee which depends on the value of your car. At that point, they will give you a license plate (if you have diplomatic status and want a DPL or FC license plate, you should take your papers to the Secretary of the Society of Foreign Consuls in New York City and not to the Department of Motor Vehicles). In Manhattan, the New York State Department of Motor Vehicles is located at 80 Centre Street at the corner of Worth Street (587–4620).

What To Do When You Have an Accident; When Your Car Is Stolen; When Your Car Is Towed Away in Manhattan. If you have an accident with another car, stop your car immediately and demand that the other driver do the same. Ask him to show you his driver's license, automobile registration, and insurance I.D. card. Write down all the necessary information as well as home telephone number and place of business. Be sure to report the accident immediately to the police and to your insurance company. They will tell you how to proceed further. If the car is rented, report the accident to the rental company.

If your car is stolen, report it to the local police. Call the Operator ("O") and ask for the police precinct nearest to where your car was stolen. You will have to go there to complete some papers. Also, call your insurance company immediately. You may have a provision in your insurance policy that allows you to rent a car for a period of time until they locate your stolen car or until they reimburse you for your loss.

It is best to remember to always lock your car when you park it. Don't keep the registration papers or insurance card in your car but with you. If the car is stolen, you will need the papers. Try not to keep packages in your car — even if it is locked. Packages attract unnecessary attention.

If your radio or any other special equipment should be stolen from your car, report this immediately to the insurance company and to the local police.

If you believe your car was not stolen but was towed away by the authorities, you will first want to call the Police Terminal at the West Side Pier, Traffic Pound (971–0770), to inquire if your car is there. To retrieve your car, you will have to go to Twelfth Avenue and 39th Street. You will need to show proof of ownership, insurance card I.D., registration, and driver's license. You will have to pay the $75 towaway charge in cash, or they will not give you back the car. They also charge you with a parking violation. In addition to the aggravation, inconvenience, and loss of time, to have your car towed away is very expensive. *Be careful. Read all parking signs.*

For information on special parking regulations, traffic, and travel conditions, call 976–2323.

A rectangular sign gives
general information

An octagonal sign
means STOP

A pennant-shaped sign
indicates a
no-passing zone

This sign means
that you are entering a
school area

A triangular sign means
that you must
yield the right of way

A round sign indicates
a railroad crossing

A diamond-shaped sign
warns of a
special hazard

Learn to recognize traffic signs by their shapes

Parking a Car in New York City. Parking a car on the streets of Manhattan, if you can find a spot, is not only frustrating but is also subject to a list of regulations. Yet these rules are always marked and posted on the signs along each street. Before you park your car in the street, be sure you read the signs carefully. Some signs read, "NO PARKING 9–11 A.M. MONDAY AND THURSDAY," and some signs state other restrictions. Always be sure of your days and times. Some streets have meters which allow you to park for periods of time ranging from twenty minutes to two hours. Always be sure the meter works when you put in your coin. If the meter is broken, don't park there. You can get a parking ticket. If you are illegally parked in Manhattan, it is very probable that you will be charged with a parking violation that can cost from $15.00 to $35.00. If there is a red and white "TOW-AWAY ZONE" sign on the same street where you park your car, you may very well be towed away. You will then have to retrieve your car at the Police Terminal at the West Side Pier, Twelfth Avenue and 38th Street. Once you have experienced this ordeal, you will never park your car again in a tow-away zone.

When you are in doubt about being able to park your car legally, the best advice is to park in a garage. There are hundreds of garages, indoor and outdoor, municipal and private, throughout the city. Their fees are always marked according to the day and time. Be sure you check them. Garaging your car in New York City is very expensive. Remember to ask for a receipt. If you use your car that day for business purposes, you can deduct the garage fee from your taxes as a business expense.

If you live in Manhattan and you garage your car regularly, the monthly rate can be very costly. Garages have been known to charge $150 to $300 per month, per car. And for these outrageous rates they have a long waiting list.

Commuters Who Drive a Car To Work. Many people prefer to drive their cars to work rather than depend on the railroad, the bus, or other public transportation. Some drivers, especially those who commute on the Merritt Parkway, benefit from the "free for three" – the free toll for cars that have at least three persons in a car pool. Some commuters need to be flexible with their work schedules and find it impossible to work according to a train schedule. And still other commuters, like those from Rockland County or parts of Westchester County, have no other choice of transportation, and their car is the only solution for commuting.

These commuters must consider what they will do with their car while they work in Manhattan:

1. They can garage it near their place of work, but that can be very expensive, especially if the commuter must pay.

2. They can garage the car in areas of New York City that are less expensive than mid-town. Such areas have low "garage real estate value": very west near Ninth Avenue, very east near York Avenue, or very north in the 90's and 100's.

3. Some people may look for even cheaper areas in which to park, in Queens (Long Island City or Astoria), the Bronx (Yankee Stadium or Riverdale), and upper Manhattan (Columbia University and Washington Heights). They may be able to park their cars on the street, if the parking sign allows it, or find a reasonably priced garage with day rates.

4. Then they can take a bus or subway to their office. If the "car commuter" has time to spare for such schemes, energy for such maneuvers, then it certainly will reduce the expense of commuting by car.

LIMOUSINES

Needless to say, there is no better way to travel in New York City than by limousine, especially if you travel with an expense account or you can decuct all fees for business purposes. Limousines can be hired by the hour or day, week or month. You can arrange for a driver and car to take you to the theatre or evening's event and then pick you up at an arranged time. You can hire just the chauffeur and supply your own car, or you can hire the chauffeur and car. You can pay by credit card or check. Prices range from $25 to $50 per hour, excluding tips and tolls. Call for the necessary information:

Farrell's Limousine Service: 988–4441; 861–6300
Fugazy Continental Corporation: 426–6600 (most reasonable rates)
Limousine Service: 279–1710
London Towncars: 988–9700

RAILROADS AND OUT-OF-TOWN TRANSPORTATION

If you should want to go to Westchester or Connecticut or Long Island, Philadelphia, Washington, D.C., or the New Jersey shore, you may want to travel by railroad or bus. This is a very pleasant way to travel, allowing you time to sightsee, relax, and read, all at the same time.

Trains leaving from New York City depart from either Grand Central Terminal (East Side at 42nd Street and Lexington Avenue) or Pennsylvania Station (West Side at 34th Street and Eighth Avenue). Trains departing from Grand Central serve Westchester County, Upstate New York, and Connecticut. Trains departing from Pennsylvania Station (known as Penn Station by New Yorkers) serve Long Island and the entire east coast of the United States from Florida to Canada, as well as Pennsylvania, New Jersey, and Washington, D.C.

Call first to check schedules, fares, and reservations. Some useful telephone numbers are:

Amtrak (for Pennsylvania, Washington, D.C., et al.): 1–800–USA–RAIL
Long Island Rail Road: 739–4200 or 1–516–222–2100
Metro-North (for Connecticut, Westchester, etc.): 532–4900
PATH (for New Jersey): 1–201–963–2558 or 466–7649
Greyhound Bus (for many destinations): 635–0800
Trailway Bus: 730–7460

Airports

New York's international airport is John F. Kennedy International Airport. It is a difficult and confusing airport, but less so than many other international airports throughout the world. Give yourself a good hour to check in before your flight's departure, and be prepared to be patient. You will have to pass through Customs, Immigration and Public Health, and to answer many questions. But, by and large, people are helpful, the airport is very well organized, and there are many multilingual hosts and hostesses. Signs are sometimes in both Spanish and English, and throughout the airport there are information booths where translators are extremely helpful. If you have any major problem, it is best to go to the ticket booth of the airline with whom you are traveling. They will speak your language and be helpful.

If you can avoid using Kennedy Airport, especially when you travel within the United States you will save yourself time and trouble. Try to book your reservation for LaGuardia Airport, which is considerably closer to Manhattan, smaller in size, and less confusing. Newark Airport is also an international airport, but it is located in New Jersey. From Manhattan, it can take you more than an hour to get to Newark Airport and vice versa. However, if you are nearer to New Jersey than to New York, and your flight can leave from Newark, it may be a good idea to use Newark Airport.

Each airport, be it Kennedy International or LaGuardia or Newark, is very well equipped with courtesy phones in all terminals. There are many banks, currency exchanges, travel insurance booths, stamp machines, credit card cash machines, information desks, restaurants, emergency care facilities, hotel reservation desks, and multi-lingual hostesses. Each airport is well equipped and well staffed.

Getting into Manhattan from each airport is not difficult, providing it is not midnight or a snowy Sunday evening. There are several options:

1. Private limousine is the most comfortable but also the most expensive way to enter New York City. You can reserve it when you arrive at the airport terminal. The advantage of this mode of travel is that you can find out the fee ahead of time, and you waste no time at all in arriving at your destination.

2. Taxis. As you leave the terminal building, you will see a sign: "TAXIS." At this designated area, there is a dispatcher who will make sure that your taxi driver understands where you are going, how much it will cost and if he is an authorized driver. Before you look for a taxi, it is a good idea to find the dispatcher and allow him to arrange your drive into the city. In this way, there will be no misunderstanding between you and the driver. At Kennedy Airport, the dispatcher hands you a card containing information about your ride from the airport to your destination. If you have any problems, there is a telephone number written on the card which you can call.

3. Bus service runs between LaGuardia and Kennedy Airports and the East Side Airline Terminal in Manhattan at 37th Street and First Avenue. For more information call Carey Bus Service at 632-0500.

4. There is also a way to enter Manhattan by subway from LaGuardia and Kennedy Airports. It is the most economical way. If you don't have many suitcases, it may also be the fastest way. But it is a little confusing, and, after a long trip, it is not the best way to terminate your travels. If you do choose this mode of travel, though, you can get all the information you may need from the ground hostess at the airport or at the information desk.

Whichever means of transportation you choose for entering New York City, be patient and be prepared to continue your voyage just a little farther.

NEW YORK BY FOOT

If you have time and you feel strong, the best way to see New York City is by foot. There is no city in the world which is easier for the pedestrian. Navigating in New York City, with its very logical and numbered streets, is perhaps the most interesting part about being in the

City. There is always a crowd to observe, a store to admire, and a beautiful structure to study. New York City is a perpetual show, and the pedestrian can participate by passing through and penetrating into the varying, dynamic sections.

Numbered Streets. New York City is divided geometrically. If you are located at 8th Street, you know you are south. The numbered streets progress in numerical order, one after the other. Many of the streets are designed for one-way traffic. They alternate, one street carrying eastbound vehicles, and the following street westbound. The main thoroughfares for two-way traffic are 14th, 23rd, 34th, 42nd, 57th, 72nd, 79th, 86th, and 96th streets.

Avenues run north and south and intersect at right angles with the streets.

East Side, West Side. New York is divided into two sides, East Side and West Side. Fifth Avenue and Central Park are the dividing lines. Building addresses are numbered according to their proximity to Fifth Avenue. On the East Side, for example, one might begin with 1 East 77th Street, 115 East 77th Street (which is further away from 5th Avenue), and so on. On the west, they may start with 10 West 77th Street, followed by 204 West 77th Street (farther away from Fifth Avenue or Central Park West on the West Side).

There are some areas of New York which are not as easily identifiable, as in the old section of the city at the southern tip of Manhattan. They do not have numbered streets or avenues. Each street has a name, or their numbered streets are not in numerical order. The best advice for one visiting this quarter is to carry a good map and to refer to it often. For all other sections of Manhattan, if you know where east and west, north and south are, you will always be able to find your way. Compared to Paris, Athens, Lisbon, or Rome, navigation in New York City is easy, and it is certainly a lot of fun.

PART III

Schools for Students of All Ages

CHAPTER 7

Public Schools in New York City

Advantages and Disadvantages of the New York Public School System
How To Find the Public School in Your District
Elementary School Programs for Gifted Children; Outstanding High
*   Schools in New York City*
General Telephone Numbers for Public Schools in Manhattan
Public High Schools in the Five Boroughs (see Appendix D)

ADVANTAGES AND DISADVANTAGES OF THE NEW YORK PUBLIC SCHOOL SYSTEM

WITHIN Manhattan proper, there are many different types of public schools, enrolled in by different types of students, founded on varying pedagogical philosophies, and comprised of faculties with diverse backgrounds. In the past several years, the public schools have re-evaluated their curriculums and have raised their academic standards. Students' reading scores have increased by two grade levels, and mathematical skills have improved. The over-all picture of New York's public education has changed, and many parents are reassessing their neighborhood schools.

The advantages of the public schools in New York City are several:

1. Students represent a microcosm of New York City. They all come together from different cultures and traditions to achieve a common goal: education. Their heterogeneous backgrounds add to the entire educational process. Parents and students bring into the classroom generations of different cultures, with the common aim of helping one another.

2. Parents are very active in the P.T.A. (Parent-Teachers Association). They help in fund raising and participate in school activities—academic as well as social and cultural.

3. In several of the elementary schools, there is one class for each grade composed of "gifted" children. These children receive special attention and are allowed to accelerate their studies on an individual basis.

4. There are special public schools for children who have specific learning problems (see the list in this chapter). The teachers are trained accordingly, and the curriculum is altered to accommodate the student.

5. There are several public high schools that specialize in one field of study such as science, math, dance, music, drama, technology, vocational skills, etc. The teachers in these schools are trained specialists, and students are admitted based on test results and achievement.

6. Public schools are tuition free. (Private schools can cost $2,000 to $6,500 per student, per year.) All children who live in the school district are automatically accepted to the school. There is no interview or testing, except for the specialized high schools.

To make the over-all picture more complete and objective, we present the negative aspects as well:

1. The average classroom has thirty students. Private schools have an average of ten to twenty students in each classroom; in the early grades, the teacher in the private school may have an assistant.

2. Sometimes the overcrowded classroom does not have enough books, supplies, desks, lockers, cafeteria facilities, or gym equipment.

3. There is a limited number of extra programs. (Private schools have well-endowed computer programs, science labs, orchestras, sports facilities, etc.) There is a limited number of special teachers such as reading specialists, math tutors, librarians, music, art, and dance instructors.

4. The curriculum is usually traditional, with a limited choice of electives and non-academic programs. Cultural enrichment and advanced courses may be more extensive in private schools.

How To Find the Public School in Your District

The best way to be sure of your school district is to call up the information headquarters of the Board of Education at 596-5030 and ask them to connect you to "Zoning." Tell the person at "Zoning" the address where you live and ask them which is your school district. Ask which elementary schools, junior high schools, and high schools are in this district and the location for each. Then go to that particular school with your child and register the child. You will need to fill out some papers, relate information about your child's medical history, and show the child's birth certificate or passport. All children five years old or more are required to attend school.

If your child has a specific problem regarding education, then one of the following telephone numbers may be useful:

Center for Multiple Handicapped Children: 369–3134
Deaf and Hard of Hearing Special Education: 349–5701
Special Education: 596–8929
Visually Impaired Special Education: 349–6907

If you know your school district, you may want to call the office directly for information regarding addresses of schools, public transportation, registration, etc.:

School District 1, District Office. 80 Montgomery Street. 577–0200.
School District 2, District Office. 210 East 33rd Street. 481–1640.
School District 3, District Office. 300 West 96th Street. 678–2800.
School District 4, District Office. 319 East 117th Street. 860–5858.
School District 5, District Office. 433 West 123rd Street. 690–5863.
School District 6, District Office. 665 West 182nd Street. 690–8900.

ELEMENTARY SCHOOL PROGRAMS FOR GIFTED CHILDREN

According to the City's annual reading scores and SAT (Scholastic Achievement Test) results, the two best elementary schools in Manhattan are P.S. 158, located on York Avenue between 78th and 77th Streets, and P.S. 6, located on Madison Avenue between 81st and 82nd Streets. Both schools have small classes for gifted children and are well endowed with supplies, equipment, and services for all their students. Parents of the students are actively involved in maintaining the high standard of scholastic achievement.

Manhattan is divided into school districts. Each district corresponds to a neighborhood. Considering the neighborhoods in which these two excellent elementary schools are located, one would correctly surmise that the students come from upper-middle-class environments. The real estate in these neighborhoods is correspondingly expensive. To rent an apartment, and especially to buy an apartment, in these areas is costly.

One pays for the option to use the public facilities. If you are planning to move into one of these two neighborhoods and you are interested in taking advantage of the public elementary school, before you sign a contract with a real estate agent or before you commit yourself to an apartment, call up the public school and verify that your address is within its school district.

The following list is an excellent reference for P.S. 6 and P.S. 158. If your home address appears on this list, then your child is eligible to attend that public school.

P.S. 6 — District Addresses. 45 East 81st Street. 737-9774.

Street	Odd Numbers	Even Numbers
East 91st	None	2-98
East 90th	1-65	2-74
East 89th	1-67	2-74
East 88th	1-57	2-123
East 87th	1-125	2-122
East 86th	1-137	2-128
East 85th	1-125	2-132
East 84th	1-133	2-170
East 83rd	1-175	2-170
East 82nd	1-167	2-180
East 81st	1-171	2-170
East 80th	1-187	2-188
East 79th	1-185	2-142
East 78th	1-129	2-138
East 77th	2-133	2-140
East 76th	1-141	2-136
East 75th	1-123	2-130
East 74th	1-135	2-140
East 73rd	1-133	2-142
East 72nd	1-125	2-140
East 71st	1-135	2-140
East 70th	1-133	2-136
East 69th	1-129	2-128
East 68th	1-99	none
Fifth Avenue	878-1098	(Odds and evens)
Madison Avenue	813-1271	814-1272
Park Avenue	681-1075	680-1130
Lexington Avenue	1143-1235	928-1320
Third Avenue	None	1392-1488

P. S. 158 — District Address. York Avenue and 77th Street. 744-6562, 744-6563.

Street	Odd Numbers	Even Numbers
East 87th	None	500-554
East 86th	501-533	500-554
East 85th	501-533	500-536
East 84th	501-533	500-534
East 83rd	501-625	500-544
East 82nd	501-625	500-544

East 81st	501–537	500–518
East 80th	501–525	500–544
East 79th	501–533	300–554
	425–435	
East 78th	301–539	300–522
East 77th	301–523	300–520
East 76th	301–519	300–520
East 75th	301–519	300–520
East 74th	301–519	300–520
East 73rd	299–511	None
East End Avenue	1–91	2–154
First Avenue	1361–1509	1370–1496
Gracie Square	None	1–12
Gracie Terrace	1	None
Second Avenue	None	1404–1510
York Avenue	1377–1491	1370–1644

Please note that these lists are subject to change. Please verify with the school before signing a lease.

Another excellent public elementary school is Hunter College Elementary School at 71 East 94th Street. Admission to this school (Nursery School to Twelfth Grade) is based on testing, not residential location. The competition for available places at Hunter is very fierce. You may need to apply when your child is three years old and hope that he scores at the very top percentile. It is best to call the school for specific information about applying and testing: 860–1259.

Outstanding High Schools in New York City. There are several excellent secondary schools that are public and available to all residents of the five boroughs. They are rated academically as high as many of the private schools in New York City. Since these public high schools charge no tuition, there are many students who would like to attend them. The policy is to accept only those students who are best qualified. Most students are accepted for the first year of high school (Ninth Grade) and remain in the same school for four years until they graduate (the exception to this is Hunter, which is also an elementary school).

The academically oriented schools such as Stuyvesant High School and Bronx High School of Science require their applicants to take a test the year before they wish to attend the school. Those students who score in the highest percentile are accepted. The artistically oriented schools – the Julliard School of Music, for example, or the High School of Music and Art – request that their students "audition" in the form of dance, drama, or music or present a "portfolio" of art work in conjunction with an interview.

If you have an artistically gifted or unusually bright child,then one of the following schools is highly recommended. Call up the school and speak to the principal's office regarding the procedure for admission and testing.

Bronx High School of Science. 75 West 205th Street, Bronx. 295–0200.
Brooklyn Technical High School. 29 Fort Greene Place, Brooklyn. 858–5150.
Chelsea Vocational High School. 131 Sixth Avenue. 925–1080.
Fiorello H. LaGuardia High School of Music and Art. West 135th Street and Convent Avenue. 926–0870.
High School of Art and Design. 1075 Second Avenue. 688–4430.
Hunter High School, Park Avenue and 94th Street. 860–1267.
Julliard School of Music. Lincoln Center Plaza. 799–5000.
Manhattan Vocational and Technical High School. 320 East 96th Street. 369–0770.
New York School of Printing. 439 West 49th Street. 245–5925.
School of Fashion Industries. 225 West 24th Street. 255–1235.
School of Performing Arts. 120 West 46th Street. 819–0197.
Stuyvesant High School. First Avenue and 15th Street. 673–9030.

General Telephone Numbers for Public Schools in Manhattan

Adult Education. 596–6196
Bilingual Office (Spanish and English). 690–8920
Center for Multiple Handicapped Children 369–3134
Continuing Education 799–6565
Deaf and Hard of Hearing Special Education 349–5701
High School Equivalency 596–6196
Information Headquarters 596–5030
Occupational Training Center 675–7926
Public Transportation 392–8855
School Volunteers Unit 921–5620
Special Education 596–8929
Visually Impaired Special Education. 349–6907
Zoning Information. 596–6113

CHAPTER 8

Private Schools
in New York City

Advantages and Disadvantages of the Private Schools
Application, Testing, and Interview
Tuition
Listing of Each Private School in New York City with Address,
    Telephone Number, Name of Headmaster or Headmistress, and
    Enrollment Figure
Pre-Nursery and Nursery Programs
Information Agencies for Counciling and Guidance
Private High Schools in New York City (see Appendix E)

ADVANTAGES AND DISADVANTAGES OF THE PRIVATE SCHOOLS

NEW YORK CITY is the extended campus for more than a hundred private schools, and each private school is different from its neighbor. Some schools are traditional in philosophy — students wear uniforms, concentrate on the three R's, and address their teachers formally; other schools are more liberal — students wear sneakers and jeans, choose their own programs from a wide gamut of courses, and joke with their teachers. Some schools are unisex — all boys or all girls; others are co-ed. Some schools include nursery programs; others begin with the first grade. Some extend their grades throughout high school; and others prepare their students for boarding schools. Some schools have indoor swimming pools, outdoor tennis courts, sophisticated computer rooms, well-endowed science laboratories, fully equipped libraries, and unending facilities for music, dance, and art studios. Whatever type of education you want your child to have, you can get it in New York City.

The only problem is that there are many students applying to the New York City private schools and sometimes the schools do not have enough spaces for all applicants. Consequently, even if you know what school you want for your child, there is no guarantee that the school wants your child. Perhaps this is the most frustrating element about the New York City private school system. To give you a complete picture of the New York City private schools, let's look at the advantages and the disadvantages.

Advantages

1. The total number of students in each class is controlled. Students get individual attention. There is a reading specialist on staff, tutors, and a wide gamut of specialty teachers and teacher assistants.

2. Teachers give regular reports to parents about students' progress. Teachers and parents communicate often and maintain a close working relationship.

3. If a student needs extra help, this is often arranged as part of the school program. If a student wants to accelerate or work independently, this, too, is easily arranged.

4. Students learn a lot. There are unending facilities, exciting electives, and up-to-date equipment. During the last year of high school, some students can take "advanced placement" (AP) courses, which are the same courses given to college freshmen.

5. There are after-school programs, sports teams, clubs, enrichment programs, and tutorial classes. Many times there is no extra fee for these activities, or the fee is nominal. All students can participate in these extra programs.

6. Schools offer scholarships and/or financial aid to families who have difficulty in paying the tuition. (Many of the private schools claim that at least 10% of their students receive financial aid or scholarship money.)

Disadvantages

1. Private schools in New York City are very expensive. Nursery programs for two-year-olds can cost between $2,000 and $3,000 per child, per year. Elementary school can cost $3,000 to $6,000. High school can cost even more.

2. Students work hard and compete with one another. In many schools, the acquisition of high grades is very important. Sometimes the grade becomes more important than the act of learning.

3. There are a good number of students in the private schools who come from very wealthy families (this can be viewed as an advantage or

disadvantage). Students' economic backgrounds sometimes influence their goals, attitudes, and behavior.

4. The schools ask overtly for contributions in addition to the tuition. Some schools are more aggressive and verbal than other schools in this request.

APPLICATION, TESTING, AND INTERVIEW

Each school has a grade into which it is easiest to enroll your child. This is usually the grade with which the schooling begins, such as Nursery or Kindegarten or First Grade; or the grade with which the school expands its facilities and enrollment, such as Seventh or Ninth Grade. It is always advisable to apply your child to the grade for which the school accepts a large number of new students. Otherwise, you will have to pray for an unexpected opening and have your child compete with many other students who covet the same opening. Traditionally, one applies before December of the previous year for admission. If you are interested in applying your child for First Grade admission for, say, September 1986, then the wisest procedure would be in September or October 1985 to call up the school and ask them for an application. You will need to fill out the application, pay a processing fee, supply the school with references and past school transcripts.

The next step is to arrange for your child to be tested by the Educational Records Bureau (E.R.B.), 3 East 80th Street (535-0307). The E.R.B. is a non-profit educational institution. Its testing programs are used in schools to assess the aptitude and achievement of individual students. All students older than four years are requested by the private schools to take this uniform test, which is only given by the Educational Records Bureau. When the student cannot read, as in the case of Nursery and Kindegarten children, the test is verbal. They test the child's I.Q., natural intelligence, ability to concentrate, and reading readiness. For primary grades, the test is longer, written, and divided into several sections: natural intelligence, reading, and mathematics. As the students get older, they take Standard Achievement Tests (S.A.T.s) which last several hours. All tests administered by the E.R.B. are corrected within a week. Copies of the grades and percentiles are sent to the schools to which the child is applying and to the child's parents. These test results are used by the private school as a guideline for admission and as part of the student's application.

Two weeks after your child takes the E.R.B. test, call the school(s) and ask the Director of Admission if your child's folder is complete. A complete folder should consist of:

1. Complete and signed application.
2. Check for application fee.
3. Letters of recommendation.
4. E.R.B. test results.
5. If the student attends school, the present school should send a copy of the child's transcript and a letter of recommendation from the Director. (If you apply to more than one school, be sure each school has a complete folder for your child.)

Once the folder is complete, you should make an appointment for an interview.

The child's interview should not be a dramatic ordeal. All New York children who attend private schools pass through this experience. Paradoxically, many of them fare better than their parents. Some hints and suggestions to make the procedure less threatening are:

1. Ideally, both parents should attend the interview with their child. Arrange times carefully so that everyone will have 1½ hours free for a tour and interview. Your child may have some further testing.
2. Dress accordingly. The child should not wear jeans or sneakers.
3. Study the school's bulletin before the interview so that you understand the school's philosophy, aims, and curriculum.
4. Come prepared with a few intelligent questions.
5. Parents should allow their child to ask questions and participate in the interview.
6. All rules of courtesy, etiquette, and good manners should be observed and applied.
7. Try to show your family unit as a strong one, wherein each member is interested in the education and development of the child.

TUITION

Most private schools will inform the parents by letter, no later than March 15, if the child has been rejected, accepted, or is on a waiting list. (If you receive no information by March 15, call the Office of Admission.) If the child is accepted, the school will ask you to sign a letter or to contact the school if you are still interested in sending your child to that school. Within a very short period of time, they will send you a contract for the new school year. When you sign the contract, you will have to include a deposit—usually $100 to $500. If this deposit is non-refundable, they will specify the details. The first tuition payment is due during the summer; they will send you the necessary information. Usually you pay one-half or two-thirds of the tuition before September; the balance is due in January or February. In addition, the scholarship office will send you a letter, or contact you during the year, for a donation. This is optional.

If you cannot afford the fees for tuition, call up the school's Accounting Office and make an appointment to speak to someone regarding financial aid. All this information is kept confidential. No one, not even your child, needs to know about your financial arrangements with the school. Many schools will have a well-endowed scholarship fund. No social stigma or additional responsibilities are imposed upon the student or parents if a student receives financial aid.

The listing below of New York City private schools specifies useful data that can serve as a guideline to understand the overall picture of New York City's unique private school system. For each school, we have included the amount of tuition costs per academic year. This figure does not include fees, which can total $100 to $1,000 extra per child per year, excluding suggested amounts for donations and contributions to the scholarship fund. Fees are calculated to include the student's use of books, supplies, physical education equipment, hot lunch, Parents-Teachers Association membership, tutorial programs, or any other extra expenses the school may incur for the year. When inquiring about tuition costs, remember to ask each school about their additional fees.

The prices we have mentioned for tuition range from the youngest grade of the school's enrollment to the highest grade. Most schools have a graduated tuition scale. As the student gets older, the school day becomes longer, the extra classes of laboratories and computers become more numerous, and, thus, tuition becomes more costly. Accordingly, fees will vary from one grade to another.

NEW YORK CITY PRIVATE SCHOOLS

Alexander Robertson School
    3 West 95th Street   Enr. 80 $2,900
    New York, N.Y. 10025   Co-ed   all grades
    663–6441   Gr. 1–6
    Rev. Thomas Wilson, Headmaster

Allen-Stevenson School
132 East 78th Street   Enr. 300 $4,700
New York, N.Y. 10021   Boys   1st Grade
288–6710   Gr. 1–9 $6,300
Desmond F.P. Cole, Headmaster   9th grade

Anglo-American School
18 West 89th Street   Enr. 300 $5,500
New York, N.Y. 10024   Co-ed   kindergarten
724–6360   Gr. K–12 $6,600
Paul Beresford-Hill, Headmaster   12th grade

Baldwin School of New York
160 West 74th Street   Enr. 170 $5,940
New York, N.Y. 10023   Co-ed   7th grade
873–4900   Gr. 7–12 $6,798
Daniel Kimball, Headmaster   12th grade

Bank Street School for Children
610 West 112th Street   Enr. 450 $4,250
New York, N.Y. 10025   Co-ed   nursery
663–7200   Gr. N–8 $5,150
Joan Cenedella, Director   12th grade
Betsy Hall, Admissions

Barnard School
554 Fort Washington Avenue   Enr. 150 $2,400
New York, N.Y. 10033   Co-ed   kindergarten
795–1050   Gr. K–12 $4,000
Eunice Latham, Headmistress   12th grade
Gloria Galle, Admissions

Birch-Wathen School
9 East 71st Street   Enr. 385 $4,025
New York, N.Y. 10021   Co-ed   kindergarten
861–0404   Gr. K–12 $6,425
Dr. Byron Wright, Headmaster   12th grade
Robert Kiessling, Admissions

Brearley School
610 East 83rd Street   Enr. 620 $4,700
New York, N.Y. 10028   Girls   kindergarten
744–8582   Gr. K–12 $6,700
Evelyn Halpert, Headmistress   12th grade
Jane Marshall, Admissions

Browning School
  52 East 62nd Street   Enr. 325 $4,640
  New York, N.Y. 10021   Boys   kindergarten
  838–6280   Gr. K–12 $6,300
  Charles Cook, Headmaster   12th grade
  Basil Campbell, Admissions

Buckley School
  113 East 73rd Street   Enr. 375 $4,600
  New York, N.Y. 10021   Boys   kindergarten
  535–8787   Gr. K–9 $6,050
  Brian R. Walsh, Headmaster   9th grade

Caedmon School
  416 East 80th Street   Enr. 150 $2,700
  New York, N.Y. 10021   Co-ed   nursery
  879–2296   Gr. N–6 $4,450
  Dr. Paul Czaja, Director   6th grade

Calhoun School
  433 West End Avenue   Enr. 430 $2,650
  New York, N.Y. 10024   Co-ed   nursery
  724–2308   Gr. N–12 $6,250
  Dr. Neen Hunt, Director   12th grade
  Sybil Schwartz, Admissions

Carnegie Hill School
  12 East 96th Street   Enr. 125 $4,125
  New York, N.Y. 10128   Co-ed   nursery
  289–6771   Gr. N–6 $5,525
  Mr. Rodman G. Pellett,   6th grade
    Headmaster

Cathedral School
  1047 Amsterdam Avenue   Enr. 200 $4,500
  New York, N.Y. 10025   Co-ed   kindergarten
  865–8400   Gr. K–8 $6,025
  Richard W. Ackerly, Headmaster   8th grade

Chapin School
  100 East End Avenue   Enr. 607 $4,600
  New York, N.Y. 10028   Girls   kindergarten
  744–2335   Gr. K–12 $6,500
  Mildred Berendsen, Headmistress   12th grade
  Mary Schumacher, Admissions

Churchill School
22 East 95th Street   Enr. 80 $9,000
New York, N.Y. 10028   Co-ed   all grades
722–0610   Gr. K–8
Mary Newmann, Director

Collegiate School
241 West 77th Street   Enr. 540 $4,800
New York, N.Y. 10024   Boys   1st grade
873–0677   Gr. 1–12 $5,900
Dr. Richard F. Barter,   12th grade
    Headmaster
James P. Jacob, Admissions

Columbia Grammar and
Preparatory School
5 West 93rd Street   Enr. 496 $4,025
New York, N.Y. 10025   Co-ed   kindergarten
749–6200   Gr. K–12 $5,616
Richard Soghoian, Headmaster   12th grade
Erika Ben-David, Admissions

Convent of the Sacred Heart
1 East 91st Street   Enr. 460 $3,600
New York, N.Y. 10028   Girls   nursery
722-4745   Gr. N–12 $6,400
Sister Nancy Salisbury,   12th grade
    Headmistress
Rozanne Edmondson, Admissions

Corlears School
324 West 15th Street   Enr. 100 $2,450
New York, N.Y. 10011   Co-ed   nursery
741–2800   Gr. N–6 $4,200
Marion Greenwood, Director   6th grade

Dalton School
108 East 89th Street   Enr. 1240 $5,100
New York, N.Y. 10028   Co-ed   nursery
722–5160   Gr. N–12 $7,300
Dr. Gardner Dunnan, Headmaster   12th grade

The Day School
4 East 90th Street   Enr. 340 $2,800
1 East 92nd Street   Co-ed   nursery
New York, N.Y. 10028   Gr. N–8 $5,950
369–8040   8th grade
John Dexter, Headmaster
Caroline M. Tripp, Admissions

Dwight School
402 East 67th Street Enr. 320 $6,100
New York, N.Y. 10021 Co-ed for all grades
737–2400 Gr. 7–12
Stephen H. Spahn, Headmaster
Constance Spahn, Elizabeth
 Callaway, Admissions

Ethical Culture Schools
Dr. H.B. Radest, Director
Mrs. Marilyn Herman, Admissions

Midtown School Enr. 500 $4,900
33 Central Park West Co-ed nursery
New York, N.Y. 10023 Gr. N–6 $5,775
874–5205 6th grade
Jane Southern, Principal

Fieldston Lower School Enr. 300 $4,900
Fieldston Road and Manhattan Co-ed nursery
 College Parkway Gr. N–6 $6,150
Riverdale, N.Y. 10471 6th grade
543–5000
David Schwartz, Principal

Fieldston School Enr. 700 $6,975
Fieldston Road and Manhattan Co-ed 7th grade
 College Parkway Gr. 7–12
Riverdale, N.Y. 10471
543–5000
Kenneth Barton, Principal

The Fleming School
10 & 35 East 62nd Street Enr. 425 $3,725
New York, N.Y. 10021 Co-ed nursery
752–3025 Gr. N–8 $5,500
Ray-Eric Correa, Director 8th grade

Friends Seminary
222 East 16th Street Enr. 550 $4,670
New York, N.Y. 10003 Co-ed kindergarten
477–9500 Gr. N–12 $5,840
Joyce McCray, Principal 12th grade
Ellen Stein, Admissions

Gateway School
921 Madison Avenue Enr. 30 $8,930
New York, N.Y. 10021 Co-ed for all grades
628–3560 Upgraded
Davida Fishbein, Director 5–10 years
Elaine Segal, Admissions

Grace Church School
86 Fourth Avenue	Enr. 309	$3,400
New York, N.Y. 10003	Co-ed	Nursery
475–5609	Gr. N–8	$5,900
Kingsley Ervin, Headmaster		8th grade
Caroline Pelz, Admissions		

Hewitt School
45 East 75th Street	Enr. 334	$4,400
New York, N.Y. 10021	Girls	Kindergarten
288–1919	Gr. K–12	$6,300
Agatha K. Crouter, Headmistress		12th grade
Lucy Littlefield, Admissions		

Horace Mann–Barnard Schools
231 West 246th Street	Enr. 885	$6,500
Bronx, N.Y. 10471	Co-ed	all grades
548–4000	Gr. 7–12	
Michael Lacopo, Headmaster		
Gary Miller, Admissions, High School		

Horace Mann–Barnard Elementary	Enr. 480	$5,100
	Co-ed	kindergarten
4440 Tibbett Avenue	Gr. K–6	$5,850
Bronx, N.Y. 10471		6th grade
(Mailing address: 231 West 246th Street, Bronx, N.Y. 10471)		
960–0600		
Norman F. Fountain, Principal		
Nancy Schulman, Admissions		

Horace Mann School for Nursery Years	Enr. 200	$4,100
	Co-ed	nursery
55 East 90th Street	Gr. N–K	$5,300
New York, N.Y. 10028		kindergarten
369–4600		
Rosemary Hutchinson, Director		

Lenox School
170 & 154 East 70th Street	Enr. 350	$4,145
New York, N.Y. 10021	Co-ed	kindergarten
288–4778	Gr. K–12	$6,425
Colin Reed, Headmaster		12th grade
Joan Miller, Admissions		

Little Red School House
196 Bleecker Street Enr. 200 $3,675
New York, N.Y. 10012 Co-ed nursery
477–5316 Gr. N–7 $5,035
James Rein, Director 7th grade
Jean Lince, Admissions

Elisabeth Irwin High School
40 Charlton Street Enr. 130 $5,175
New York, N.Y. 10014 Co-ed 8th grade
477–5316 Gr. 8–12 $5,500
James Rein, Director 12th grade
Mary Alfano, Principal

Loyola School
980 Park Avenue Enr. 190 $4,100
New York, N.Y. 10028 Co-ed all grades
288–6200 Gr. 9–12
Father James Fox, Headmaster

Lycée Français de New York
3 East 95th Street Enr. 950 $3,000
New York, N.Y. 10028 Co-ed nursery
369–1400 Gr. N–12 $5,225
Maurice Galy, President 12th grade
Mme. Cerisoles, Admissions
There are several locations in the City for the different grades, such as 72nd Street and Fifth Avenue.

Manhattan Country School
7 East 96th Street Enr. 188 Sliding scale
New York, N.Y. 10028 Co-ed tuition for
348–0952 Gr. N–8 all grades
Augustus Trowbridge, Director

McBurney School
15 West 63rd Street Enr. 300 $5,400
New York, N.Y. 10023 Co-ed 7th grade
362–8117 Gr. 7–12 $6,150
Lawrence Pallamy, Headmaster 12th grade
Scott White, Admissions

Marymount School
1026 Fifth Avenue Enr. 320 $3,700
New York, N.Y. 10028 Girls nursery
744–4486 Gr. N–12 $6,200
Sister Kathleen Fagan, RSHM, 12th grade
 Headmistress
Miss Barbara Scott, Admissions

Montessori Family School
   323 East 47th Street   Enr. 125 $3,600
   New York, N.Y. 10017   Co-ed   nursery
   688–5950   Gr. N–6 $3,900
   Lesley Haberman, Headmistress   6th grade
   Ann Reed, Admissions

New Lincoln School
   210 East 77th Street   Enr. 300 $4,100
   New York, N.Y. 10021   Co-ed   kindergarten
   879–9200   Gr. K–12 $6,100
   Verne Oliver, Director   9th grade–
                                                          12th grade

Nightingale–Bamford School
   20 East 92nd Street   Enr. 470 $5,000
   New York, N.Y. 10028   Girls   kindergarten
   289–5020   Gr. K–12 $6,600
   Mrs. Edward B. McMenamin,   12th grade
      Headmistress
   Patricia Wainwright, Admissions

Professional Children's School
   132 West 60th Street   Enr. 215 $4,370
   New York, N.Y. 10023   Co-ed   4th grade
   582–3116   Gr. 4–12 $5,280
   Carol M. Lane, Director   12th grade
   Twinky Otis, Admissions

Ramaz School
   (Upper School)   Enr. 900 $2,725
   60 East 78th Street   Co-ed   nursery
   New York, N.Y. 10021   Gr. N–12 $6,000
   427–1000   12th grade
   Rabbi Joshua S. Bakst, Dean
   Ruth Ritterband, Headmistress

   (Lower School)
   125 East 85th Steet
   New York, N.Y. 10028
   Rabbi Mayor Moscowitz, Head,
      Judaic Studies
   Sandee Brickman, Head, General
      Studies
   Daniele Lassner, Admissions

Rhodes School
212 West 83rd Street   Enr. 220 $5,300
New York, N.Y. 10024   Co-ed   6th grade–
787–4300   Gr. 6–12   8th grade
Donald Nickerson, Headmaster $5,800
         9th grade–
         12th grade

Riverdale Country School
5250 Fieldston Road   Enr. 990 $4,900
Bronx, N.Y. 10471   Co-ed   nursery
549–8810   Gr. N–12 $7,200
Roger Boocock, Headmaster   12th grade
Scott Reed Smith, Admissions

Robert Louis Stevenson School
24 West 74th Street   Enr. 125 $9,500
New York, N.Y. 10023   Co-ed   all grades
787–6400   Gr. 7–12
Lucille Rhodes, Director

Rodeph Sholom Day School
10 West 84th Street   Enr. 250 $2,990
New York, N.Y. 10024   Co-ed   nursery
362–8800   Gr. N–6 $5,895
Mr. Irwin Sclachter, Director   6th grade
Alice Barzilay, Admissions

Nursery School   Enr. 100 $2,990
7 West 83rd Street   Co-ed   nursery
362–8800
New York, N.Y. 10024
Bernice Kaufman, Director

Rudolf Steiner School
15 East 79th Street   Enr. 300 $2,940
New York, NY. 10021   Co-ed   nursery
535–2130   Gr. N–12 $5,075
Raymond Schlleben,   12th grade
  Administrator
Diana Bethke, Admissions

St. Bernard's School
    4 East 98th Street   Enr. 335 $4,765
    New York, N.Y. 10029   Boys   1st grade
    289-2878   Gr. 1-9 $6,075
    Richard H. Downes, Headmaster   9th grade
    Elizabeth H. Forster, Courtney G.
      Iglehart, Admissions

Saint David's School
    12 East 89th Street   Enr. 380 $3,240
    New York, N.Y. 10028   Boys   nursery
    369-0058   Gr. N-8 $5,860
    David D. Hume, Headmaster   8th grade
    Richard Dryzga, Admissions

St. Hilda's and St. Hugh's School
    619 West 114th Street   Enr. 525 $2,750
    New York, N.Y. 10025   Co-ed   nursery
    666-9645   Gr. N-12 $4,675
    The Rev. Mother Ruth,   12th grade
      Headmistress
    Dr. Louise Lee Nettler,
      Admissions

St. Luke's School
    487 Hudson Street   Enr. 200 $3,200
    New York, N.Y. 10014   Co-ed   nursery
    924-5960   Gr. N-8 $4,500
    Barbara Belknap, Principal   8th grade

St. Michael's Montessori School
    225 West 99th Street   Enr. 140 $2,350
    New York, N.Y. 10025   Co-ed   nursery
    663-0555 $2\frac{1}{2}$-12 $4,000
    Ravi Romano, Director   years   7th grade

Searing School
    20 West 23rd Street   Enr. 50 $10,800
    New York, N.Y. 10010   Co-ed   all grades
    929-5454   Gr. 6-12
    Elizabeth Duda, Head

Spence School
    22 East 91st Street   Enr. 525 $4,860
    New York, N.Y. 10028   Girls   kindergarten
    289-5940   Gr. K-12 $6,740
    Eve Gilbert, Headmistress   12th grade
    Teresita S. Currie, Admissions

Town School
540 East 76th Street   Enr. 350 $3,000
New York, N.Y. 10021   Co-ed   nursery
288–4383   Gr. N–8 $6,200
Mrs. Gillian duCharme,   8th grade
  Headmistress

Trinity School
139 West 91st Street   Enr. 930 $6,630
New York, N.Y. 10024   Boys,   kindergarten
873–1650   K–12 $7,545
Dr. Robin Lester, Headmaster Co-ed,   9th grade–
G. Wells McMurray, Admissions K–4, 9–12   12th grade

United Nations International School
24–50 East River Drive   Enr. 1460 $3,100
New York, N.Y. 10010   Co-ed   kindergarten
684–7400   Gr. K–12 $5,500
Robert Belle-Isle, Director   12th grade
Barbara Chlanda, Admissions
There is another school in Jamaica, Queens (380–5260).

Village Community School
272 West 10th Street   Enr. 245 $3,730
New York, N.Y. 10014   Co-ed   kindergarten
691–5146   Gr. K–8 $4,630
Sheila Sadler, Director and   8th grade
  Admissions

Walden School
1 West 88th Street   Enr. 535 $2,800
New York, N.Y. 10024   Co-ed   nursery
787–5315   Gr. N–12 $6,300
Stephen Clement, Director   12th grade

York Preparatory School
116 East 85th Street   Enr. 385 $5,900
New York, N.Y. 10028   Co-ed   6th grade
628–1220   Gr. 6–12 $6,300
R. P. Stewart, Head   12th grade·
Mrs. Clark, Admissions

Pre-Nursery and Nursery Programs

There are several excellent private pre-nursery programs for children aged six months to three years. They combine the theory and practice of play groups and day care centers. Some programs are held two times a week, two or three hours each day. Other programs are longer. Some pre-nursery and nursery programs are small programs that are part of the larger, ongoing school, such as at Town School, Dalton, and Horace Mann. If you are interested in applying your child to one of these three schools, it will certainly be easier if you first enroll him in the pre-nursery or nursery program. If you are looking only for a pre-nursery or nursery program, then the most practical thing to do is to find a qualified program near your home. The following list represents toddler programs in New York City. Call them for information regarding availability of space, application, interview, etc.

Toddler Programs (Under Three Years)

All Souls School. 1157 Lexington Avenue (79th Street). 861–5232. Ages 2½–6.

Brick Church. 62 East 92nd Street. 289–4400. Ages 2–6.

Broadway Presbyterian. 601 West 114th Street. 749–4635. Ages 2 yrs. 9 mos. to 5 yrs.

Brownstone School and Day Care Center. 128 West 80th Street. 874–1341. Ages 2–10.

Central Synagogue. 123 East 55th Street. 838–5122. Ages 2–5.

Child Development Center. 120 West 57th Street. 582–9100. Ages 2–6.

Children's All Day School. 109 East 60th Street. 752–4566. Ages 6 mths. to 6 yrs.

Christ Church Day School. 520 Park Avenue. 838–3036. Ages 2–5.

Columbia Greenhouse Nursery School. 424 West 116th Street. 666–4796. Ages 2–5.

Elisabeth Seton. 1175 Third Avenue (68th Street). 879–2215. Ages 2 yrs. 3 mos. to 5 yrs.

Emanu-el Midtown Nursery. 344 East 14th Street. 674–7200. Ages 2–6.

Epiphany Community Nursery School. 1393 York Avenue (74th Street). 737–2977. Ages 2–5.

Episcopal School. 35 East 69th Street. 879–9764. Ages 2–6.

First Presbyterian Church Nursery School. 12 West 12th Street. 691–3432. Ages 2½–4.

International Play Group. 330 East 45th Street. 371–8604. Ages 6 mos. to 6 yrs.

Learning Environments for Children. 593 Park Avenue (64th Street). 421–3282. Ages 2–6.

Madison Presbyterian Day School. 921 Madison Avenue (73rd Street). 288–9638. Ages 2–6.

Marble Hill School. 5470 Broadway (West 230th Street). 562–7055. Ages 2 yrs. 9 mos. to 6 yrs.

Medical Center Nursery School. 60 Haven Avenue (169th Street). 568-0564. Ages 2 yrs. 9 mos. to 6 yrs.

Merricat's Castle. 316 East 88th Street. 831-1322. Ages 2-5.

Montessori Family School. 323 East 47th Street. 688-5950. Ages 18 mos. to 12 yrs.

Multimedia Preschool. 40 Sutton Place (59th Street). 593-1041. Ages 2½-6.

Park Avenue Christian Church Day School. 1010 Park Avenue (84th Street). 535-5012. Ages 2½-6.

Park Avenue Synagogue Early Childhood Center. 50 East 87th Street. 369-2600. Ages 2-5.

Red Balloon. 560 Riverside Drive. 663-9006. Ages 2-6.

Riverside Church Weekday School. 490 Riverside Drive (120th Street). 749-7155. Ages 2½-6.

Rockefeller University Children's School. 1230 York Avenue (64th Street). 570-8580. Ages 2 yrs. 9 mos. to 6 yrs.

Roosevelt Island Day Nursery. 545 Main Street, Roosevelt Island. 752-1754. Ages 2 yrs. 9 mos. to 6 yrs.

Temple Emanu-el Nursery School. One East 65th Street. 744-1400. Ages 2½-5.

Temple Israel Early Childhood Learning Center. 112 East 75th Street. 249-5000. Ages 2½ + .

Town School. 540 East 76th Street. 288-4383. Ages 2-13.

Union Theological Day Care Center. 527 Riverside Drive (122nd Street). 663-5930. Ages 6 mos. to 5 yrs.

West End Collegiate Playschool. 368 West End Avenue (77th Street). 787-1566. Ages 1½-4.

William Woodward, Jr. Nursery School. 436 East 69th Street. 744-6611. Ages 2-4.

YM and YWHA Nursery School. Lexington Avenue and 92nd Street. 427-6000. Ages 2-5.

Nursery Program (three, four and five years old)

The schools that are listed for the Toddler Programs also have Nursery Programs. Refer to both lists.

Acorn School. 330 East 26th Street. 684-0230. Ages 3-5.

Bellevue South Nursery School. 10 Waterside Plaza (25th Street). 684-0134. Ages 3-5.

Community Nursery School. 28 East 35th Street. 686-2699. Ages 3-6.

Dalton School. 108 East 89th Street. 722-5160. Ages 3-17.

Horace Mann Nursery Years. 55 East 90th Street. 369-4600. Ages 3-5.

Jack and Jill School. 209 East 16th Street. 475-0855. Ages 3-6.

Mandell School. 127 West 94th Street. 222-1606. Ages 3-5.

New York Hospital Nursery School. 435 East 70th Street. 472-6859. Ages 3-4.

Park Avenue Methodist Church Day School. 106 East 86th Street. 289-6997. Ages 3-5.

St. Bartholomew Community Preschool. 109 East 50th Street. 751-1616. Ages 2-5.

Spuyten Duyvil Infantry. 3041 Kingsbridge Avenue. 549-1525. Ages 3-4.

Tompkins Hall Nursery School. 21 Claremont Avenue. 666-3340. Ages 3-5.

West Side YMCA Co-Op Nursery. 5 West 63rd Street. 787-4400. Ages 3-6.

INFORMATION AGENCIES FOR COUNSELING AND GUIDANCE

1. A.W.S. — American Welcome Services (734-9210). This organization has all information related to schools — private and public, applying, testing, and interviewing. They have extensive information on all activities, cultural programs, and sports-related activities for children of all ages.

2. E.R.B. — Educational Records Bureau, 3 East 80th Street (535-0307). All children who apply to New York private schools need to take the uniform entrance exam administered by the E.R.B. As soon as you receive an application for a private school, you should call the E.R.B. office and make an appointment for your child to be tested. Within one week you should have the results. You can make an appointment with a consultant from the same office, for an additional fee, to discuss the results and interpretation of the test. At the same time they will advise you about schools for your child, based on the child's test scores.

3. Parents League of New York, 115 East 82nd Street (737-7385). They are very good for obtaining information about private schools, camps, after-school activities, babysitters, and all other information related to your children. For the annual membership fee of $18.00, you can make appointments for private consultation to discuss testing, interviewing, and applying for schools.

CHAPTER 9

Boarding Schools on the Eastern Coast of the United States

Advantages and Disadvantages of Boarding Schools
Application
Financial Aid
Agencies for Further Information

ADVANTAGES AND DISADVANTAGES OF BOARDING SCHOOLS

M ANY parents who are not satisfied for one reason or another with the New York private day schools send their children to boarding schools. The student lives in a dormitory or house at the school, dines with the other students, attends classes, and participates in sports and extra-curricular programs. On weekends, students remain at school. They may participate in programs or attend classes. They do their homework at the library or enjoy their free time with colleagues. During vacations, students return home to spend the holidays and summers with their families.

To give you a better picture of what a boarding school is, we have analyzed the advantages and disadvantages of the system.

Advantages

1. Students learn excellent study habits. They are taught individually how to study and how to organize their free time. Their study time is supervised, and all assignments are checked by a member of the faculty.

2. Classes are very small, on the average of five to twenty students in a class. There is a great deal of extra individual attention. Teachers and supervisors can extend the school day for a student who needs tutoring, special attention, or acceleration.

3. The child learns to develop independently. Since the family is not

139

near, the child makes decisions, may make mistakes, learns, and matures accordingly. The child becomes very responsible.

4. Friends and peers inherit the role of family. Children learn to get along with all types of people. They are exposed to a more heterogeneous group of students than in the traditional private day schools. They learn to get along with faculty members and authority figures. There is a set of rules that must be observed and upheld.

5. Foreign students who want to receive an American education enjoy living with other students. Most boarding schools have a percentage of foreign students.

6. Parents who travel extensively may find it advantageous to have their child supervised and taken care of by a very competent faculty and school.

7. Sports activities and programs may be more extensive at a boarding school than at a day school. Most boarding schools are located on large campuses in rural settings and have excellent sports facilities. Not many urban day schools can offer skiing or ice skating on campus.

Disadvantages

1. Some students are not mature enough to live away from their families. They may have a difficult time resolving their own problems.

2. Some students may experience loneliness and isolation.

3. Boarding schools may be more expensive than private day schools. At the boarding school you pay for room and food in addition to the tuition.

4. It may be difficult for the faculty and staff to supervise each child all day and all night. Some students may take advantage of their new freedom and the absence of parental authority.

Deciding to send a child to boarding school is a very important decision. It is necessary that the entire family, including the child, agrees on this decision. Parents should try to be objective about their child's needs, capabilities, and level of maturity before they dispatch the child to live and study away from home. It is advisable to seek the counseling of a professional to get a very complete picture of the specific school being considered.

APPLICATION

The process of applying to a boarding school is the same as applying to Manhattan's private day schools. Inquire specifically about what type of entrance tests are required. Is the interview on campus? How many letters of recommendation are needed? What information is needed to make the student's folder complete? Each school has different requirements. Satisfy each school individually.

FINANCIAL AID

Most boarding schools have significant amounts of financial aid, some awarding as much as $1,000,000 annually. These funds are available not only to lower income families but to middle and upper income households. Some schools that are very well endowed, such as Phillips Academy, provide assistance to families with incomes of up to $60,000.

Most boarding schools use the Parents' Financial Statement, which is completed by the parents and then processed by the School Scholarship Service in Princeton, New Jersey. Based on an analysis of income, expenses, assets, and liabilities, the S.S.S. will make a recommendation to the boarding school concerning the amount a parent should be expected to contribute toward the child's tuition.

If the family's financial situation changes after the application has been sent in and filed, the parents should feel free to discuss the need for financial aid. Schools do not base their decisions of acceptance or rejection on the family's ability to pay. Indication of intent to apply for financial aid does not affect the admissions decision or the student's responsibilities once admitted.

SOURCES OF FURTHER INFORMATION

1. Parents League of New York, 115 East 82nd Street (737-7385). They are very good for giving information about boarding schools as well as private day schools. For the annual membership fee of $18.00, you can make appointments for private consultation to discuss testing, interviewing, and applying to boarding schools.

2. Advisory Service on Private Schools, 18 East 41st Street (696-0499). This agency gives information about private day schools as well as boarding schools.

3. The Peterson's *Annual Guide to Independent Secondary Schools,* Princeton, New Jersey, gives a detailed analysis of the private boarding schools in the United States and abroad. The book has been compiled from information submitted by each school. There is information about financial aid, tuition plans, military schools, schools with religious affiliations, schools for students with special needs, etc. This book is very helpful for all families and students who are interested in boarding schools.

CHAPTER 10

Universities and Colleges

Admissions Policies, Application, Interviews, Tests
Tuition and Expenses
Scholarships and Financial Aid
Why Are the Major Universities in New York Famous?
Where Can You Find the Best Programs in New York for
    Specific Studies?

ADMISSIONS POLICIES, APPLICATION, INTERVIEWS, TESTS

To enter an American university is a major project. It takes time, planning, and money. For some Americans, it is the culmination of their education and of their dreams; for others, it's just the beginning. For the foreigners who study in the United States, it becomes even more special. The realm and the depth of their education spreads to the intangible. It's the exposure to a different way of living. Students, American or foreign, who want an American college education, must make their plans a year or two before they plan to attend college. Each step should be carefully understood and executed.

The first question to ask is: Which college do you wish to attend? The gamut of choice is overwhelming. There are large universities with impressive campuses, unending facilities, modern equipment, varied programs, and several degrees and diplomas. There are urban colleges that embrace an entire city as the campus. And there are small, protective rural schools, where individual attention is not a luxury but a common part of the curriculum.

142

The next question to ask relates to programs and courses of study. It's a good idea to be familiar with what courses are required for specific areas of concentration. In this way, you can better assess your own capabilities and compare them with your academic goals. Other questions, perhaps less scholastic but equally important, should be considered. Do you want to live in a student dormitory or have your own apartment? Do you like large lecture classes or individual tutoring and private seminars? Is the library an important factor? Do you need foreign books, art studios, computers, science labs for your area of concentration? Make a list of priorities and try to match the college with the list.

When an American student applies to colleges, he is advised by his guidance counselor to apply to at least three choices. The first choice may be within his capabilities. The second choice should be attainable. The third choice should be the "safe" choice. This is a good guideline to follow.

The first step in your investigation is to write to the Office of Admissions of several schools for their bulletins and to ask for an application. Take note of the deadline for applications and testing dates. All high school transcripts, letters of recommendation, tests, essays, and applications should be completed and put on file by a certain date. If you have the opportunity to visit the college, you should try to do that also. Sometimes, by visiting the college and speaking to students and faculty members, you will have a clearer idea if the school is for you.

At the time you visit the college, you should arrange an interview with the Director of Admissions. At this time, you can ask questions and learn more about programs of study and college life. Many colleges require an interview, either on campus or off campus. If you can't visit the school, an alumnus or faculty member may interview you at your high school or home. Whichever way you decide, you should be sure of the deadline for the interview.

Some students are very set on a specific college. They have known for years that a certain school is their "first" choice. If this is the case, inquire if that college has an "early decision" policy and apply early. You will also need to take the standardized tests early.

Standardized tests can include the S.A.T. (Scholastic Aptitude Test), Achievement Tests, English Composition Test of the College Board, and Test of English as a Foreign Language (T.O.E.F.L.). This last test is required of all foreign students. Standardized tests are used frequently by colleges and universities in the United States as a means to evaluate applicants. They are by no means the only criterion or the ultimate means of judging a student, but are accepted as one of the tools for assessment.

They are also used by the colleges to place freshmen in English classes. All these standardized college board tests are given frequently during the school year, either at a student's high school, testing center, or American Embassy. It is best to inquire specifically the dates and location. Reservations are necessary, and one must include a check for the test. The S.A.T. costs $10.50 or $11.00, and the Achievement Tests cost from $16.75 to $18.25. There is a guidebook for taking these tests which also includes some sample examinations. If your high school does not have these books, write to the main testing center for them. This information is invaluable.

There are some courses available to prepare the student for these College Board Standardized Tests. Stanley Kaplan's Center is just one of the many programs available. American students understand the importance of scoring well on these tests, and American businessmen are satisfying this market.

The Scholastic Aptitude Test (S.A.T.) is composed of two sections: a verbal section and a mathematical section. The verbal section consists of multiple-choice questions and is designed to test students' understanding of what they read and the extent of their vocabulary (studying vocabulary lists beforehand could help). The mathematical questions test students' ability to solve problems involving arithmetical reasoning, algebra, and geometry. The S.A.T. score level ranges from 200 to 800 on both sections. Many schools will mention in their booklets what their students "usually" have scored prior to admission. This gives the applicant some guidelines. The Ivy League schools usually like to see scores above 650 in both sections.

Achievement tests are designed to test students' knowledge in specific academic areas. The Office of Admissions will specify which achievement tests are required.

After the major preoccupation of applying, being interviewed, and tested, the student and family must next consider a very important subject — finances and expenses.

TUITION AND EXPENSES

An American college education can be very expensive. Some families begin saving for their children's college when they are just toddlers. Trust funds and custodial accounts are set up by parents and grandparents to cover the exorbitant costs of an American college education.

There are some families that even choose where they will live based on the fact that some cities or states offer very good college educations to their residents at nominal fees. California is such a state. California's fine universities are very reasonably priced at $200 for the yearly tuition as compared to a private university such as Stanford University, in the same state, which charges $10,105 for its annual tuition and housing.

New York State is another example. The State Universities of New York are considerably less expensive than the private universities. The State University of New York at Stony Brook costs $1,155 for the annual tuition for New York State residents (housing is extra). Columbia University is ten times more expensive at $10,052 per year.

Other State Universities are also less expensive compared to private institutions. Arizona State University charges $650 for the year's tuition and fees for Arizona residents (non-residents are not much more expensive at $1,475). And New Mexico State University can cost $744 for a resident student and $2,256 for a full-time non-resident. One must add housing, food, books, and supplies to these figures. Choice of housing facilities includes on-campus dormitories or apartments that may not be on-campus. In the case of the latter, transportation costs must also be considered.

City Universities, like State Universities, are also inexpensive. New York City has many such institutions, undergraduate as well as graduate, in all the five boroughs. The City University of New York at Queens College charges $1,260 a year for a state resident and $1,650 for a non-state resident. The City University of New York, Hunter Campus, is $925 a year for a state resident and $1,425 for a non-resident (of course, the classes are larger than they would be at Barnard College or Marymount Manhattan College).

Not only are the New York City Universities inexpensive, but they are relatively easy to enter. For the past ten years, they have had an admissions policy called "open admission." All residents of the City can enter the college if they have graduated from high school. Grades and test scores do not become a competitive factor.

Privately owned colleges and universities are different. They are difficult to enter, and they are expensive. New York University charges $8,820 for its annual tuition. Yale is $10,340. Princeton is $10,045. Columbia University is $10,052, etc., etc. The prices are high, and they seem to get more and more expensive each year.

SCHOLARSHIPS AND FINANCIAL AID

Yet the situation is not so bleak. The concept of scholarships and financial aid in the American universities is a common one. Aid is available to all students, to the wealthy as well as to the less wealthy. One out of every three students at Harvard received a scholarship last year, and the school has listed more than 5,000 part-time jobs on and off campus. Low-interest loans, which do not have to be paid back until after graduation and after the student begins work, are also available to all students at American colleges. There is no shame, no social stigma against the student who works part-time to help pay for tuition or books. On the contrary, it is a status. And many jobs are located on the college campus.

Some colleges offer a College Work-Study Program, which is a federal program through which students may work for pay in non-profit agencies.

When the student applies for admission, he may also apply for financial aid. It must be remembered, however, that a student's acceptance or rejection to the college does not depend upon the family's ability to pay. A student will not be penalized for submitting a financial aid form along with the application.

If an applicant applies for scholarship or financial aid, he may be required to submit a family financial statement and a federal income tax form. A student over 21 years old may be legally and financially independent of the family and can then submit an independent financial statement and income tax return. At the time of completing the financial aid application, take note of the deadline. If it is submitted late, the student may not be eligible for financial aid.

The foreign student may apply directly to the American university for financial aid, scholarships, or work-study options. But the student may also apply to the foreign educational programs unique to his country. His Embassy will provide all information related to which scholarships and stipends are available.

WHY ARE THE MAJOR UNIVERSITIES IN NEW YORK FAMOUS?

New York City has become the international capital of not only banking, finance, art, design, and media, but of education as well. Many students who want to study in the United States come first to study in New York—rightly so, for their entire educational experience is completed and complemented by the rich cultural and artistic life New York City can offer. Fifty years ago, Columbia University was the most popular and the best known university in New York for foreign students.

But today, New York University and Pace University are equally appreciated. All three major universities have excellent housing facilities for foreign students. Foreign undergraduate 'and graduate students get priority for rooms in the dormitories. If a student attends classes full-time (a minimum of twenty hours per week), the student is eligible for a student visa. A good number of foreign students come to New York with such visas. Each year the visa must be renewed, and the student must continue to matriculate as a full-time student.

If a student just wants to study the English language, he can enroll full-time at one of the English language centers and be eligible for a student visa (again he must take a minimum of twenty hours per week). The most recommended programs in New York for this type of study are those at New York University, Columbia University, Pace University, and Hunter College of the City University of New York.

Columbia University, traditionally popular with foreign students, offers superb undergraduate and graduate programs in *all* fields of study. The undergraduate school has an enrollment of 2,800. The total university enrollment, which is co-educational and includes all graduate schools, has 18,050 men and women. Particularly sought-after programs are at the School of Medicine (affiliated with Columbia–Presbyterian Hospital), the School of Dentistry, the School of Law (which has an excellent International Law division), the School of Journalism, the Teachers College, the Union Theological Seminary, the Jewish Theological Seminary, the School of Engineering and Applied Science, and the School of Nursing.

New York University is equally diversified and complete as an undergraduate and graduate institution. For many generations, foreign students have studied in the Schools of Medicine (part of New York University Medical Center and University Hospital), Veterinary Medicine, Dentistry, Law, Engineering, Business, Nursing, Education, Arts and Sciences, Journalism, and Film. Much larger than Columbia, New York University has 13,500 men and women enrolled in its undergraduate program and many more in all the graduate schools.

Pace University in the past decade has known a great surge in reputation and growth in facilities. The Lubin School of Business has attracted many foreign students. Pace has three campuses, all part of the main University, but each campus is independent and geographically separate: Lower Manhattan, White Plains, and Pleasantville. The Schools of Education, Nursing, and Law, the Dyson College of the Arts, the Lubin School of Business, and the School of Journalism are very popular with foreign students.

For specific information regarding admission, expenses, financial aid, special programs, housing, and application, write directly to the college of your choice.

Barnard College. 3009 Broadway. 280–5262.
City University of New York, Hunter College. 695 Park Avenue. 570–5566.
Columbia University. New York, N.Y. 10027. 280–1754.
New York University. New York, N.Y. 10003. 598–1212.
Pace University. New York, N.Y. 10038. 488–1200.

WHERE CAN YOU FIND THE BEST PROGRAMS IN NEW YORK FOR SPECIFIC STUDIES?

For specific interests and areas of study, the following colleges are very popular. Write or call them for a bulletin and application, and direct all questions about housing, financial aid, and programs to the Office of Admissions.

Academy of Aeronautics. LaGuardia Airport, Flushing, Queens. 429–6600.
Bank Street College of Education. 610 West 112th Street. 663–7200.
City University of New York: Graduate School and University Center. 33 West 42nd Street. 790–4395.
City University of New York: John Jay College of Criminal Justice. 444 West 56th Street. 489–5183.
College of Insurance. 123 William Street. 962–4111.
Cooper Union (Art, Architecture, Design). 41 Cooper Square; 254–6300.
Fashion Institute of Technology. 227 West 27th Street. 760–7642.
Jewish Theological Seminary of America. 3080 Broadway. 678–8000.
The Juilliard School (Music). 144 West 66th Street. 799–5000.
Katherine Gibbs Secretarial School. 120 Claremont Avenue. 749–2802.
Mannes College of Music. 150 West 85th Street. 580–0210.
New School for Social Research. 66 West 12th Street. 741–5600.
New York College of Podiatric Medicine. 53 East 124th Street. 427–8400.
New York State University of Maritime College. Ft. Schuyler, Bronx. 409–7200.
Parsons School of Design. 66 West 12th Street. 741–8900.
School of Visual Arts. 209 East 23rd Street. 679–7350.
State University of New York: Agricultural and Technical College at Farmingdale. Melville Road, Farmingdale. 516–420–2000.
Stern College for Women. 245 Lexington Avenue. 481–0560.
Taylor Business Institute. One Penn Plaza, 34th Street and Eighth Avenue. 279–0510.
Technical Career Institutes. 320 West 31st Street. 594–4000.
United States Merchant Marine Academy. Kings Point, Long Island.
Yeshiva University. 245 Lexington Avenue. 481–0560.

CHAPTER 11

Where To Find
Adult Education Courses
in Manhattan

What Is Adult Education?
List of Adult Education Programs in the Universities and Colleges of New York City
Museums, Clubs, and Organizations That Have Adult Education Programs
Continuing Education Programs Sponsored by the City
Career and Vocational Courses Sponsored by the City
High School Equivalency Programs

WHAT IS ADULT EDUCATION?

ADULT EDUCATION is just what it says—a form of education devoted to adults. Students of all ages take courses at local universities, clubs, and associations. They attend lectures, participate in workshops, and study either for pleasure or for a possible change in career. They do not have to be full-time students, nor do they need to be high school or college graduates. They don't have to take a minimum number of courses per semester, nor do they have to take courses in succeeding semesters. They can register in a formal, vocational program or simply take one or two courses that they enjoy.

Many universities and colleges offer adult education courses within their continuing education departments. Each college has a bulletin or list of courses that they make available to potential students, indicating which courses are being given, when, where, and by whom. Instructors and lecturers may be part-time, or full-time faculty members or pro-

149

fessionals who work in the fields they are lecturing about. Courses are usually scheduled in the evenings or on weekends.

Admission to adult educational courses is not difficult. It is usually on a "first-come first-served" basis. You do not have to be admitted formally to the college or university as does the undergraduate or graduate student. You don't have to be a high school graduate or a college graduate. You don't have to take any tests or be interviewed.

An adult educational course is also less expensive than a formal three-credit course in an undergraduate or graduate school. For adult courses there is a small tuition fee or registration fee in addition to the price per course. Senior citizens may receive a discount. In some of the leading universities you can register and pay by mail, often with a credit card.

Adult education is a new concept of learning. In the past decade, many adults have participated in taking courses as a way of continuing their interests in a structured fashion. To be a part of an adult education program is an excellent way to continue learning and to make friends at the same time.

LIST OF ADULT EDUCATION PROGRAMS IN THE UNIVERSITIES AND COLLEGES OF NEW YORK CITY

Manhattan Universities and Colleges

Baruch College, C.C.N.Y. Dept. of Continuing Education. 17 Lexington Avenue. 725-3000.

Columbia University, Dept. of Continuing Education. 208 Hamilton Hall. 280-1754.

Cooper Union, Dept. of Continuing Education. 41 Cooper Square. 254-6300.

Fordham University, Dept. of Continuing Education. Columbus Avenue and West 60th Street. 841-5100.

Hunter College, Dept. of Continuing Education. 695 Park Avenue. 570-5566.

Marymount Manhattan, Dept. of Continuing Education. 221 East 71st Street. 472-3800.

New School for Social Research. 66 West 12th Street. 741-5600.

New York University, Dept. of Continuing Education. 70 Washington Square. 598-1212.

Pace University, Dept. of Continuing Education. 1 Pace Plaza. 488-1200.

MUSEUMS, CLUBS, AND ORGANIZATIONS THAT HAVE ADULT EDUCATION PROGRAMS

American Museum of Natural History. Central Park West and 79th Street. 873-4225. There are courses and lectures in biology, zoology, archaeology, history, anthropology, marine navigation, piloting, astronomy, etc. There are also special movies, exhibits, and presentations. Hayden Planetarium, associated with the Museum of Natural History, offers courses in the evening as well as during the day.

Ethical Culture School. 33 Central Park West. 874-5200.

Geothe Haus. 1014 Fifth Avenue (84th Street). 744-8310. There are courses given in language, literature, and art in German and English. The Video Club is very popular. For a nominal fee per year, members can view and hear original German productions of opera, theatre, and concerts taped the season before in Germany. There is an extensive library of German books, conferences, exhibitions, and receptions weekly.

Institute for Asian Studies. 619 Lexington Avenue. 535-7496. This organization specializes in Asian culture, art, archaeology, history, religion, and philosophy. Courses, lectures, and seminars are related to these areas of study.

L'Alliance Française. 22 East 60th Street. 355-6100. Courses and lectures are held in French and English. There is a large selection of French films presented each week. There are language classes in French, cultural and social events.

Metropolitan Museum of Art. Fifth Avenue and 82nd Street. 535-7710. There is a very extensive list of cultural and artistic activities available to members and non-members as well as an excellent lecture series related to art, music, and literature. There are concerts of chamber music. The Children's Museum has a very interesting program for children.

Museum of Modern Art. 11 West 53rd Street. 708-9400. There are lectures on key artistic figures related to current exhibitions. The foreign and American movies are also very popular. The museum has an extensive library available to members. During the summer there are musical groups, modern and classical, performing in the courtyard.

Nippon Club. 145 West 57th Street. 581-2223. At this club, mostly for Japanese nationals who are living and working in New York, there is an abundant choice of courses, lectures, and workshops in Japanese. This is the cultural and social club for the Japanese community. There is also a program of luncheons and dinners accompanied by speeches from Manhattan's leading political and social figures.

The Coast Guard. 668-7000. This United States government agency offers comprehensive courses in navigation, boating (power or sail), and safety.

The Italian Cultural Institute. 686 Park Avenue. 879-4242. This government agency specializes in offering Italian language classes for all levels. In addition, there is a complete program in cultural affairs.

The Ulpan Center. 515 Park Avenue. 752-0600. All levels of Hebrew are taught during the day and evening, and on Sunday. In addition, there are lectures and guest speakers related to Israeli affairs.

YMHA. 92nd Street and Lexington Avenue. 427-6000. They have courses in sports, gymnastics, music, art, language, and writing. They have a very extensive program of concerts and lectures. Workshops for senior citizens, children, and adults.

YWCA. 610 Lexington Avenue. 755-4500. Their programs are diversified, ranging from sports to culture. It is best to call or write for a brochure.

CONTINUING EDUCATION PROGRAMS SPONSORED BY THE CITY

Continuing education programs in the public schools offer courses in basic education, remedial reading, mathematics, English as a second language (ESL), Elementary School Equivalency leading to an Elementary Education Diploma, Citizenship Education, and High School Equivalency preparation. For information regarding times and places, call 596-3907, 596-3906 or 596-6943.

In the public high schools there are also many courses of diverse interest offered in art, music, and hobbies. These courses are less expensive than those offered in the colleges and universities. Call them for a list of courses, dates, and registration:

Stuyvesant Adult Center. 345 East 15th Street. 254-2890.
Washington Irving Adult Center. 40 Irving Place, Room 350. 674-5000.
Julia Richman Adult Center. 317 East 67th Street. 879-6866.
Murry Bergtraum. 411 Pearl Street. 233-1533.
J.H.S. 104 Adult Center. 330 East 21st Street. 254-2890.
J.H.S. 147. 225 East 23rd Street. 254-2890.
P.S. 40. 320 East 20th Street. 254-2890.

CAREER AND VOCATIONAL COURSES SPONSORED BY THE CITY

Career and vocational training sessions are held during the day, five days a week, in New York's public schools. For information regarding places and times, the number to call is 596–3424 or 596–4404. Courses are available in air conditioning and refrigeration, air pollution control, automotive trades, aviation trades, beauty culture and cosmetology, building maintenance, business training, electrical trades, fashion trades, food trades, health care, machine shop, oil heating, printing trades, radio and television repair, welding, and woodworking.

Adult consumer and homemaking education courses are also offered in the New York public schools. For information regarding programs and schedules, call 596–2129 or 596–2219. Courses are given in family money management, housing and equipment, personal and family relationships, child development and parenting, textiles and clothing, nutrition and community health. The following centers are just a couple of the many in New York:

Chinatown ACE Center. 70 Mulberry Street. 233–2174.
West Harlem ACE Center. 231 West 151st Street.

HIGH SCHOOL EQUIVALENCY PROGRAMS

There are some adults who have not had the opportunity to finish their high school studies. Years later, they may wish to do so.

New York City has several programs which allows adults to fulfill the necessary requirements in order to receive a high school diploma. Spanish speaking candidates can participate in a Spanish-speaking program.

Day Centers
Forsyth Street. 198 Forsyth Street. 982–5660.
93rd Street School. 257 West 93rd Street.
Spanish Language Equivalency Examination (in Spanish). Board of Education, Room 832. 110 Livingston Street, Brooklyn. 522–7530.

Evening Centers
Louis D. Brandeis High School. 145 West 84th Street. 874–1005.
Julia Richman High School. 317 East 67th Street. 472–1588.
Spanish Language Equivalency Examination. 110 Livingston Street, Brooklyn. 522–7530.

PART IV

What To Do When You Are Ill

CHAPTER 12

Medical Care in New York

What is the Procedure When You Need To See a Private Doctor? How To Find a Specialist; How To Make an Appointment; How To Pay
What Types of Hospitals Are There in New York City?
What To Do in an Emergency: What To Do in Case of a Heart Attack; List of Emergency Heart Care Stations in the Five Boroughs; What To Do in Case of a Non-Hospital Emergency
What Is the Procedure for Hospital Admission?
How To Arrange To Give Birth
What Is the Best Form of Medical Insurance?
List of Specialized Clinics
Where To Go with Sick Animals
Emergency Telephone Numbers

WHAT IS THE PROCEDURE
WHEN YOU NEED TO SEE A PRIVATE DOCTOR?

BEING ill in a new city can be complicated. Being ill in New York City can be awesome. But if you proceed logically and unemotionally, you can eliminate a great deal of unnecessary apprehension.

The first step is to find a good internist. An internist is a "board-certified" specialist in internal medicine who by years of education, training, and a series of examinations has the most complete knowledge of general medicine in comparison to other physicians. The same doctor may also be a sub-specialist in cardiology, gastroenterology, hematology, or other sub-specialities of internal medicine. But first the internist must qualify for the exams in internal medicine.

157

How To Find a Specialist. How to find this well-qualified doctor? You can ask your friends if they have an internist whom they recommend. Be sure his office is not far from your home or place of work. You can also telephone the university hospital nearest you and ask the secretary of the department of internal medicine to recommend several internists on their staff. By nature of teaching assignments and clinical appointments, attending physicians at university hospitals are encouraged to maintain a high standard of medical ethics and knowledge.

If you need a foreign-speaking internist, you can call your consulate and ask them to recommend one. You can also call the Medical Society of the County of New York at 399–9040. They have a panel of internists they can recommend.

If you have children, you will also need to have the name of a pediatrician. Even if you do not need a pediatrician immediately, you should have the doctor's name available in case of an emergency. However, it would be wise to call the doctor first, before any emergency occurs, and ask if he accepts new patients. Ask if you can introduce yourself to the doctor. This is proper protocol, so he will know who you are if you need him. In any event, you will need to visit a pediatrician with your child at the beginning of the school year. All schools require a health report and examination from a pediatrician before the child begins school.

To start you off, we can recommend several Manhattan specialists who are board certified in their field of medicine, are university trained, who teach at leading Manhattan medical schools, have academic titles, and also see private patients in their offices.

Internist: Dr. M. Bayer, 969 Park Avenue (517–7300)
Ophthalmologist: Dr. J. Eichenbaum, 1050 Park Avenue (289–7200)
Pediatrician: Dr. R. Moloshok, 73 East 90th Street (SA 2–7840)

How To Make an Appointment. Ask the secretary first if the doctor accepts new patients, and what is the fee schedule and format of payment. At the time of your appointment, always plan some extra time, for you may have to wait. That is why a doctor's reception room is called a "waiting room."

If you have a specific problem and you know you will need a specialist other than an internist, such as a plastic surgeon, orthopedist, ophthalmologist, etc., you can ask your internist to recommend one. But if you are unsure of your diagnosis or symptoms, it may be safer to go see your internist first and let him suggest what you should do.

For elective (nonemergency) medical care, it is always better, if you can afford it, to make an appointment with a private doctor rather than at a clinic. At a clinic, be it hospital or private, you will also have to pay a fee. You will have to wait a good deal of time, and you may be seen by an intern or resident and not by the attending physician.

If you have a specific ailment or disease and you have been under the care of a doctor in another country or city, it would be wise, before you relocate, to ask your first physician for all your records. No doctor will refuse to give you records of your tests, X-RAYS, laboratory reports, hospital findings, etc. And if they were properly done, it makes no sense to repeat them, especially within a short period of time.

How To Pay. When you make an appointment to see a private doctor, ask the secretary on the telephone what the doctor's fees are and if the doctor accepts insurance. Some physicians in New York City will not accept insurance payment for office work (they may for hospital work). They will sign all the necessary forms your insurance company requires, and then the insurance company will reimburse you (the reimbursement can be 50%–100% of the doctor's bill, depending on your policy and coverage). The Manhattan physician likes to be paid the day you come to the office, so as to eliminate paperwork. But if you did not bring enough money or your checkbook, you can ask the secretary to mail you the bill. Remember to get a receipt for all payments. Doctor bills are tax deductible, an important point to remember at the time of completing your tax returns.

WHAT TYPES OF HOSPITALS ARE THERE IN NEW YORK CITY?

The New York hospital structure is unique. There are many hospitals in New York City, but each institution fits into a specific category.

University Hospitals. These are teaching hospitals that are affiliated with a medical school. The students, interns, residents, and fellows rotate through the different wards, sections, and clinics of the hospital. Each area constitutes part of their learning experience. The advantage for the patient is that these students are smart, dedicated, available, and supervised by attending physicians who admit and oversee the patients. The faculty is comprised of full-time and volunteer doctors. The disadvantage of being a patient in a university hospital is that there is always someone near your bedside asking questions. The house staff is there to learn.

In a university hospital, the equipment is always of the finest quality. For difficult diagnostic work or sophisticated treatment, this may be essential for the patient's prognosis. A small, private hospital is not equipped to handle transplants, major surgery, or sophisticated diagnostic procedures.

The following is a list of some of the major university hospitals in the five boroughs:

Manhattan
Columbia–Presbyterian Hospital. 622 West 168th Street. 694-2500.
Memorial Sloan Kettering Hospital. First Avenue and 69th Street. 794-7722.
Mount Sinai Hospital. Fifth Avenue and 100th Street. 650-6500.
New York Hospital. 525 East 68th Street. 472-5454.
Roosevelt-St. Luke's Hospital. Ninth Avenue and 58th Street. 554-7000.
New York University Medical Center-University Hospital. 560 First Avenue. 340-1999.

Bronx
Albert Einstein College of Medicine. 1825 Eastchester Road. 430–2000.
Montefiore Hospital and Medical Center. 111 East 210th Street. 920–4321.

Queens
Long Island Jewish Hospital. 270–05 76th Avenue. New Hyde Park. 470–2000.

Brooklyn
Downstate Medical Center, State University Hospital. 445 Lenox Road. 270-2401.
Maimonides Hospital. 4802 Tenth Avenue. 270-7679.

Staten Island
St. Vincent's Medical Center of Richmond. 355 Bard Avenue. 390-1234.

Private Hospitals. At a private hospital, the medical staff is "voluntary." This means that the physicians receive no payment from the hospital. On the contrary, they volunteer their services to the clinics, wards, teaching programs, and administration. In return, the hospital allows the attending physicians to admit patients. At a private hospital, there is no house staff—no interns, no residents. There is usually a house physician who takes care of immediate problems when one's private doctor is not available. Usually there is an emergency room. The private doctor is responsible for the patient, while in a university hospital the intern or resident oversees the patient's welfare. In a private hospital, the nurses are usually very competent. For the patient, a stay in a private hospital is as pleasant as a hospital experience could be.

City Hospitals. These are city-run and city-funded public hospitals. Anyone can go to the clinics for a nominal fee. All elective, non-emergency care, for children and adults, is administered here. X-rays, laboratory work, and minor procedures can be performed by specialists in these clinics. The only problem is that the patient must be forbearing. There is sometimes a long wait. The physicians on staff are paid a salary by the hospital and usually do not see private patients in the hospital, although in the past couple of years this has been changing.

Veterans' Administration Hospitals. These hospitals are federally, nationally, and city funded for American veterans who have fought in past wars. Veterans are eligible to enter the hospital at any time in their lives, free of charge. Some of these institutions have out-patient clinics, where patients can be cared for during the day and do not have to stay overnight. Veterans' hospitals usually have very well qualified physicians. Many of these doctors share their time and interest between research projects and patient care. Their research and teaching assignments, however, may leave them with not enough time for clinical patient care. Most of the patients stay in wards; there are a few private rooms available.

What To Do in an Emergency

For emergency care, you would be wise to go to a university hospital located near your home or place of work. Sometimes it is not possible to reach your private doctor, or he may not be available. In that case, you would do best to go directly to the emergency room of a university hospital. It may be that your private doctor will be on staff at the same hospital. If he is, they will try to locate him. If he is not, the emergency room physician will give you immediate care and recommend the necessary specialist according to your ailment. The specialist may come to see you immediately at the emergency room or shortly afterward.

If the patient needs to get to the hospital immediately and cannot walk, especially in the case of a heart attack or when he needs oxygen, it is best to call a private ambulance. The following private ambulances will give you immediate service:

Empire State Ambulance: 794–3200.
Keefe and Keefe Ambulance: 988–8800.

There are also city ambulances you can call (telephone 911). But if it is a question of time and urgency, you may not want to wait for them.

You can also take a taxi if the patient is able to walk. But no patient should go alone if there is a choice. All hospitals ask for papers to complete and questions to answer. Someone in a great deal of pain may not be able to take care of this properly.

What To Do in Case of a Heart Attack. In the past ten years, heart attacks, which used to be the No. 1 cause of death in America, have decreased greatly. There has been a 25% reduction in the number of deaths due to heart attack in the United States. This can be attributed to advances in emergency heart medicine and the rigid standards of "emergency heart care stations" in hospital emergency rooms. In most cases of heart attack, it is not the actual attack that kills the patient but the two to five hours after the attack. It is during this period that the heart's electrical rhythms change. Also, the heart muscle becomes damaged by a lack of oxygen and deprives the rest of the brain and body organs. It is during these hours that the patient needs intensive care. And not all 87 hospitals in the five boroughs are equipped for heart attack victims. A good heart attack emergency room has two cardiologists always on duty or easily reached, the proper equipment, an emergency room cardiac staff, and a coronary care unit for closely watched follow-up care.

In the case of a heart attack, it is of the utmost importance to go immediately to the nearest emergency heart care station. The following list can be of great service in such cases.

Manhattan
Bellevue Hospital Center. 27th Street and First Avenue. 561–4347.
Beth Israel Medical Center. 16th Street and First Avenue. 420–2000.
Cabrini Medical Center. 227 East 19th Street. 725–6000.
Lenox Hill Hospital. 100 East 77th Street. 794–4567.
New York University Medical Center. 560 First Avenue at 33rd Street. 340–7300.
Roosevelt Hospital. 58th Street and Ninth Avenue. 554–7000.
St. Luke's Hospital. 114th Street and Amsterdam Avenue. 870–6000.
St. Vincent's Hospital. 153 West 11th Street. 790–7888.

Bronx
Bronx Municipal Hospital Center. Pelham Parkway and Eastchester Road. 430–5000.
Montefiore Medical Center. 111 East 210th Street. 920–4321.
North Central Bronx Hospital. 3424 Kossuth Avenue. 920–7171.
St. Barnabas Hospital. 4422 Third Avenue. 960–9000.

Brooklyn
Brookdale Hospital Medical Center. Linden Boulevard and Rockaway Parkway. 240-5000.
Catholic Medical Center, St. Mary's Hospital. 1298 St. Mark's Avenue. 774-3600.
Kings County Hospital. 451 Clarkson Avenue. 735-3131.
Long Island College Hospital. 340 Henry Street. 780-3000.
Lutheran Medical Center. 150 55th Street. 630-7000.

Queens
Booth Memorial Medical Center. 56-45 Main Street. 670-1231.
Catholic Medical Center of Brooklyn, Mary Immaculate Hospital Division. 152-11 89th Avenue, Jamaica. 291-3300.
City Hospital Center at Elmhurst, affiliated with Mt. Sinai Hospital. 7901 Broadway. 830-1515.
Long Island Jewish–Hillside Medical Center. Lakeville Road and 76th Avenue. 470-2000.
Queens Hospital Center. 82-68 164th Street. 990-3377.

Staten Island
Richmond Memorial Hospital and Health Center. 375 Seguine Avenue. 317-2000.
St. Vincent's Medical Center of Richmond. 355 Bard Avenue. 390-1234.
Staten Island Hospital. 475 Seaview Avenue. 390-9000.

What To Do in Case of a Non-Hospital Emergency. If you need emergency medical care but you do not feel your case warrants a visit to the hospital or to the emergency room, you may just want to call a physician. If you do not have a private physician, or if your physician does not make house calls, you can call one of the following. They will send a doctor to your house within two hours. Most of these doctors will also perform routine diagnostic tests, and they will arrange for any ambulance service that may be needed.

American Housecalls: 238-1800 for New York City; 222-0850 for Long Island; and 965-2500 for Westchester.
Housecalls Unlimited: 939-0700.
Doctors on Call: 238-2100 for New York City; 944-7200 for Bergen County, New Jersey.
Doctors Home Referral: 745-5900.
Housecalls, Inc. 853-1500.

For a dental emergency, the best thing to do is to proceed to the emergency room of a leading university hospital. They will have an oral surgeon on duty or available. An oral surgeon is the specialist you will need in case you have an accident to your mouth or jaw.

If you have an abscessed tooth or severe pain due to a cavity or an exposed root or nerve, you will want to call a private dentist. The following group offers such services:

Diversified Dental Service. 30 East 40th Street. 679-7770.

WHAT IS THE PROCEDURE FOR HOSPITAL ADMISSION?

It is never a pleasant experience to have to go to a hospital. No matter what kind of accommodations or what kind of doctors you have, being in a hospital is no vacation. But for those who need hospital care, being in New York City is a great advantage. There are more than 85 hospitals in the five boroughs, and several of them are considered to be the best in the world. In these leading university hospitals, you can find the most sophisticated equipment. Every procedure, technique, and operation can be done. The doctors are the best trained in the United States, and competition has kept them abreast of new procedures and modern equipment. In New York City there is every type of clinic available for elective or emergency care, and no one needs to fear the unknown. Everything is explained and nothing is left unexplored.

For those people who have to spend a period of time in a hospital, it is helpful to understand the procedures for admission. Each hospital may have its unique system, but basically they share common ground.

When you enter the hospital, you proceed directly to the Admitting Office, which should be on the first floor. There you have to expect to spend some time completing the large number of papers the hospital needs for its records. Everyone who is admitted must fill out:
1. an admission application form;
2. a consent for general medical treatment;
3. a room and floor card;
4. a telephone request;
5. a consent to release information to the Medical Department of New York State for its records;
6. a financial agreement.

The financial agreement is important for the hospital's business office. If you have American medical insurance, which covers you for hospitalization, you will not need to give a deposit for a semi-private room (two people in a room). However, if you want a private room (whether you do or do not have insurance), you will have to give a general deposit. This could be at least $500 for a week's stay. The deposit is to cover the difference between the rate for a semi-private room, for which your insurance company pays, and that for a private room.

If you do not have American medical coverage, you will have to leave a large deposit, be it for a semi-private or a private room. The hospital will request a deposit based on a daily rate. If you don't know how long you will be staying in the hospital, the admitting office may request a deposit of $3,000 to $4,000 a week. If you plan to stay three days, the deposit could be between $1,500 and $2,500. This is to insure the hospital that you will pay your bill in full at the time you are discharged. Bearing in mind these figures, it is undoubtedly true that a stay in an American hospital is a costly affair.

You can pay your deposit in the form of a personal check, money order, cash, or perhaps even a charge card. Doctor's Hospital accepts MasterCard. Other hospitals may also accept a charge card. It's best to call and inquire what your expenses will be before you go to the hospital. You are responsible for paying the total hospital bill the day you are discharged. Your original deposit may have covered a large portion of the bill, but then again it may not.

If you do not have any American medical coverage, you will be personally responsible for the hospital bill. If you have insurance coverage in your home country, don't forget to keep all your receipts. Perhaps you can be reimbursed.

If you work in New York or the United States for a large company or organization, most likely they will give you "benefits." This includes medical and hospital health insurance. You can now understand why this is an important detail to discuss with your employer as soon as you come to New York. It is a good idea to bear in mind that medical care in the United States is costly and that, if you can take care of certain tests or procedures in your home country, it may be wise to do so before you come to the United States. This includes dental care, eye examinations, and eyeglasses.

When you do come to the United States, ask your employer or personnel officer to explain to you your medical coverage. Ask specifically about hospital care, elective surgery, plastic surgery, dental care, corrective lenses, maternity, and psychiatry. Be sure your family is covered in the policy as well, especially if you have children who are over eighteen years old and live with you.

How To Arrange To Give Birth

The most traditional way to give birth is to deliver in the maternity ward of a hospital with an obstetrician in charge. The obstetrician is the doctor who has followed the patient during pregnancy, and it is the obstetrician who will deliver the baby. It is also the obstetrician who makes all the necessary arrangements with the hospital for delivery and stay and who reserves the delivery room and nursery. In New York, the maternity wards of the hospitals are very well equipped, intensive care units and pre-natal emergency sections very modern. Both mother and child are supervised regularly and carefully.

For an anticipated uncomplicated birth, there are other ways to deliver. In the past several years, delivering in a non-hospital setting with a midwife, rather than at the hospital with an obstetrician, has become popular. The Maternity Center at 48 East 92nd Street (369–7300) is such an institution. The Maternity Center is a birth center that holds classes in pre-natal care and prepared childbirth. They have a staff of very professional and experienced midwives. Members of the family, including brothers and sisters, are encouraged to participate in the delivery. Mother and baby can go home twelve hours after delivery instead of staying the traditional four to seven days in a hospital. If there is an emergency, for either baby or mother, the obstetrician or pediatrician on staff at the Maternity Center is also on staff at Lenox Hill Hospital and will admit the mother or baby at Lenox Hill.

What Is the Best Form of Medical Insurance?

There are several major medical insurances. Some are supported by the national or state government, while others have been established by private companies. Medicare is a nationally supported insurance for American citizens or permanent residents aged 65 or older. To be eligible, you need a Social Security number, and you must file an application with any Social Security office. Medicaid is a state-supported insurance for those individuals who earn less than $2,500 per year. To be eligible for either Medicare or Medicaid, you must live in the United States for at least six months and be a permanent resident or have those papers on file. Medicare and Medicaid are as close to a nationalized medical program as the Americans have come. Medicare pays 80% of all hospital bills, based on the rate of a semi-private room, and 80% of the "allowed" and "approved" doctor bills. There is a nominal annual fee for the insurance and a $75.00 deductible for the year (this amount changes each year). For more information regarding Medicaid, call 594-3050.

Private medical insurances which offer coverage for hospital and office care are:

> Blue Cross - Blue Shield: 490-4141
> Prudential Life Insurance: 210-6400
> G.H.I. (Group Health Insurance): 760-6400
> Traveler's Insurance: 516-294-5573
> Aetna Life Insurance: 766-2000

If you need to get insurance for yourself and your family, it is best to call up a few of the above companies and ask what types of policies they have and their fees for specific coverage. You may have to "shop and compare." But if you cannot get insurance with a group (a group policy is less expensive than an individual policy), you will have to make sure you have some form of medical insurance.

Dental care in the United States has always been considered expensive. Traditionally, dental care has not been covered by any medical insurance policy. But now there is the availability of dental insurance for private individuals as well as for groups. The best people with whom to discuss the various policies are the people from the New York State Dental Society at 986-3937.

LIST OF SPECIALIZED CLINICS

It is good to have the telephone numbers of specialized clinics in case a certain problem arises. These are the best known in New York City:

Abortion Advisory Service: 729-0230

Abortion Information Service: 1-800-321-0575

Alcoholics Anonymous: 473-6200

Associated Psychiatric Services of New York County. 242 East 72nd Street. 288-5583.

Drug Abuse Program: 488-3954.

Executive Health Group. 777 Third Avenue. 486-8900.

Fertility Institute of New York. 42 East 65th Street. 734-5700.

Margaret Sanger Center (birth control, pregnancy detection, abortion, gynecological services, infertility treatment, special services for teens) 380 Second Avenue. 677-6474.

Park Avenue Family Health Care Services. 58 East 116th Street. 289-4500.

Preventive Medicine Institute-Strang Clinic (cancer detection clinic). 55 East 34th Street. 683-1000.

WHERE TO GO WITH SICK ANIMALS

New Yorkers like animals. Newcomers to the city are always surprised to see such a large number of dogs in the streets of New York. In spite of the relatively small apartments in Manhattan, the scarcity of green parks, and the busy pace most New Yorkers keep, there are a good deal of household pets. Therefore, New Yorkers are organized to be sure that there are medical facilities for their pets. When an animal gets sick, there are several options: (1) You can take the animal to a private veterinarian or (2) you can take the animal to an animal hospital. The following addresses and telephone numbers are useful to have.

Private Veterinarians
   Animal Emergency Clinic. 240 East 80th Street. 988-1000.
   The Veterinary House Call Group. 692 Columbus Avenue. 431-1015.
   The Animal Clinic of New York. 1623 First Avenue. 628-5580.

Animal Hospitals
   American Animal Welfare Association Hospital. 47 East 30th Street. 685-2857. They have other locations in all five boroughs.
   Animal Medical Center. 510 East 62nd Street. 838-8100. This is an animal university hospital with specialists in many areas and complete medical and surgical facilities.
   A.S.P.C.A. Animal Hospital. 441 East 92nd Street. 876-7700.

EMERGENCY TELEPHONE NUMBERS

Abortion Advisory Services 729-0230
Abortion Information Service 1-800-321-0575
Alcoholics Anonymous 473-6200
Ambulance (public and city service) 911
Ambulance, Empire State (private 24-hour emergency service) . . .
. . . 794-3200
Ambulance, Metropolitan (Brooklyn) 633-5002
Animal bite 566-7105
Battered women 577-7777
Child abuse 431-4680
Coast Guard 668-7936
Crime Victims Hotline 577-7777
Deaf emergency teletypewriter 1-800-342-4357
Dental Society of New York 889-8940

Doctors on Call (house calls) . . . . 737–2333 (for New York City)
. . . 201–7200 (for New York State)
Doctors Home Referral (house calls) 745–5900
Drug Abuse Program 488–3954
Electrical emergency 683–8830
F.B.I. 553–2700
Gas and steam leaks 683–8830
Mayor's Office for the Handicapped 566–3913
New York City Fire Department 628–2902
New York City Police Department 911
    To obtain local precinct number 374–6700
New York County Medical Society 399–9040
New York League for the Hard of Hearing 741–7650
Poison Control Center 340–4494
Rape Help Line 777–4000
State Commission for the Blind and Visually Handicapped 678–2500
Suicide Prevention 532–2400
United States Secret Service 466–4402
Veneral Diseases Hotline. 734–6010

PART V

The World of Work in New York

CHAPTER 13

How To Prepare
for a Job Interview

How To Write a Résumé
How To Be Successful at an Interview
What Are Employment Agencies?

I F you are interested in getting a job in New York, it would be useful to know the American system for doing so. It doesn't matter if the job is part-time or full-time, with a high-paying salary or volunteer work. It doesn't matter how you get the opportunity to apply for the job, be it through a friend, or an agency, or a newspaper advertisement. You will still have to know how to write a résumé, what to include in a cover letter with that résumé, and how to prepare and present yourself for an interview. This chapter will give you some ideas about these steps. Everything is very logical and systematic, but these steps are to be considered as guidelines. The most important element is how *you exercise* these guidelines.

HOW TO WRITE A RÉSUMÉ

Your résumé consists of several parts that show at a glance your education, work experience, and special qualifications. It should be easy to read and logical to follow. It is what represents you, and it is what allows you to have an interview for a potential job. It is the first tangible expression of your work. Before the interviewer has the opportunity to speak to you, he will have your résumé in front of him.

173

If your past jobs have been varied, you may want to write several résumés, each one emphasizing different areas of expertise. The multi-résumé approach is also useful if you are not sure about what field in which you want to work. Each résumé can emphasize a different objective or work experience, depending upon which job you are seeking.

How To Prepare a Résumé

1. Ideally, your résumé should be one typewritten page, double spaced, or even single spaced if you have a lot of information. If you have an unusually strong background, or many years of experience, or a great number of publications, then certainly use two or more pages. But remember, recruiters and interviewers have a lot of résumés to read and verbose résumés are counterproductive.

2. Your résumé should be professionally typed on standard white paper, 8½ inches by 11 inches. Type always on one side only. You should use black ink, for that will photocopy well.

3. Ideally, make many copies, either to be immediately used or to be kept for further use. When you Xerox your résumé, use the best quality machine available. Offset printing will give better quality than a photocopy.

4. It is very important that you proofread your résumé several times and have someone else proofread it as well. It would be very embarassing if you misspell a name or date. Take time to edit your résumé.

5. The content of your résumé should be factual, positive, to the point, and brief. You do not have to write your descriptions in full sentences, but you should have consistency and parallelism in your grammar and parts of speech. Once you start with a certain style, keep it. Don't change in the middle of the résumé to another style.

What Should Be in a Résumé?

1. At the top of the page put your name, phone number (with area code) and a complete mailing address. Women do not have to write *Mrs.* or *Miss.* They may not want their interviewer to know initially that they are single, married, or divorced. It is not necessary to include how old you are.

2. It is better not to use full sentences. Short, concise phrases are easier and quicker to read. Keep everything ordered and easy to find. Be consistent with your grammar.

3. Reverse chronological order. For your entries about education and work experience, put the most recent first and list the rest going back in time. To a recruiter, your last job and your latest schooling are more important than the earlier ones.

4. There are potentially eight parts to a résumé. However, if one part does not pertain to your background or your job, don't use it. Eliminate it altogether. The eight parts are the following:

a. Address
b. Objective
c. Education
d. Employment experience (c and d can be reversed; use the one which is most important or most prestigious)
e. Publications, or writing samples, or portfolio
f. Special skills such as languages, computer knowledge, etc.
g. Personal information or hobbies
h. References available upon request

Sample Résumé Format

Name:
Address:
Telephone Number:

Objective:

Education:	(Most recent first. Include name of school, degree graduation date.)
Employment Experience:	(Put last position first. Put job title, name of company, dates, name of supervisor. Put duties, accomplishments, responsibilities, etc.)
Publications:	(Most recent first. Use standard entry for a bibliography. *Media Coverage* may be a substitute entry.)

Special Skills:

Personal:	(Hobbies, awards, scholarships, special accomplishments, etc. should go here.)

References Available Upon Request

Sample Résumé

GREGORY BAYER, Ph.D
400 East End Avenue
New York, New York 10028
212-696-1024

OBJECTIVE:
   To teach English literature at the College level.

EDUCATION:
Ph.D., Department of Comparative Literature, New York University, 1974.
M.A., Department of French, New York University, 1970.
B.A., New York University, 1968.
Program of Study Abroad, Faculté des Lettres; Nice, France, 1966–1967.
Cours d'été, Faculté des Lettres; Nancy, France, 1966.
Cours d'été, Sorbonne University; Paris, France, 1965.

EMPLOYMENT EXPERIENCE:
Adjunct Associate Professor, Department of Humanities, Pace University, 1979–1983.
Adjunct Instructor, Department of English, Hunter College, 1976–1979.
Instructor, Department of English, Marymount Manhattan College, 1974–1978.
Instructor, Department of English, Briarcliff College, 1973–1974.

PUBLICATIONS:
"Hermann Hesse: Author of Two Modern Kunstlerromane." Mid-Hudson Modern Language Association; December 2, 1980.
"English Majors and Internships." White Plains Community Council; November 13, 1980.
"Literature and Medicine." The School of Medicine at C.C.N.Y., May 8, 1980.

FELLOWSHIPS:
Pace University Teaching Stipend, Coordinator of Internships, English Department, 1980.
Carnegie–Mellon Teaching Fellowship, Hunter College, 1977–1978.
New York University Tuition Fellowship, Graduate School of Arts and Science, 1969–1974.
Foreign Students Study Abroad Fellowship, 1966–1967.

LANGUAGES:
Fluent French, Spanish and Italian.

References Available Upon Request

What Should You Include in a Cover Letter?

1. If you are mailing your résumé, you should always include with it a cover letter. The cover letter can be informal, just reiterating your interest in a specific position or type of work, and where you can be contacted so as to arrange an interview. Or the cover letter can be formal, in which you give yourself another opportunity to show yourself as a specially trained and qualified person for the future job. You can point out one or two skills from which your employer can benefit and which were not mentioned in the résumé. Give your telephone number and the time when you can be reached.

2. Put the potential employer's name and title on the top left-hand corner of the letter.

3. If you can be personal, it is better. If you know someone who works in the organization, use his name. Or if "you know someone who knows" the person you are writing to, use that person's name: "Mr. David Stone in your Accounting Department suggested that I write you regarding the job opening for Computer Programmer."

4. Type your cover letter, double spaced, and sign it with a pen. If you are sending out many résumés and requests for employment, take extra time to be sure that each cover letter is the original copy and that you sign each copy individually. Do not send a Xeroxed copy of a cover letter.

5. After you mail out your cover letter and résumé, one week later phone the person to whom you sent it and inquire if the letter was received. This is your follow-up. At this point, try to arrange an interview.

6. At the interview, bring two extra copies of your résumé. Someone else may interview you, or they may want to forward your résumé to another person.

The résumé and cover letter are merely tools to get you an interview. It is at the interview that you show how indispensable you are.

How To Be Successful at an Interview

1. Once you have arranged the interview, begin an in-depth research about the company or organization. Call the public relations section of the company and ask them for some literature. The public library may have some additional information about the organization or about the area of work in which you are interested. Try to speak to someone at the company before you have your interview, or try to speak to someone at a competing organization.

2. Prepare some questions as well as some hypothetical answers, and prepare to play the "devil's advocate" if need be.

3. Possible questions which you may be asked are the following:
- What was your last job? What were your responsibilities?
- Why did you leave your last job?
- What are your career goals?
- What would you like to do with us?
- What can you offer us?
- Why do you want this job?
- Where else are you seeking employment?

4. Dress is important at the time of an interview. Men should wear a suit and tie and women should wear a dress or suit. Come prepared with a pen and a pad, in case you have to write something down.

5. The very beginning of the interview is the most important part because it determines the tone for the remainder of your meeting. Try not to talk too much at first. Let the interviewer talk. But be prepared to come with a comment or question or answer as the interviewer talks and use it as you see fit. Convey the feeling to the interviewer that you know about the company and you are knowledgeable about the type of work you are applying for. If you listen carefully, the interviewer might mention the skills he is looking for. Try to speak of your skills in terms of what the interviewer is seeking. If you can, draw parallels between your past experience and education with the position you are seeking.

6. At the end of the interview, the interviewer will ask if you have any questions. Have some specific questions prepared. Try to have the questions memorized and not written. It is practical to have a good number of questions in your mind, as several of them may have already been answered during the interview. Don't ask too many questions. Three is a safe number. Avoid interrogating your interviewer.

7. It may be in bad taste to ask about the salary during the first interview. You will have to decide this at the time of the interview.

8. After the interview, send a follow-up letter thanking the interviewer for the meeting and pleasant conversation. Then one week later, if you haven't heard from the interviewer, call and express your continued interest in the position and in the organization. Be polite, but persistence in the proper amount may be useful.

WHAT ARE EMPLOYMENT AGENCIES?

The problem of how and where to get work are questions that many newcomers ask all the time. Once in New York, the woman of the family may want to work, for she feels she needs to help financially. Life in New York is more expensive than anyone suspects until he spends some time living here. Other newcomers who are relocated with a company or organization may want to change jobs once they are in New York. And still other newcomers come to New York City specifically to work here. Whatever the reason, to find a job may be complicated. After you have talked to your friends and relatives and investigated all leads, you may want to go to an employment agency. There are many in New York City, some specialized for specific areas of work, others more general. There are agencies for accountants, bankers, teachers, health professionals, secretaries, executives, computer programmers, bilingual people, temporary workers, domestics, etc.

To find which agency would be appropriate for your profession, you should telephone the national organization for your area of work. If you are a doctor, for example, you should call the American Medical Association or the New York Medical Society. Ask them to recommend a specific agency. You can also get information from the New York Public Library at 40th Street and Fifth Avenue. The reference librarian will be able to direct you to the proper source.

You may want to try several agencies. Most agencies have similar procedures in assisting prospective employees.

1. Make an appointment to speak with a person at the agency who will first want to interview you.

2. You may have to fill out forms. Read them carefully. The papers will explain the agency's policy for payment. Before you sign the papers, be sure you understand the terms and fee you must pay the agency. If you are not sure, you can ask the interviewer or secretary to explain them to you.

3. The agency will make appointments for you with several potential employers. The agency may give you the names and telephone numbers and have you make the appointments.

4. Go for the interview and keep in touch with the agency with all follow-up information. If you have any questions or problems, direct all your inquiries to your counselor at the agency.

5. If you take a job that the agency recommended to you, you will have to pay them a fee. Make sure from the beginning that you understand the financial commitment which will be expected of you.

Finding a job in New York City is very similar to finding a place to live. Both demand persistence, constant investigation, and courage. New York is a large city. It is true that there is a lot of competition and that there are many well qualified people, but this is still the city for opportunities. If you really want to succeed in New York and you are willing to work hard and make compromises, you will find a way to succeed.

Getting a good job is the first step.

PART VI

For the Foreign Newcomer

CHAPTER 14

Etiquette

How To Dine and Talk Business at the Same Time
Reservations and Reconfirmations
Follow-Up Information for All Appointments
Women in the World of Work
New York Concepts: Time; Competition
Small Talk
What Types of Conversation To Avoid
How To Dress: Different Occasions Imply Different Types of Dress
Entertaining at Home: Invitations; Brunch; Cocktail Party; Sit-Down
    Dinner Party; Buffet
When You Are Invited to a Party
When You Are Invited as a House Guest
When You Invite Someone to a Restaurant or Theatre
Special Occasions for Gift Giving
Christmas Gifts
Tipping

HOW TO DINE AND TALK BUSINESS AT THE SAME TIME

IN New York City, entertaining is an important part of one's lifestyle. In the business and professional world, the act of entertaining is done on many levels and in many guises. Inviting a client or colleague for lunch, or taking that person to the opera or a sports event, or arranging for husband and wife to attend a seminar in Hawaii, are effective ways to entertain. Trips, presents, and charge accounts are other imaginative fringe benefits that fit into the entertainment category.

183

Corporations and companies arrange receptions, dinner dances, country club sports events, and gala evenings at the opera or museums, all as ways to entertain clients, colleagues, and special guests. Executives, bankers, and business people attest to the value of entertaining and regularly support the time and expense needed to execute minute details and varied programs. These efforts must be effective or they wouldn't be so popular. Everyone in New York wouldn't be doing it, if it didn't work.

A popular form of entertaining is to lunch or dine out during the work week. This gives you the opportunity to talk leisurely and establish a personal rapport.

If you go for lunch or dinner, geographical location may be important. Choose a restaurant that is located near your guest's place of work (with luck, it will be convenient for you, also). Considering the number of fine restaurants in New York City, it shouldn't be difficult to find something within two to five blocks of your guest's office. Ask your guest what type of cuisine he prefers. If there is a specific food that the guest doesn't eat, he will mention it unabashedly at this point.

If you entertain often at lunch or dinner, an excellent way is to invite a guest to your club. There are many private clubs in New York City that have luncheon and dining rooms as well as sports facilities—gyms, sauna, swimming, squash, tennis, etc. At a club, one is always sure of friendly, efficient, and consistently good service. Some clubs are more social and snobby and difficult to join than others. Some clubs do not allow the "group" to join (bank, company or organization) but only the "individual." Some memberships are not transferrable to your colleagues in your organization. (Refer to Chapter 19 for more information on how to join a club.)

How To Mix "Small Talk" with "Big Talk." Never begin your meal by talking about business. Your guest may not be ready for it. He may first need a cocktail to quench his thirst or an appetizer to feed his appetite. Your guest may need to relax and unwind from a difficult day or he may just want to learn a little about the person he is dining with. Thus, with the first dish indulge in your opening—small talk. Chat about New York, sports, hobbies, movies, theatre, etc. (not the weather!). Try to understand the psyche of your guest and his way of thinking. This information will help you phrase, package, and present the reason for your dining together. Give yourself at least fifteen minutes before you say anything about business.

During the middle of your meal, look for the appropriate moment to discuss business. Your guest is very much aware of why you invited him for lunch or dinner. The fact that he accepted your invitation means that he is ready to hear what you wish to say. Know beforehand what you want to discuss. Be prepared with the proper documents and papers, figures, and data. If you sense that your guest feels you are coming across too strong, quiet down. Don't take out all your papers or give all your data. You can always send some follow-up information the next day. You want your guest to have a pleasant reaction to your meeting. It is your introductory step. You can always arrange another appointment. You don't have to say everything at one time. Too much "big talk" can be counterproductive. Try to feel what would be the best combination.

RESERVATIONS AND RECONFIRMATIONS

One of the preliminary steps in entertaining is to take care of the reservations. If you are dining out, you must reserve in advance—be it for lunch or dinner. You may need to reserve further in advance for dinner than for lunch, especially at some of the very sought-after restaurants. Sometimes you need to give a week's notice. It may be advisable on the day of your reservation to reconfirm your table. At this time, you may want to request a special table in a specific room or you may want to order a special dish in advance.

If you have invited a guest to meet you at the restaurant, you may arrive separately. Leave your guest's name with the maître d'hôtel and let him lead your guest to where you will be. You may have a choice of waiting at the bar or at your table. It may be wiser to wait at the bar. If your guest is more than half an hour late and you feel you don't want to wait longer or you don't want to eat alone, it is easier to exit from the bar than from a table. (Unfortunately, these embarrassing moments happen to all of us.)

It may be a good idea to reconfirm your appointment with your guest on the same day. Always give the exact address. Some restaurants may share the same name but are at different locations.

If you invite someone to a sports event, theatre, concert, or opera, you may have to reserve seats a good deal in advance, depending upon availability of tickets. Check that your seats are good. If they are not, your invitation may be counterproductive. Work out the details if you are also going to invite your guest for a snack—when and where. Make all reservations. Take into consideration transportation and time. Reconfirm the day of the event with your guest regarding where to meet, at what time, appropriate attire, etc.

FOLLOW-UP INFORMATION FOR ALL APPOINTMENTS

When you meet with a colleague or guest, either formally at the office or informally at a club or restaurant, always have a pen and pad available, so you can write down some personal notes. Your guest may ask for some specific information, or may phrase a request in a certain way that you wish to remember. If you can get the information that your guest requires, inform him when he can expect to receive the information. Take care of all requests immediately. The longer the lapse of time, the less important appears to be the task. You want to show that you consider the request for information very important.

It may be a good idea to include with the follow-up information a handwritten note saying how much you enjoyed the lunch or dinner or meeting, and it would be your pleasure to have the chance to repeat it. A few lines written by hand shows a personal touch—the natural continuation of your acquaintanceship.

A week after you mail out the material, call the person and inquire if the information was received. If you want to be sure that the material arrives quickly, use a messenger service or "Express Mail Delivery." The regular mail delivery in New York City has an infamous reputation for unnecessary delays.

WOMEN IN THE WORLD OF WORK

Many foreigners may be surprised to see such a large number of women working in New York. Some foreigners may even find difficulty in doing business with a female colleague. It has taken American men a good number of years to accept women as colleagues and even competitors. Newcomers to the United States will have to be patient with their initial feelings regarding this situation. Try to hide your surprise if a female colleague invites you to lunch and signs the check. Try to be very indifferent if a female is called in as a consultant or professional advisor.

In the past fifteen years, the role of the American woman has undergone a series of changes. Due to equal opportunities for education and career choices, increased rates of inflation and cost of living, and a high rate of divorce, women feel the need and the opportunity to work outside of the home more than in past generations. Today, it is not unusual to find a woman in a very competitive, traditionally male-dominated world. This same woman works as hard and as efficiently as her male counterpart.

Newcomers to the United States may wonder what happens to the American family structure if so many women are working. Women with young children may work part-time or may work from their homes. Child care facilities, nurseries, and babysitters help those women who work full-time. Family members such as grandparents, spouses, and older children share in child-rearing and domestic responsibilities.

Americans seem to have accepted the concept that a woman can work and have a family at the same time. The key is organization and support from the entire family. Paradoxically, the American family structure seems to become tighter in these circumstances. Everyone must help one another to attain a certain goal. Women are morally and emotionally more satisfied, children are less dependent, and men have fewer financial pressures.

New York Concepts

Time. New Yorkers are obsessed by time. They never have enough time to see everything, do everything, accomplish everything, and enjoy everything that they may want. They can't stand to "waste" time, and they are impatient with those who don't seem to organize time to its maximum. All New Yorkers seem to pulsate at an accelerated level.

If a colleague asks you to take care of doing research, or obtaining information, or following through a project, time may be an important factor. Many business deals or contracts can be lost because of "slow timing." It is always more circumspect to get all data and information required of you submitted "early" than "on time" (just be sure that it is done thoroughly). For New Yorkers, time has become a commodity — even a luxury — that may be more coveted than wealth or power. For if you don't have the time to exercise your wealth or power, you are not benefiting from your work and sacrifices.

Taking into consideration the importance of time, Americans have devised sophisticated labor saving devices — devices that allow them more free time: telephones, Telexes, Xerox machines, computers, etc.

Time is so important that Americans, generally speaking, tend to be punctual. Keep this in mind when you have appointments, deadlines, and contracts. In New York City, time is one thing that cannot be wasted.

Competition. Competition in New York City is fierce, poignant, and sometimes obvious. Everyone competes for everything. Infants compete with one another to get admitted to certain nursery schools. Students compete with one another to get high grades. Adults compete with one another to earn more money, to amass more material rewards, to secure power, clout, and influence. Companies compete with each other to collect more clients, control more shares, earn more profits. Even New York City competes with other cities to be more powerful, to increase population, to enhance its image, to receive more state and federal money.

New York attracts people from all over the world. They all want to become successful. To achieve this, the individual will ultimately have to make sacrifices. He will also have to compete with others who are equally competent, equally trained, and equally ambitious. Hard work, long hours, nervous stomachs, and unending compromises are only a few of the things that New Yorkers must experience when they become part of the New York syndrome to succeed.

Small Talk

Another important aspect of social etiquette in New York City is small talk. For New Yorkers, this is not a small matter. On the contrary, small talk governs conversations and molds New Yorkers' thinking. Be it for social or business purposes, small talk is a big "must" in New York society.

What is small talk? Why do New Yorkers indulge so often in it?

Small talk is the art of saying something superficial and light, but interesting, without burdening the listener with something too intelligent or too reflective. The Americans are famous for their small, light chatter. The British are probably even better in this art, for they add to it their acerbic sense of humor. In this instance, the Americans tend to imitate the British.

Why Do New Yorkers Indulge So Often in Small Talk? Small talk is a "game." The game is to give an opinion as infrequently as possible; to reveal one's real thoughts and one's real personality as little as possible.

1. For New Yorkers, it is considered bad taste to express a strong opinion to someone you have just met. They are not sure of the other person's opinions, and they don't want to offend.

2. It's bad business for them to express the opposite point of view from the person with whom they are speaking. People trust people who think like them, dress like them, and share common values.

3. Small talk allows the speaker to wait until he understands the other person's opinions and strategy—the other person's "game." While the speaker is waiting and talking rather mechanically, he has time to analyze the person with whom he is talking. This gives the speaker time until he is ready to say what will be advantageous to him.

4. When a New Yorker talks to someone at a cocktail party or reception, he wants the person to like him, to trust him, and to do business with him, or to continue a relationship that can develop from a superficial acquaintance to a meaningful friendship.

5. New Yorkers try to make friends. Small talk allows them to "break the ice," to be inoffensive and pleasant, from the very beginning.

WHAT TYPES OF CONVERSATIONS TO AVOID

Religion and politics are the two "no-nos" in social etiquette. New York is such a vast city, populated by so many ethnic groups, that it is very hard to know exactly with whom you are talking. You don't want to say something wrong. The best advice is to act like a diplomat and to be circumspect in your opinions and careful in your choice of topics.

You may be asked about your home country, the politics and the lifestyle. Again, be careful what you say. It would be in bad taste to talk badly against your own country. If someone asks you about the politics in your country, you can't leave the question unanswered. Give your listener some interesting, tangible thoughts to hold on to—but not an opinion or an idea that your listener would resent or you would regret saying.

HOW TO DRESS:
DIFFERENT OCCASIONS IMPLY DIFFERENT TYPES OF DRESS

New Yorkers are very concerned about how they dress and how they appear to others. It is not so much that they want to wear the latest fashion and newest style, but they do take care to dress neatly and properly, depending upon the occasion.

For business purposes, men wear jackets and ties; women wear dresses or skirts and stockings. There are some restaurants and clubs that will not serve gentlemen if they don't have a tie and jacket, nor women who wear slacks.

For women, a basic dress that can be made simpler or dressier, according to the occasion, is always a safe choice for cocktail parties, dinner engagements, or business appointments. Formal attire usually means a full-length gown or a very elegant mid-calf dress.

Men in New York tend to dress conservatively. Dark shirts, white ties, and loud colors may not be appropriate for those who work on Wall Street or Park Avenue. Casual attire, such as sneakers and jeans, don't belong at board meetings or conferences. Formal wear — "black tie" — means a black tuxedo with bow tie. If an invitation specifies "black tie," the gentleman should dress accordingly, or he may be embarrassed. If the invitation is written "Black tie optional," the choice is the gentleman's.

ENTERTAINING AT HOME

Many companies and organizations have public relations departments, and members of these sections are trained to handle entertaining on a grand scale. They are organized and competent to deal with large numbers and elaborate plans. However, there are times when entertaining extends to the home and involves the entire family. It is then that the mistress or the gentleman of the house takes over the public relations. All the details regarding invitations, menu, wine, preparation, and execution fall into their domain. And so this chapter has some hints that may be helpful.

Invitations. When you invite guests to a gathering, it is more effective to send out invitations than to telephone the guests. Something written becomes more important than something said on the telephone. There is also less room for error. Invitations can take many forms, from the packaged style to the professionally printed. Whichever style you choose, there is some essential information that should not be omitted: date, time, address, who is giving the party, if there is a special event such as birthday party or Christmas celebration, and R.S.V.P. *"Répondez s'il vous plait"* — R.S.V.P. — means "please respond." You can give your home telephone number or office number, or, if you don't want the telephone to ring at all, you can print your address next to the R.S.V.P.

You may want to write on the invitation if it is a cocktail party (which will hint to your guests that they will not have a complete dinner), or a buffet, or a sit-down dinner. If it is a formal reception, be sure to write "Black tie required" or "Black tie optional."

Some hosts and hostesses prefer their guests to leave at a certain time. There is nothing wrong in printing: "Buffet Dinner 7:00 P.M. to 10:00 P.M." The laws of protocol dictate that your guests have a half-hour of grace; they should leave by 10:30. This detail may be important if the hosts and guests must vacate a premises at a certain time.

There are different types of dining, and each one has its own rules and subtleties. A brief description of each may be helpful—brunch, cocktail party, sit-down dinner, and buffet.

Brunch. Brunch is the American cross between *br*eakfast and *l*unch. It is something enjoyed by New Yorkers because it is a "non-traditional" meal. It satisfies the New Yorkers' desire to do something different. It is usually served on Saturday or Sunday, when some New Yorkers may wake up too late for breakfast and too early for lunch. It is a nice way to begin a special weekend.

Restaurants and hotels have taken advantage of the idea and offer special brunches that begin with alcoholic fruit juices or champagne cocktails. Some cafés offer music or jazz as an extra attraction.

In Chinatown, from 10:00 A.M. to 2:00 P.M., the "Dim Sum" meal is very popular for brunch. You choose what you want from an assortment of twenty or thirty dishes. The waiters parade through the restaurant carrying different appetizers, and you signal them when you like what you see. You are charged "per plate" and in this way can sample many new foods from various regions of China. It is a fun type of brunch to share with a group of friends.

Cocktail Party. A cocktail party is a way of inviting a large group of people without having to serve a formal sit-down dinner. Cocktail parties can be scheduled any time between 5:00 P.M. and 9:00 P.M.

Guests usually stay a couple of hours, have a couple of drinks, and mix with as many people as they can. A cocktail party is a "free" form of socializing (the fact that they have all been invited is an adequate introduction). Everyone talks to everyone, regardless of traditional protocol. The concept of a cocktail gathering is that invited guests should meet one another.

And yet, under this guise of relaxed informality, the hosts have a difficult role. There may be some guests who require special attention, and some ulterior motives may need to be satisfied. Subtly and smoothly the hosts circulate, making sure that the right people meet each other.

For a cocktail party, invitations and R.S.V.P.s are in order. The hostess always needs to know how many glasses are necessary and how much food and drink is needed. For the drinks, a large selection should be available, including Scotch, gin, vodka, rum, wine (white and red), soft drinks, water, fruit juice, and a large supply of ice. For food, hors d'oeuvres and a selection of appetizers are popular. Consider that some people may be standing while they eat and won't be able to cut tough meat.

Sit-Down Dinner Party. A sit-down dinner party is more formal than a cocktail party. Plans for the party begin with the same protocol of invitations and R.S.V.P.s. Guests adhere more carefully to punctuality than they would for a cocktail party.

The sit-down dinner usually begins with an informal cocktail and hors d'oeuvre session. After half an hour, when all the guests are present, everyone is seated. Sometimes there are nameplates at specific seats; sometimes the host or hostess will designate where guests should sit. Sometimes spouses may not be seated next to each other. This is not done to be impolite but to give everyone the opportunity to speak to as many new people as possible.

Your cue to go home is when the other guests leave, unless you have a specific reason or invitation to stay longer. Dinner parties during the workweek tend to end earlier than those on the weekends.

It is always appreciated if you send a thank-you note the next day to your host or hostess, or if you telephone or send flowers if you didn't come with a gift. The few minutes it takes to say thank you will reinforce the friendship.

Buffet. A buffet, be it for breakfast, lunch or dinner, is a practical way for a host and hostess to serve a large number of people. Each guest is expected to feed himself from a choice of different dishes. Usually at a buffet, guests can sit or stand where they please and they are encouraged to be mobile.

It is not considered impolite if you return to the buffet table to help yourself to more food. And it is not considered impolite to circulate from one group of people to another group. Invitations, R.S.V.P.s, and thank-you's are all part of the protocol.

When You Are Invited to a Party

The first and most logical thing to do is to R.S.V.P. If you are not sure how to get to the party, ask your host or hostess at this time. You may also want to ask what type of attire would be appropriate.

"What time to arrive?" is a question that is often asked. Generally, Americans are punctual. For a sit-down dinner party or a buffet, try not to be more than fifteen minutes late. For a cocktail party, the time of arrival is rather flexible, but don't come at the very end. If you are invited to a reception where there is a planned guest speaker or a show, punctuality is important.

"What time to leave?" Sometimes this can present a problem. One never wants to leave too early, for fear of insulting the hosts, or too late, for fear of boring the hosts. If the invitation specifies the time, then your problem is easily resolved. If not, you have to use your best judgement. It is always helpful to take a cue from some other departing guests.

The next question is, "Should I bring a gift to the host or hostess?" Yes, Americans are generous people. They like to give gifts, and, like children, they like to receive gifts. Chocolates or wine or flowers or something from your home town are nice presents. With any token of your appreciation—be it a cake you baked or a piece of art work you designed—the thought makes a nice gesture. Don't forget to enclose a handwritten note with a few personal words.

When You Are Invited as a House Guest

If you are invited for the night or weekend as a house guest, again take along a small gift for the host or hostess or the children, if there are any, as a token of your appreciation. Try to make the gift personal and meaningful.

In New York, families may have fewer domestics than in other countries. It is not unusual, or considered out-of-place, to see the man of the house and the children helping with the dishes and other domestic responsibilities. As a house guest, you become one of the family, and thus you may want to offer to do something also. If there is no domestic, make your bed the way you found it and keep tidy your room and bathroom.

After you return to your own home, send a thank-you note. You may also want to reciprocate. You will certainly want to continue the personal friendship that was extended to you.

When You Invite Someone to a Restaurant or Theatre

In New York, with the large selection of restaurants and evening entertainment, the lack of domestic help, and the busy life-style of both spouses, it is not unusual for your host to invite you "out" rather than "home." At "home" one may give a cocktail party or buffet dinner, but, when it is a question of entertaining one or two couples, it may be more enjoyable and easier for your hosts to dine out than at home.

Formal or written invitations are not necessary if you invite people out for dinner or to the theatre. A telephone call may be enough. But make sure your guests write down all the information as to time, address of meeting, attire, and what type of event. Ask them to call you back after they have checked their schedule and they are sure they are free. The invitation should be given at least ten days in advance, if you can, and even more if you have tickets for an event. Call up your guest a day before your appointment to reconfirm that you will be going out together the next evening.

If you can pick up your guests at their home with a car or taxi, that makes the evening's preparation easier for your guests. Arrange your time so you can arrive at a theatre or concert ten or fifteen minutes before the performance. In this way, you have ample time to read the program. If you are dining, arrive a few minutes before your reservation.

If you cannot travel together (your guests may live very far from you and take other means of transportation), arrange to meet them beforehand at a specific meeting place and at a specific time. At a restaurant, the rendezvous meeting is the obvious one. If you arrive early, you can choose to meet them at the table, leave their name with the maître d'hôtel, and have the maître d' lead them to your table. If you have tickets for an event, meet them at the box office fifteen minutes before the performance (there is always only one box office, even in the largest concert hall). Explain to them beforehand where you will be waiting. Also tell them that, if they are late, you will leave their tickets for them at the box office in their name. In this way, you will not miss the performance. Most concerts and operas and some shows do not permit members of the audience to take their seats after the performance begins. You may not mind waiting for your guests, and you may even think that it would be more polite to do so. But you must think about your guest's honor. How are they going to feel if they were delayed in traffic or blocked in a garage and caused you to miss the beginning of the performance? You don't want your guests to be placed on the defensive. They will feel less embarrassed if you are *not* late because of them.

If you are planning a combination of events and places to go during the same evening, make sure all your plans are made in advance. The details may be very important to the success of the entire evening.

SPECIAL OCCASIONS FOR GIFT GIVING

Americans like to give gifts on all kinds of occasions because they are a giving people and because of the utilitarian value it holds for them. Traditionally, Americans have an unending list of celebrations that call for merriment, sharing, friendship, and, also, gift giving.

An *engagement party* is usually given by a relative or a close friend to celebrate the engagement of a couple before they get married. A proper gift is something that the couple as a new family unit can enjoy together. If they have any hobbies or special interests, the choice of a gift is easier. You may want to share the gift with common friends or relatives.

A *shower* is another occasion for gifts. It is a party given to the future bride by a relative or close friend and reserved for women. The future bridegroom may be invited to join in the festivities as well. The gift one gives, traditionally, is something the new bride will need for her house. Sometimes all the invited guests contribute a certain amount of money and buy one large present. Sometimes the shower is a "surprise party," and the hostess may suggest ideas for presents.

The *wedding* is the culmination of this nuptial celebration. Again you can share the gift with another guest, or you can make something yourself. The gift does not have to be expensive. Close relatives sometimes give the new couple money as a present, but, if you are not part of the family, this would not be recommended.

At the time of a *baby's birth* there is usually a celebration. This time the gift is for the baby. It is always a good idea to ask the parents what they need, or what they have already received.

Birthday celebrations, wedding anniversaries, Christmas gatherings, graduation parties, and many other celebrations are reasons for gaiety, friendship, and sharing of happiness. To arrive "empty-handed" could be embarrassing, so prepare to have something to give. A book or record, something made by you, or a small work of art, is always appreciated. One doesn't have to spend a lot of money to offer a token of friendship.

CHRISTMAS GIFTS

Christmas is a very special holiday all over the world. But, unfortunately, in New York, the concept of giving gifts at Christmas time has lost its levity and merriment, lost its philosophical symbol. In the past years, there have been too many Santa Clauses, too many requests for gifts. Yet if one lives or works in New York City, it is difficult to avoid this season. Even if one vacations during the holiday, one does return, and one doesn't wish to be snubbed or blacklisted for a few negligent oversights.

There is no clear-cut rule about what or how much to give employees for a Christmas present. According to Letitia Baldridge, who revised *The Amy Vanderbilt Complete Book of Etiquette,* the more personal the relationship the more appropriate it is to give a present instead of cash. Somebody you have tipped regularly probably should get less than the neglected samaritan who has gone unrewarded all year long.

Cash or presents? If the former, how much? The following information should only be used as a guideline:

1. Residential building employees: In luxury rentals, co-operatives, and condominiums with more than six staff members, tips usually average between $10.00 and $40.00 per employee. The Superintendent is at the higher scale. Seniority of employment and those who do special favors for you may become favorites. In smaller buildings with one or two employees, tips may run a bit higher, $20.00 to $50.00. Apartment house staff tipping is considerably lower outside of Manhattan.

2. Mail and delivery men: It is illegal to tip the postman. However, those delivery men who go to the same homes on a regular basis do sometimes receive from $5.00 to $10.00 per family.

3. Household helpers: For housecleaners who work for you once or twice a week, the average Christmas present is the equivalent of one week's pay. For babysitters, double the night's salary. For the regular housekeeper, depending on how extravagant you are, give a present or a week's salary.

4. Garages: Many garages have one "pot" for all the workers. The total tips could range from $20.00 to $50.00 for the group. If your garage's tradition is separate presents, you should tip them as you would one of the building's employees.

5. Restaurants: In the business district, approximately 10% of the regular customers give a Christmas tip in an envelope and have the maître d'hôtel divide it among the service staff.

6. Beauty salons: For those who regularly use a single salon, Christmas tips and gifts are practically a convention. The range varies

from a basket of fruit to lavish presents, depending on how important one's hair is.

In New York City, anyone who renders a regular service and sends a Christmas card is usually hinting for a gift. They may also wish you Christmas cheer, but clearly their request is obvious. Christmas in New York City can be a very expensive season.

TIPPING

New Yorkers, with their business-oriented mentality and their service-oriented city, tend to tip heavily. Their practical sense tells them that subtle gifts and tips increase efficiency.

Tipping is always a delicate question. How much to tip? Whom to tip? And how to avoid the problem altogether? There is no clear-cut rule on how much to tip someone who offers you a service. But there are some general guidelines among New Yorkers.

Whom To Tip

Taxi drivers get 15% of the total bill. If they go over a bridge or a tunnel, you have to pay the toll.

Waiters in restaurants get 15%. A maître d'hôtel can receive 5% of the total bill or a few dollars, but you're not obliged to pay him. If he gets you a table when there's a big wait, or if he does you a favor, or if you want him to remember you for the next time you dine there, you can tip him when he leads you to your table or after your dinner when you are leaving the restaurant.

Barbers, beauticians, manicurists, and the person who washes your hair get 15% of their particular bill. If it is the owner who renders the service, you can choose to tip or not; but practically it may be a good idea to tip the owner also.

Doormen at an apartment building or restaurant get 50¢ when they get you a taxi.

The garage attendant receives a tip if he did something special for you such as washing your car or changing a flat tire. The amount of the tip varies according to what he did. But it's not necessary to give him a tip every time he gets you your car.

Coat check attendants at restaurants and clubs receive $1.00 per coat unless there is a sign saying "NO TIPPING" or "NO GRATUITIES."

Tip the delivery boy when you don't pay extra for a delivery service.

Whom Not To Tip

Salespeople in a department store or shop.

Theatre attendants who escort you to your seat at the movies or theatre or concert or opera.

Gas station attendants when they pump your gas or clean your windows or put air in your tires.

Coat check attendants at museums. When in doubt, ask.

People who work at a dry cleaning establishment or laundromat.

Guides when you take a trip or tour of the city.

Delivery boys when they deliver your groceries and you pay extra for that service at the market. (In New York City, the markets charge an extra $1.00 for delivery. If you wish to tip the boy in addition and personally, that depends on you.)

CHAPTER 15

Where To Go for Courses in English as a Second Language (E.S.L.)

Manhattan
Brooklyn
Queens
Bronx
Staten Island
Public Schools

MANHATTAN

American Business Institute. 1657 Broadway, New York 10019. 582–9040.

E.S.L. classes meet Monday through Thursday in the late afternoon and evening. There are four levels: advanced elementary through advanced intermediate. Also courses in business skills. Classes are held in four 13-week quarters, 16 hours a week, 4 hours a day. Students must take a placement test. Courses start September, January, April, and June.

American Language Communication Center. 875 Avenue of the Americas, New York 10001. 736–2373.

Ten levels of E.S.L. Each course is for 12 weeks. Morning classes 8:00–10:00 A.M. and 10:00 A.M.–1:00 P.M. Evening classes 6:00–9:00 P.M. Saturday program 11:00 A.M.–5:00 P.M. Courses in T.O.E.F.L. Program (Test of English as a Foreign Language), required by all American Universities, Monday-Friday 10:00 A.M.–2:00 P.M. for six weeks. Courses for groups and private individuals.

199

American Language Institute, New York University. 1 Washington Square North, New York 10003. 598-3931.

There are more than 25 courses for basic, intermediate, and advanced students which meet from 2 hours a week to a full-time program of 20 hours a week. Courses meet weekdays, evenings, and Saturdays. Call for an appointment for placement exam ($10.00). Fees range from $60.00 to $1,900. Classes start September, February, June. Registration fee $20–$35.

American Language Program, Columbia University. 505 Lewisohn Hall, New York 10027. 280-3584.

E.S.L. classes meet during the day for 20–22 hours per week or 5–10 hours per week during the evenings. Placement test. Full-time 14-week session $1,920. Part-time 10 hours per week $950 and for 5 hours per week $455. Courses start September, January, May, July.

Community English Program, Teachers College, Columbia University. Main Hall, Room 311, 525 West 120th Street, New York 10027. 678-3279.

E.S.L. classes on three levels held in one morning and two evenings per week. Placement test $10.00. Courses start September, November, January, March, July.

Dulac Schools of Language. 3 East 63rd Street, New York 10021. 759-7720.

Comparable to Berlitz. As a big business they accept MasterCard and Visa and teach more than 37 languages. Private lessons are $16.50 per hour. Group lessons of 3-4 students are a lot less. Each session lasts two hours. You can also arrange lessons at your home or office. Their method is the oral, practical approach.

E.S.L. School at Riverside. Riverside Drive at 120th Street, New York, 10027. 222-5900, ext. 350.

Offers intensive English classes (5 hours daily) and part-time classes (2½ hours daily) for 30 days. Students must be at least 17 years old and have been in the United States for less than one year. For intensive classes, students must have at least a high school education from their own country. Telephone for registration dates. Classes start every 3-4 weeks. No charge for daytime classes Monday–Friday. Night classes Monday, Tuesday, Thursday from 6:30 to 9:00 for 6 weeks. Fee is $100.00.

English Conversation Program, International Center in New York. 119 West 40th Street, New York 10018. 921–8205.

Conversations in English in one-on-one tutoring one hour per week; weekdays, some weekend hours. Clubs and social activities also offered. Must become member of International Center and have been in the U.S. no longer than seven years. Fee $40.00 for course. Rolling admission.

English-in-Action. 16 East 69th Street, New York 10021. 734–9273.

One-on-one conversation and tutoring. No beginners. Registration 10:00 A.M.–4:30 P.M. weekdays; Wednesdays 10:00 A.M.–7:00 P.M. $50.00 annual registration fee. No charges for classes. Rolling admission. Classes in 20 different locations.

English Language Institute, The New School. 66 West 12th Street, New York 10011. 741–5676.

E.S.L. classes offered Monday and Thursday evenings and Saturdays with sections from beginner to advanced. Classes meet for 12-week sessions, 6 weeks in the summer. Classes start September, January, June.

International English Language Institute, Hunter College. 695 Park Avenue, New York, New York. 772–4290.

E.S.L. taught on all levels in five 8-week sessions and in a 6-week TOEFL program. Classes are held days and evenings for 4–20 hours a week, Monday to Saturday. Call for dates of placement test. Students must be 18 years or older. $10.00 registration fee. Tuition per 8-week session: for 4 hours $162.00; for 8 hours $315.00; for 10 hours $390.00; for 16 hours $620.00; for 20 hours $770.00. Courses start September, November, January, March, June. Monday–Thursday 9:00 A.M.–8:00 P.M.; Friday 9:00 A.M.–5:00 P.M.; Saturday 9:00 A.M.–5:00 P.M.

International Mission. 1 World Trade Center, Suite 103, New York 10048. 432–1088.

Group classes of 5–15 students. They do not offer private lessons. They do not charge tuition because this is a community service of the Churches of Christ. There is, however, a one-time registration fee of $60.00, and students buy their own books for $20.00.

Language Lab. 501 Madison Avenue, New York 10022. 697–2020.

E.S.L. classes in basic or advanced communication, writing and comprehension as well as an intensive remedial program. Courses offered days, evenings and Saturdays, $280.00 for 30 hours in group lessons; $550.00 for 30 hours in private lessons. Classes start late September and late January.

Language Guild Institute. 75 East 55th Street, New York 10022. 679-7171.

Classes run for 60 minutes. Instruction can be arranged privately. For a 20-hour course, 4-10 students in a group at $160.00. For a 20-hour course, 2-3 students in a class at $180.00. For a 20-hour course, private rate is $275.00. For a 50-hour course, 4-10 students in a group is $375.00. For a 50-hour course, 2-3 students in a group is $425.00. For a 50-hour course, private rate is $650.00.

Owen School. 871 Seventh Avenue, New York 10019 (55th Street). 586-8098.

$25.00 application fee. 10-week courses, 2 hours daily at $350.00. 3 hours daily at $500.00. 4 hours daily at $700.00. T.O.E.F.L. Program of two 2-hour classes for 4 weeks at $150.00.

Spanish-American Institute. 215 West 43rd Street, New York 10036. 840-7111 or 279-0376.

E.S.L. instruction offered on six levels in day and evening classes Monday through Friday. Also secretarial and office skills instruction. Placement test and interview. Courses start last Monday of each month for 3 months, 2 hours a days at $300.00.

YM/YWHA. Lexington Avenue and 92nd Street, New York 10028. 427-6000.

Elementary and intermediate classes meet three times a week for 1½ hours per class, days or evenings, for 12 weeks. Placement interview. Registration $7.50, tuition $130.00. Fall registration September. No membership needed.

YWCA. 610 Lexington Avenue, New York 10022. 755-4500.

Classes offered on three levels as well as in speech, writing and conversational English. Day and evening classes run for 5- to 10-week sessions, depending on the level. Placement test and interview. $35.00 annual membership dues. $60-95 per course. New classes are about every 4, 5, or 8 weeks.

BROOKLYN

Adult Education Program, Brooklyn College. Bedford Avenue and Avenue H, Brooklyn, New York 11210. 780-5184.

E.S.L. classes on three levels plus a workshop with emphasis on conversation. Classes meet 2 evenings a week 6:30-9:30 P.M. Workshop meets 10:00 A.M.-3:00 P.M. Saturdays. Students must take a placement test at the Adult Education Office, Room 1212, Boylan Hall. $125.00 per 8-week course; $7.00 registration fee; $85.00 for workshop. Courses start October, March.

Long Island University. Brooklyn Center, University Plaza, Brooklyn, New York 11201 (De Kalb Avenue and Flatbush Avenue). 403-1010.

Tuition, including registration fee, is $920.00 for 20 hours a week of intensive program; $460.00 for 10 hours a week of semi-intensive; $235.00 for 5 hours a week of specific skills.

QUEENS

English Language Program, Fiorello H. LaGuardia Community College. Executive Building, Room 339A, 31-10 Thomson Avenue, Long Island City, New York 11101. 626-2718.

Intensive E.S.L. classes meet Monday–Friday 9:00 A.M.-2:00 P.M. Non-intensive classes meet 2 days a week in 2-hour classes or Saturdays 9:00 A.M.-1:00 P.M. Three levels. $95.00 for non-intensive course; $675.00 for intensive course. Courses start every two months.

English Language Institute, Queens College. 65-30 Kissena Boulevard, Flushing, New York 11367. 520-7495.

E.S.L. classes meet 5 days a week for 18 hours of class at beginner, intermediate, and advanced levels. Interview and placement test. Students must be at least 18 years old and secondary school graduates. Tuition is $800.00 for U.S. residents; $1,000.00 for foreign students. Courses start in September, January, June.

Queens Borough Public Library. 89-11 Merrick Boulevard, Jamaica, New York 11432. Also at Broadway, Elmhurst, Flushing, and Jackson Heights branches.

E.S.L. classes are offered in two 10-week sessions of two 2-hour classes per week. Registration is in September and February. No fee.

St. John's University. Evening Division, Room 103, St. John Hall, Grand Central and Utopia Parkways, Jamaica, New York 11439. 969–8000.

E.S.L. courses at beginner, advanced I and II levels are offered Monday evenings in 10-week sessions.

Understanding the World of Work: A Program for Foreign Adults, York College. Division for Adult and Continuing Education, 150–14 Jamaica Avenue, Jamaica, New York 11451. 969–4175.

E.S.L. classes on three levels meet 5 hours weekly, Tuesday and Thursday evenings in 10-week cycles. Also five work-oriented seminars meet Wednesdays 7:00–9:00 P.M. Walk-in counseling available (bilingual Spanish and English). Students must be at least 25 years old and Queens residents. $95.00 fee for course. Classes start in October, January, April. Rolling admission.

Adult Basic Skills Program, York College. 150–14 Jamaica Avenue, Jamaica, New York 11451. 969–4175.

Morning and evening classes on two levels meet 4 days a week. Participants use Language Lab once a week. Also courses in Basic Education which includes bilingual counseling and instruction in survival skills. Students must be at least 16 years old. No charge. Rolling admission.

Continuing Education Courses, York College. 150–14 Jamaica Avenue, Jamaica, New York 11451. 969–4175.

E.S.L. courses on three levels meet Tuesday and Thursday evenings in 2-hour sessions. Classes start in September, February.

BRONX

City University of New York, Bronx Community College. West 181st Street and University Avenue. 220–6227.

City University of New York, Hostos Community College. 475 Grand Concourse. 960–1200.

City University of New York, Lehman College. Bedford Park Boulevard West. 960–8511.

Part-time 10-week, 2 evenings a week programs for $120.00.

College of Mount Saint Vincent. Riverdale. 549–8000.

STATEN ISLAND

City University of New York, College of Staten Island. 130 Stuyvesant Place, Staten Island. 390-7733.

Classes begin each semester of the college year. One course is less than $200 per semester.

PUBLIC SCHOOLS THAT HAVE E.S.L. PROGRAMS

Central office: 596–5030; 695–8929. These courses are sponsored by the Board of Education; therefore, they are either free or have nominal fees for registration. They are in the form of group classes. It is always a good idea to inquire about the sizes of the groups and their levels.

Washington Irving High School. 40 Irving Place, New York 10003. 414–4116.

Forsyth Street School. 198 Forsyth Street, New York 10022. 982–5660.

93rd Street School. 257 West 93rd Street, New York 10025.

Louis D. Brandeis High School. 145 West 84th Street, New York 10024. 874–1005.

Julia Richman High Schol. 317 East 67th Street, New York 10021. 472–1588. E.S.L. classes for beginners, intermediate, and advanced meet Mondays and Wednesdays 7:00–9:00 P.M. Classes start in October, January, April, July.

Stuyvesant Adult Center. 345 East 15th Street, New York 10003. 254–2890. E.S.L. classes offered 2 evenings a week 6:30–8:30 P.M. for 8-week session.

Murray Bergtraum. 411 Pearl Street, New York 10038. 233–1533.

J.H.S. 104 Adult Center. 330 East 21st Street, New York 10010. 254–2890.

P.S. 40 320 East 20th Street, New York 10010. 254–2890.

CHAPTER 16

Organizations Offering Help to the Foreigner and Newcomer to New York City

Foreign Consulates and Permanent Missions in New York City
New York City Organizations
Religious Organizations; Churches; Synagogues; Mosques

FOREIGN CONSULATES AND PERMANENT MISSIONS IN NEW YORK CITY

IN case of an emergency or other problem, the foreigner who lives in New York City does not have to despair. There are several organizations that have been established to assist the foreigner and newcomer in case of need.

There are more than 150 foreign consular offices and permanent missions located in New York. Their function is to serve and protect nationals of their countries who live and work in the area. The following list will be helpful. Call first to inquire about their hours.

Algeria. 15 East 47th Street. 750–1960.
Argentina. 12 West 56th Street. 397–1400.
Australia. 636 Fifth Avenue. 245–4000.
Austria. 31 East 69th Street. 737–6400.
Bahamas, Commonwealth of The. 767 Third Avenue. 308–2244.
Bahrain, State of. 2 United Nations Plaza. 223–6200.
Bangladesh. 821 United Nations Plaza. 867–3434.
Barbados. 800 Second Avenue. 867–8435.
Belgium. 50 Rockefeller Plaza. 586–5110.
Bolivia. 10 Rockefeller Plaza. 687–0530.

206

Brazil. 630 Fifth Avenue. 757–3080.
Burma. 10 East 77th Street. 535–1310.
Burundi. 201 East 42nd Street. 687–1180.
Canada. 1251 Avenue of the Americas. 586–2400.
Central African Republic. 386 Park Avenue South. 689–6195.
Chile. 360 Madison Avenue. 370–1455.
China, People's Republic of. 520 Twelfth Avenue. 279–4275.
Colombia. 10 East 46th Street. 949–9898.
Congo. 14 East 65th Street. 744–7840.
Costa Rica. 211 East 43rd Street. 986–6373.
Cuba. 315 Lexington Avenue. 689–7215.
Cyprus. 13 East 40th Street. 686–6016.
Denmark. 280 Park Avenue. 697–5101.
Djibouti. 866 United Nations Plaza. 753–3163.
Dominican Republic. 17 West 60th Street. 265–0630.
Ecuador. 1270 Avenue of the Americas. 245–5380.
Egypt. 1110 Second Avenue. 759–7120.
El Salvador. 46 Park Avenue. 889–3608.
Estonia. 9 Rockefeller Plaza. 247–1450.
Ethiopia. 866 United Nations Plaza. 421–1830.
Fiji Mission. 1 United Nations Plaza. 355–7316.
Finland. 540 Madison Avenue. 832–6550.
France. 934 Fifth Avenue. 535–0100.
Gabon. 820 Second Avenue. 867–3100.
Gambia. 19 East 47th Street. 752–6213.
German Democratic Republic. 58 Park Avenue. 686–2596.
Germany, Federal Republic of (West). 460 Park Avenue. 940–9200.
Ghana. 19 East 47th Street. 832–1300.
Great Britain. 845 Third Avenue. 752–8400.
Greece. 69 East 79th Street. 988–5500.
Grenada. 141 East 44th Street. 599–0301.
Guatemala. 57 Park Avenue. 686–3837.
Guinea. 820 Second Avenue. 697–6330.
Guyana. 622 Third Avenue. 953–0930.
Haiti. 60 East 42nd Street. 697–9767.
Honduras. 18 East 41st Street. 889–3858.
Hungary. 8 East 75th Street. 879–4127.
Iceland. 370 Lexington Avenue. 686–4100.
India. 3 East 64th Street. 879–7800.
Indonesia. 5 East 68th Street. 879–0600.
Iran. 622 Third Avenue. 687–2020.
Ireland. 580 Fifth Avenue. 382–2525.
Israel. 800 Second Avenue. 697–5500.
Italy. 690 Park Avenue. 737–9100.
Ivory Coast. 46 East 74th Street. 988–3930.
Jamaica. 866 Second Avenue. 935–9000.
Japan. 280 Park Avenue. 986–1600.
Jordan. 866 United Nations Plaza. 752–0135.
Kenya. 866 United Nations Plaza. 421–4740.

Kuwait. 801 Second Avenue. 661–1580.
Lebanon. 9 East 76th Street. 744–7905.
Liberia. 300 East 44th Street. 687–1025.
Lithuania. 41 West 82nd Street. 877–4552.
Luxembourg. 801 Second Avenue. 370–9850.
Madagascar. 801 Second Avenue. 986–9491.
Malaysia. 140 East 45th Street. 986–6310.
Malta. 249 East 35th Street. 725–2345.
Mauritania. 600 Third Avenue. 697–2490.
Mexico. 8 East 41st Street. 689–0456.
Monaco. 20 East 49th Street. 759–5227.
Morocco. 437 Fifth Avenue. 758–2625.
Nepal Mission. 711 Third Avenue. 986–1989.
Netherlands. 1 Rockefeller Plaza. 246–1429.
Nicaragua. 1270 Avenue of the Americas. 247–1020.
Niger. 575 Lexington Avenue. 935–6100.
Norway. 825 Third Avenue. 421–0280.
Pakistan. 12 East 65th Street. 879–5800.
Panama. 1270 Avenue of the Americas. 246–3771.
Paraguay. 1 World Trade Center. 432–0733.
Peru. 805 Third Avenue. 644–2850.
Philippines. 556 Fifth Avenue. 764–1330.
Poland. 233 Madison Avenue. 889–8360.
Portugal. 630 Fifth Avenue. 246–4580.
Qatar. 747 Third Avenue. 486–9335.
Saint Lucia. 41 East 42nd Street. 697–9360.
Saint Vincent and the Grenadines. 41 East 42nd Street. 687–4490.
Samoa. 820 Second Avenue. 599–6196.
San Marino. 109 East 79th Street. 737–3749.
Saudi Arabia. 866 United Nations Plaza. 752–2740.
Senegal. 392 Fifth Avenue. 947–7355.
Singapore. One United Nations Plaza. 826–0840.
Somali Democratic Republic. 711 Third Avenue. 687–9877.
South Africa. 425 Park Avenue. 838–1700.
Spain. 150 East 58th Street. 355–4080.
Sri Lanka. 630 Third Avenue. 986–7040.
Sudan. 210 East 49th Street. 421–2680.
Suriname. 1 United Nations Plaza. 826–0660.
Sweden. 825 Third Avenue. 751–5900.
Syrian Arab Republic. 820 Second Avenue. 661–1313.
Switzerland. 444 Madison Avenue. 758–2560.
Thailand. 53 Park Place. 732–8166.
Trinidad and Tobago. 420 Lexington Avenue. 682-7272.
Tunisia. 405 Lexington Avenue. 557–3344.
Turkey. 821 United Nations Plaza. 247–5309.
Union of Soviet Socialist Republics. 136 East 67th Street. 861–4900.
Uruguay. 301 East 47th Street. 752–8240.
Venezuela. 7 East 51st Street. 826–1660.
Viet Nam. 20 Waterside Plaza. 685–8001.
Yugoslavia. 767 Third Avenue. 838–2300.

Zaire. 767 Third Avenue. 754–1966.
Zambia. 237 East 52nd Street. 758–1110.
Zimbabwe. 19 East 47th Street. 980–5084.

NEW YORK CITY ORGANIZATIONS

Institute of International Education. 809 United Nations Plaza, New York 10017. 883–8470.

All foreign students who study in New York should become familiar with this organization and what it offers. A telephone call or visit would be worthwhile. They have literature and books available that may be very informative for the foreign student.

New York Association for New Americans (N.Y.A.N.A.). 225 Park Avenue South, New York 10003. 674–7400.

New York's agency for refugees, especially for Russians, Eastern Europeans, Cambodians, Indo-Chinese, Cubans, and Haitians. This agency does a great deal to help the refugee get settled. They help with housing, schools, English language, medical care, and all the details of resettlement.

New York Chamber of Commerce and Industry. 200 Madison Avenue, New York 10016. 561–2020.

This organization serves large companies and middle-sized businesses from Europe, especially the United Kingdom and West Germany, that want to set up subsidiaries and offices in New York. The role of this Chamber is to act as the business's voice before the government and provide many services a firm cannot afford to offer on its own, such as real estate planning, financial and political details.

New York City Commission for the United Nations and for the Consular Corps. 2 United Nations Plaza, New York 10017. 319–9300.

Affiliated with the United Nations, this organization serves the delegates of the United Nations and the diplomats who come to live and work in New York City. If there are any questions about housing, schools, English language, law, diplomatic immunity, etc., this organization is prepared to help the families of the diplomatic corps — but not the staff members.

New York City Office of International Business. 17 John Street, New York 10038. 566–3812.

This is a very new office that was formed to satisfy the needs of the foreign business community in New York City. Activities and interests are directed toward American trade and business with the leading Western European countries.

New York City Visitors Bureau. 2 Columbus Circle. 397–8222.

This organization takes care of visitors, tourists, and conventions. All information in brochure form regarding what to see and do in New York is available for the visitor. Participants in conventions who have free time to spend in New York should also contact this office, for the Visitors Bureau can arrange guided tours with translators, excursions outside New York, and programs in New York City.

RELIGIOUS ORGANIZATIONS

Catholic Charities of the Archdiocese of New York. 1011 First Avenue. 371–1000.

This is an organization which helps Catholic refugees who emigrate from all over the world to the United States.

Hebrew Immigrant Aid Society (H.I.A.S.). 200 Park Avenue South. 674–6800.

This is an organization which helps Jewish refugees leave their countries and immigrate to the United States. They take care of passports and visas, transportation from the country of origin to the actual destination. They work in conjunction with N.Y.A.N.A., which takes care of the refugees once they are in New York.

In the five boroughs there are more than 2,250 churches and 600 synagogues. This list is just a small sampling.

Churches
  Brick Church (Presbyterian): 1140 Park Avenue
  Broadway United Church of Christ: 211 West 56th Street
  Buddhist Temple: 64 Mott Street
  Calvary Baptist Church: 123 West 57th Street
  Christ Church (Methodist): 520 Park Avenue
  Christian Science 1st Church: Central Park West at 96th Street
  Church of All Nations (Methodist): 48 St. Mark's Place

Church of Notre Dame (Roman Catholic): 405 West 114th Street
Church of the Ascension (Episcopalian): Fifth Avenue at 10th Street
Church of the Covenant (Presbyterian): 310 East 42nd Street
Church of the Divine Paternity (Unitarian): Central Park West and 76th Street
Church of the Holy Apostles (Episcopalian): Ninth Avenue and 28th Street
Church of Our Lady of Victory (Roman Catholic): 60 William Street
Church of the United Nations (nonsectarian): 77 United Nations Plaza
Fifth Avenue Presbyterian: Fifth Avenue at 55th Street
Friends Meeting House (Quakers): 15 Rutherford Street
Grace Church (Episcopalian): Broadway at 10th Street
Greek Cathedral of the Holy Trinity: 319 East 74th Street
Holy Trinity Lutheran Church: Central Park West at 65th Street
Judson Memorial (Baptist): 55 Washington Square
Marble Collegiate (Reformed Church): Fifth Avenue at 29th Street
Park Avenue Christian (Disciples of Christ): 1010 Park Avenue
Riverside Church (Congregational): Riverside Drive at 122nd Street
St. Bartholomew's Church (Episcopalian): 109 East 50th Street
St. Francis of Assisi Monastery and Church (Roman Catholic): 135 West 31st Street
St. John The Divine, Cathedral of (Episcopalian): Amsterdam Avenue at 110th Street
St. Malachy's (Actors) Church: 239 West 49th Street
St. Patrick's Cathedral (Roman Catholic): Fifth Avenue at 51st Street
St. Paul's Chapel (Episcopalian): Broadway at Fulton Street
St. Vincent De Paul Church (Roman Catholic): 116 West 24th Street
Serbian Orthodox Cathedral of St. Lava: 15 West 25th Street
Seventh Day Adventist Manhattan Church: 232 West 11th Street
Trinity Church (Episcopalian): Broadway at Wall Street
Unitarian Church All Souls: 80th Street and Lexington Avenue

Synagogues
Beth Hamedrash Hagsdol Synagogue: 60–64 Norfolk Street
Bialystoker Synagogue: 7–17 Willett Street
Central Synagogue: 123 East 55th Street
Fifth Avenue Synagogue: 5 East 62nd Street
Park Avenue Synagogue: 50 East 87th Street
Spanish and Portuguese Synagogue: 8 West 70th Street
Stephen Wise Free Synagogue: 30 West 68th Street
Temple Emanu-El: Fifth Avenue at 65th Street
Wall Street Synagogue: 47 Beekman Street

Mosques
Islamic Center in New York. 1 Riverside Drive. 362–6800
Islamic Council of America. 401 East 11th Street. 533–5060

There are many mosques located in the five boroughs. For a complete list, call the Islamic Center at 362–6800.

CHAPTER 17

Taxes

Prepared by Joseph Graf & Co.,
Certified Public Accountants:
Peter G. Graf, C.P.A., J.D.
Edward Gross, C.P.A.
Henry Scheinkman, C.P.A., J.D.

A FOREIGN NATIONAL who is planning to reside in the United States, either for a temporary period or as a permanent resident, is faced with a maze of tax laws and regulations which, without proper interpretation and careful planning, can make his move to the United States far more costly than it should be.

It is also important that the foreign national examine the terms of the tax treaty between his country and the United States, if one exists, since the terms of the treaties vary from country to country. It is possible that a proposed plan that may be favorable under the terms of the treaty with one nation will not be so beneficial under the terms of the tax treaty with another.

It is not the purpose of this chapter to set forth in detail the provisions of the Internal Revenue Code of the United States governing the taxation of non-resident and resident aliens. Similarily, no attempt is made to compare the tax laws of the United States with the tax laws of the country of the foreign national or the effects of different tax treaties.

It is the purpose of this chapter to give the foreign national an awareness of the tax provisions to which he will be subject in the United States, and to serve as a preliminary introduction and guide. It is emphasized that proper planning is essential before any irreversible steps are taken, since such actions will carry far more weight in the determination of status than any oral testimony.

The United States tax law classifies non-citizens as being either *resident aliens* or *non-resident aliens* and applies a different manner of taxation to each. The differences in the manner of taxation are material, and a change from a non-resident status to that of a resident can have severe tax consequences.

The new law includes provisions for a specific definition of an alien. Any alien not meeting this definition will be considered a non-resident alien. The bill defines a resident alien as any national who is:

1. A lawful permanent resident of the United States (the green card test); or

2. Present in the United States for more than thirty days during the current calendar year; and had been present in the United States for at least 180 days during a three-year period weighted toward the present year (substantial presence test). The weighted average is the sum of (a) the days spent in the United States during the current year; (b) $\frac{1}{3}$ of the days present in the United States during the preceding year; and (c) $\frac{1}{6}$ of the days present in the United States during the second preceding year.

An exception to the substantial presence test is provided so that an alien who otherwise meets the requirements of the substantial presence will not be considered a resident alien, if he is:

1. Present in the United States for fewer than 183 days during the current year; and

2. Has a tax home in a foreign country and has a closer connection to the foreign country than to the United States.

Once the status of an alien in the United States has been determined, the tax laws are very definite as to which taxes should be paid by non-resident aliens and which by resident aliens.

RESIDENT ALIEN

A resident alien is taxed on his income from *all* sources, including income from outside the United States, in the same manner as a United States citizen. The resident alien is allowed the same exclusions, exemptions, deductions, and credits permitted a United States citizen. The resident alien uses the same tax form, Form 1040, as the United States citizen for the filing of his income tax return.

The estate of a resident alien is subject to federal estate tax in the same manner as a deceased United States citizen. The taxable estate of a resident alien includes all personal and real property located both inside and outside the borders of the United States.

Taxation of United States Citizens and Resident Aliens: Income Tax Form. A United States citizen or resident must file income tax returns annually, using Form 1040 to do so. His return, except for his initial return, must cover an accounting period of twelve months, and he may elect to use either a calender year or a fiscal year for filing. The choice is made on the initial return filed. The requirements for filing on a fiscal year basis state that the taxpayer must keep books and records which clearly reflect his annual income. The taxpayer may choose to report his income on either a cash method or under an accrual method, but he must be consistent in his treatment of income and deductions under either method. The taxpayer may use the cash method to report salary and non-business income and expenses, and use the accrual method to report his income from his business.

Filing of Return. The filing date of the return is no later than 3½ months after the close of the tax year (for a taxpayer using the calendar year this date is April 15). A four-month automatic extension of time to file may be secured, if requested before the due date of the return. A further extension of two months will be granted for good cause. A taxpayer who is outside the United States on the date for the original filing is permitted a two-month additional period for the filing of his return. Further extensions of up to four months may be requested. Extensions of time to file do not relieve the taxpayer from his responsibility to make full payment of any balance due by the original filing date. Penalties are provided for failure to pay, and interest, presently at 11% compounded daily, is charged on the unpaid balance. This interest rate is subject to adjustment twice during a calendar year in accordance with the average adjusted prime rate charged by commercial banks.

A taxpayer is required to estimate his tax liability for the year and to pay the amount of such estimated tax in installments during the year. Penalties are imposed if the estimated tax is less than 80% of the tax liability and if the estimated payments are not timely made, with certain exceptions.

The Internal Revenue Code contains provisions for imposing both civil and criminal penalties for violation of the filing regulations. Civil penalties may be added for the filing of negligent returns. Both civil and criminal penalties may be imposed where fraudulent returns are filed.

Filing Status. There are five different filing classifications for United States citizens and resident aliens, and the graduated tax rates for the classifications differ.

1. Single
2. Married — Filing jointly
3. Married — Filing separate returns
4. Head of Household
5. Qualified Widow or Widower with Dependent Child

The filing status of the taxpayer is determined by his marital status on the last day of his tax year. There is no dual status for the year except in the case where an individual has been both a non-resident and resident alien in the same tax year. In such event, separate returns will have to be filed covering the respective periods of non-residence and residence.

Taxpayers who on the last day of the tax year are married but not legally separated may elect to file a joint return or to file separate returns as being married but filing separately. This choice can be changed by filing a joint return within three years after the due date of the separate returns. A United States citizen or resident alien, who has a spouse who is a non-resident alien, may file a joint return with his spouse provided she agrees to be taxed on her worldwide income. Where one spouse has higher taxable income than the other, a tax savings will result from the filing of a joint return.

Exemptions. A taxpayer filing as a single individual is permitted a $1,000 deduction as exemption for himself. An additional $1,000 is allowed if he reaches the age of 65 at any time during the tax year, plus an additional $1,000 if he qualifies as being blind. On a joint return, similar deductions are permitted for the spouse whether or not she has any income.

Taxpayers filing joint tax returns or head of household returns are permitted an additional $1,000 deduction as exemption for each individual who qualifies as a dependent. There are five tests that must be met for a person to qualify as a dependent:

- Support Test
- Gross Income Test
- Member of Household or Relationship Test
- Citizenship Test
- Joint Return Test

The Support Test requires that the taxpayer furnish at least one-half the total support of the dependent for the calendar year in which his tax year begins.

The Gross Income Tests requires that the dependent have less than $1,000 gross income for the calendar year in which the taxpayer's year begins. Tax-exempt income is not included in determining gross income. A child of the taxpayer, who is under nineteen or is a full-time student, does not have to meet the Gross Income Test.

The Member of Household or Relationship Test requires that the dependent either be related to you or be a member of your household for the entire year. A dependent who is related to you does not have to live with you or be a member of your household. Related persons include parents, grandparents, children, grandchildren, great-grandchildren, brothers, sisters, aunts, uncles, nieces, nephews, step-children, step-parents, and in-laws.

The Citizenship Test requires that the dependent be a United States citizen, resident, or national of Canada or Mexico for some part of the calender year in which the taxpayer's tax year begins.

The Joint Return Test requires that the dependent not file a joint return with his spouse.

Finally, a taxpayer is permitted to list his spouse as a dependent on his return only if she has no gross income and is not taken as the dependent of another taxpayer. If the taxpayer can take his spouse as an exemption he can also take the deductions for age and blindness if they apply to his spouse.

Tax Exempt Income. The Internal Revenue Code specifically excludes certain items from income. The most important of such exclusions are the following. The taxpayer does not pay taxes on:

• Interest on the obligations of a state or one of its political subdivisions.

• The first $100 of total qualifying dividends ($200 on a joint return).

• Accident and health insurance proceeds.

• Gifts, bequests, and inheritances.

• Life insurance proceeds.

• Social Security payments (beginning with 1984, the exclusion is limited based on income).

• Workmen's compensation.

• Child support payments.

• Unemployment insurance (exclusion limited based on income).

• Relocation payments.

• First $125,000 of gain on the sale of the principal residence if the taxpayer has reached the age of 55 prior to the date of sale and other requirements are met.

• Receipts that represent the return of cost or investment (such costs or investment must be reduced by any tax benefits taken or required to be taken by statute).

A United States citizen who works abroad in 1985 and receives $80,000 as foreign earned income can exclude that amount if he meets the test of either being a *bona fide* resident of a foreign country for an uninterrupted period that includes a full tax year or having been physically present in a foreign country 330 full days out of a consecutive twelve-month period, and the portion to be excluded from 1984 is limited to the amount earned in 1984. The exclusion of $80,000 remains at $80,000 per year through 1987 and is then increased by $5,000 each year thereafter until a maximum exclusion of $95,000 is reached in 1990. In addition to the exclusion of foreign earned income, a United States citizen, who meets the *bona fide* residence or physical presence test, may elect to exclude excess housing costs incurred and also the value of meals and lodging provided by an employer in a foreign country under certain hardship conditions.

Income Tax Form 1040. The United States Individual Income Tax return consists of nine subdivisions of information which the taxpayer must complete in order to determine his correct income tax.

1. Personal information.
2. Gross income.
3. Adjustments to gross income.
4. Tax computation.
5. Credits against income tax.
6. Other taxes.
7. Payments.
8. Balance of tax due or overpayment.
9. Signatures.

Explanations of the more important items, indicated below by an asterisk (*), are set forth beginning on p. 221.

1. Personal Information. Name of Taxpayer (Taxpayers if Joint Return)

      Social Security Number of Taxpayer(s)

      Address of Taxpayer(s)

      Occupation of Taxpayer(s)

      Filing Status (see paragraph on Filing Status, above)

      Exemptions Claimed (see paragraph on Exemptions, above)

2. Gross Income. As stated before, all income received by a United States citizen or resident alien is taxable unless the income is specifically

excluded by statute. Form 1040 lists the income to be reported by category as follows:

Wages, salaries, tips, etc.

Interest income.

*Dividends.

Refunds of state and local income taxes.

Alimony received.

*Business income.

*Capital gains and losses.

Supplemental gains or losses.

*Fully taxable pensions, I.R.A. distributions, annuities.

Other pensions and annuities.

Rents, royalties.

*Partnership, small business corporations.

Estates and trusts.

Farm income.

Other income.

*Exclusion of foreign earned income.

Other income includes prizes, awards, fees, commissions, and income not covered under the listed categories. The exclusion of foreign earned income is to be entered in parentheses so as to offset the foreign earned income included in reported income.

A taxpayer who had business or casualty losses in past years may be able to deduct all or part of these losses in the current tax year.

The regulations pertaining to the computation and allowance of the loss deductions is explained later in this chapter.

3. Adjustments to Income. After a taxpayer has computed the total amount of income to be included on his tax returns, he is allowed by statute to make certain adjustments to this total. These adjustments are in effect *deductions* taken directly from the total income for the purpose of arriving at an adjusted gross income total which then serves as the base for limiting certain itemized deductions. The adjustments to gross income are:

*Moving expenses.

*Employee business expenses.

*Payments to individual retirement account.

*Payments to a Keogh (Self Employment) Plan.

Penalty on early withdrawal from Time Savings Account.

Alimony paid.

*Deduction for married couple when both work.

Disability income exclusion.

4. Tax Computation. After the amount of adjusted gross income has

been determined, it is reduced by (1) the excess of itemized deductions over a zero bracket amount and (2) by $1,000 for each of the exemptions claimed. The zero bracket amount represents the blanket allowance under the tax laws in lieu of itemizing deductions.

The zero bracket amount varies depending on the filing status of the taxpayer.

Married filing jointly	$3,400
Qualifying widow (or) with dependent child	3,400
Single taxpayer	2,300
Head of household	2,300
Married filing separate returns	1,700

A taxpayer has the right to itemize his deductions when the total of these deductions exceeds the zero bracket allowed by his filing status.

Itemized deductions consist of non-business expenditures which the tax laws permit as deductions against adjusted gross income. They are:

Medical and dental expenses.

Taxes.

Interest expense.

Charitable contributions.

Casualty and theft losses.

Miscellaneous deductions.

Miscellaneous deductions include certain deductible employee expenses, expenses incurred in the production of income, tax assistance fees, certain adoption expenses, and certain appraisal fees.

5. Credits. The credits that a taxpayer may deduct from his income tax liability are particularily valuable since they are deducted "in full" directly from income tax and are not "deductions from adjusted gross income." They are:

Credits for the elderly.

*Foreign tax credit.

*Investment credit.

Partial credit for political contributions.

*Credit for child and dependent care expenses.

Jobs credit.

*Residential energy credit.

Other credits.

6. Other Taxes. A United States citizen, in addition to paying income taxes, is required to include on his income tax return other taxes which, while related to income, are not income taxes:

*Self-employment tax.

*Alternative minimum tax.

Tax from recapture of investment credit.

Social Security tax on income from tips.

Tax on individual retirement account.

Advance earned income payments.

7. Payments. The total tax liability of the taxpayer (income tax less credits plus other taxes) is reduced by amounts withheld as income tax at source and by payments made directly by the taxpayer.

Federal income tax withheld.

Estimated payments made and credit from prior year.

Earned income credit.

Payment made with request for extension of time for filing.

Excess social security withheld.

Credit for federal tax on special fuels.

Regulated investment company credit.

8. Balance of Tax Due or Overpayment.

　　a) Amount due (income tax and other taxes exceed the amount of credits, withholding and prior payments)

　　b) Overpayment (credits, withholding and prior payments exceed the amount of income tax and other taxes)

A taxpayer who has made an overpayment in estimated tax may elect to have the overpayment refunded to him or to have the overpayment applied to the following year's estimated tax.

A taxpayer who has an amount due in excess of 20% of his total tax liability (income tax less credits plus other taxes) is subject to penalty for underpayment of estimated tax unless he can avail himself of one of the exemptions to the penalty. The computation of the penalty and the exemptions thereto are set forth on Form 2210, which should be completed by the taxpayer and attached to the return.

9. Signatures. The return must be signed by the taxpayer. In the case of a joint return, *both* husband and wife must sign, even though only one had income. A guardian of a spouse who is mentally ill may sign the return as guardian. A taxpayer who has a power of attorney from his spouse to sign the return may sign the return on her behalf and must attach the power of attorney to the return.

If the return is prepared by a preparer who charges for his work, the preparer must fill in the required information and sign the return.

Signatures need not be notarized, but, nevertheless, any false statements contained in the return are subject to penalities for perjury.

Detailed Explanations of Income Tax Return Form

　*Dividends. Dividends are distributions to a taxpayer by a corporation which may be taxable in full as ordinary income or as capital gains or

which may be non-taxable in full or in part. The taxable status of the distribution is determined by the paying corporation subject to review by the Internal Revenue Service. Taxpayers who recieve dividends through a partnership, an estate, a trust, or an association that is taxed as a corporation must include such dividends in their income. The first $100 or total qualifying dividends may be excluded from income. The exclusion is $200 if a joint return is filed. Qualifying dividends include ordinary dividends from taxable domestic corporations; dividends from foreign corporations do not qualify.

Business Income. Net earnings from a self-employed business constitute business income. A net operating loss in a taxable year which is in excess of other income may be carried back as a deduction to the preceding three years before the taxable year, and only the loss still remaining can then be carried forward for fifteen years. The net operating loss to be carried forward or carried back, as the case may be, is the excess of the allowable deductions over gross income with certain adjustments. A taxpayer may elect to forego the three-year carryback provision and elect to carry the net operating loss forward only.

Capital Gains and Losses. All assets, both tangible and intangible property, are capital assets with the following exceptions:

1. Property held for sale to customers.

2. Accounts or notes receivable acquired in the normal course of a trade or business.

3. Depreciable property used in a trade or business.

4. Real property used in a trade or business.

5. Copyrights, literary, musical, artistic compositions; letters created by the taxpayer's personal efforts.

6. Short-term obligations of the United States, state and municipal governments issued on a discount basis and payable without interest at a fixed date not more than one year from the date of issue, if the obligations were acquired before June 24, 1981.

Net income from the sale of capital assets is taxable, but the portion of the net gain to be included in income depends on the holding period of the capital assets. Capital assets acquired by the taxpayer after June 22, 1984, and held for more than six months are considered to be long-term capital assets, whereas those held for less than one year are classified as short-term capital assets. Capital assets acquired before June 22, 1984, must be held for more than one year in order to be classified as long-term capital assets. A taxpayer at the end of his taxable year must net all his long-term capital gains with his long-term capital losses. The excess of net long-term capital gains over net short-term capital loss is subject to a 60% reduction, so that only 40% of the net capital gain is taxed at ordinary income rates. An excess of net short-term capital gains over net long-term capital rates is fully taxed as ordinary income. Where there are both net long-term capital gains and net short-term capital gains, the net long-term capital gains are reduced by 60% and the net short-term capital gains are taxable in full. Where capital losses exceed capital gains, as determined by grouping all long-term and short-term gains and losses, the resultant net loss may be deducted from gross income to a maximum amount of $3,000, and any loss then remaining may be carried over to future years until the loss is exhausted. In computing the amount of net long-term capital loss to be deducted, only 50% of the net long-term capital loss is allowed. Any excess of net short-term capital loss over net long-term capital gains is deductible in full up to $3,000 and the excess over $3,000 can be carried over.

While depreciable personal property and depreciable real property used in a trade or business are excluded from the definition of capital assets, a special provision of the tax law permits the net profit on the sale of depreciable personal property and real property acquired after June 22, 1984, used in a trade or business, and held for more than six months, to be taxed as long-term capital gains. A portion of the net profit realized on the sale of personal or real property, on which depreciation has been deducted prior to the sale, may be taxed as ordinary income under recapture depreciation rules. Net profit on the sale of such assets held less than six months is taxed as ordinary income, and a net loss on the sale of such property, regardless of the holding period, is deductible in full from gross income. Depreciable personal property and real property acquired before June 22, 1984, must be held for more than one year to be accorded long-term capital asset treatment.

Fully Taxable Pensions, I.R.A. Distributions, and Annuities. Distributions received from employee pension plans and annuities to which the taxpayer did not contribute are taxable in full. Where the taxpayer paid part of the cost of the pension or annuity, only the additional amount over the money contributed by the taxpayer is taxable.

Lump sum distributions received from a qualified retirement plan may be given special tax treatment, whereby the income portion of the payment is taxed under a special ten-year averaging method. Lump sum distribution is defined as the payment of the entire amount due to the taxpayer within one year. This special ten-year averaging treatment cannot be used for distribution from Individual Retirement Accounts.

Lump sum distributions from qualified pensions may be deposited (rollover) into an Individual Retirement Account without being subject to tax, if the transfer is completed within 60 days after the distribution is received. "Rollover" privileges apply to the transfer of funds from one I.R.A. account into another I.R.A. account. Such deposits or transfers serve to defer payment of tax on the funds until distribution is made from the account into which the funds were transferred.

Partnership and Small Business Corporations. Partnerships are not treated as separate taxable entities, but the income or loss from a partnership, the capital gains and losses, and the various tax credits are passed through to the individual partners to be reported on their respective tax returns. A small business corporation is a corporation that has filed election to be taxed in the same manner as a partnership. By doing this, the corporation retains the advantage of limited liability on the part of its shareholders but avoids the separate corporation taxes applicable to income.

Exclusion of Foreign Earned Income. A citizen of the United States who works abroad may qualify, for exclusion from income in 1984, $80,000 of foreign earned income. This exclusion remains at $80,000 each year through 1987 and then is increased by $5,000 each year until a maximum exclusion of $95,000 is reached. To qualify for this foreign earned income exclusion and excess foreign housing costs, the U.S. citizen must meet a *bona fide* residence test or a physical presence test. A resident alien may qualify for the exclusions if he meets the requirements of physical presence.

Moving Expenses. A taxpayer who changed jobs, and has incurred moving expenses in connection with such change, may be able to deduct such expenses if the move meets certain eligibility, time, and distance tests.

Employee Business Expenses. A taxpayer who is an employee, and is required to make expenditures for travel, entertainment, and gifts, may deduct the excess of such expenditures over reimbursement received from his employer.

Payments to Individual Retirement Accounts. A taxpayer who earns compensation may set up an Individual Retirement Account and deduct the amount of his contribution from gross income. By doing this, the taxpayer will defer the tax on the contribution to the amount until a later year when he can expect to be in a lower tax bracket. The tax on all interest and dividends earned on the account during its existence is similarily deferred. The amount that can be contributed annually to an I.R.A. account is limited to the lesser of $2,000 ($2,250 if a non-employed spouse is involved) or 100% of the compensation included in the taxpayer's gross income. The taxpayer *may* commence withdrawals without penalty upon reaching the age of $59\frac{1}{2}$ but *must* commence withdrawals upon reaching the age of $70\frac{1}{2}$.

Payments to a Keogh (Self Employment Plan). In addition to the I.R.A. account, a self-employed individual may set up a qualified retirement plan and deduct contributions to the plan. All eligible full-time employees of the business must be included in the plan. The contribution on behalf of the self-employed individual is limited to the lesser of 15% of earned income of $15,000 for the year 1984. For the year 1985, the maximum contribution limit is $30,000.

Deductions for Married Couples Who Both Work. Where a husband and wife file a joint report and each person reports an earned income, a special deduction is permitted. The amount of the deduction for 1983 and later years is the lesser of 10% of $30,000, or the earned income of the lower earning spouse's income.

Foreign Tax Credit. A taxpayer who has paid foreign income taxes on income earned in a foreign country may claim credit for such payment on his return. Any unused foreign credit may be carried back and carried forward in the same manner as net operating loss.

Investment Credit. A taxpayer who is self-employed may deduct as a credit as much as 10% of the cost of tangible property used in business. Real property does not qualify for the credit. A taxpayer who is a member of a business partnership, or a shareholder in a small business corporation, may deduct as a credit his pro-rata portion of such 10% credit. Any unused investment credit may be carried back and forward in the same manner as a net operating loss.

Credit for Child and Dependent Care Expenses. A taxpayer who maintains a household for a dependent individual who is either under fifteen years of age, or is physically or mentally incapable of self-care, and who incurs expenses for household services and for the care of such an individual, may deduct a limited credit in connection with such expenses. The taxpayer's spouse qualifies for dependent care expense if she is physically or mentally incapable of caring for herself.

Residential Energy Credits. A taxpayer who incurs expenditures in connection with purchasing and installing qualifying insulation and other energy saving components for his residence may claim a 15% credit on the first $2,000 of such expenditures. The residence must be located in the United States and must have been substantially constructed before April 20, 1977.

A separate credit is allowed for the cost of purchasing and installing renewable energy source property in the taxpayer's residence. The credit is 40% of expenditures up to $10,000 and is available through 1985.

Self-Employment Tax. A taxpayer who is self-employed or is a member of a business partnership is required to pay self-employment tax based on the net earnings from the self-employment. The maximum amount of income subject to tax for 1984 is $37,800 and the rate of tax is 11.3%. Compensation received by the taxpayer which is subject to Social Security tax is deducted from this maximum amount.

Alternative Minimum Tax. A taxpayer is subject to the alternative minimum tax to the extent that it exceeds his regular tax. The alternative minimum taxable income in excess of $30,000 for single taxpayers, $40,000 for married taxpayers, or $20,000 for married taxpayers filing separately, is taxed at 20%. The alternative minimum taxable income is computed by adding preference amounts to adjusted gross income and then subtracting the allowable deductions. The principal preference amounts to be added include deductions for capital gains, accelerated depreciation, exclusion of dividends and interest, depletion, intangible drilling costs, and certain research and development costs. The allowable deductions are: charitable contributions, medical expenses in excess of 10% of adjusted gross income, casulty losses, wagering losses, other interest to the extent of net investment income included in the minimum tax base, interest on mortgage and housing interest on any debt incurred before July 1, 1982 that is secured by a principal residence regardless of purpose.

Estate or Gift Tax. Estate taxes are imposed on transfers of property of deceased persons who were either United States citizens or resident aliens of the United States at the time of death.

Gift taxes are imposed on the transfers of gift of property by living individual donors who were either United States citizens or resident aliens of the United States at the time of transfer.

The rates for estate and gift taxes are similar, and a unified credit is allowed which is first applied against the gift tax and the balance against the estate tax. The unified credits allowed are as follows:

1984	96,300
1985	121,800
1986	155,800
1987 and thereafter	192,800

An individual donor can make annual gifts of $10,000 to a donee and exclude that amount from gift tax. The maximum gift, in the case of an individual donor whose spouse consents to the gift, is $20,000 for each donee per year. These exclusions are not charged against the unified tax credit.

An estate tax is computed on the value of the taxable estate transferred. The taxable estate consists of all the assets reduced by:

1. Debts, claims, expenses and losses.
2. The marital deduction.
3. The charitable deduction.

The marital deduction allowed is equal to the value of the qualifying property left by the deceased to his surviving spouse.

The charitable deduction is allowed for bequests to public, charitable, or religious purposes and is not limited to any percentage of the net value of the estate.

A tentative tax is computed on the taxable estate using graduated tax rates beginning at 18% and rising to 55% for those dying in 1984 through 1987. This tax percentage is reduced to 50% for the year 1988 and thereafter.

This tentative tax is reduced by the amount of unused unified credit available and by credits for state death taxes and foreign death taxes. The foreign death taxes arise when the taxable estate included property located in a foreign country upon which death tax was required to be paid to such foreign country.

Estates of decedents who were neither U.S. citizens not resident aliens at the time of death are taxed only on the property situated within the United States. The tax rates are lower, beginning at 6% and rising to 30%. Deductions for funeral and administrative expenses, claims against the estate, unpaid taxes and mortgages, and losses are limited to the percentage that value of the gross United States property bears to the value of the total estate. No marital deduction is permitted, but charitable bequests are allowed in full. The amount of the unified credit is $3,600.

Tax Conventions. Income Tax Treaties and Death Tax Conventions have been concluded between the United States and a number of foreign countries. The purpose of the treaties and the conventions is to avoid double taxation, to give credit for foreign taxes paid, and to insure that the citizens of the United States and of the signatory foreign countries will receive equitable tax treatment. The terms and conditions of the respective treaties vary, and it is therefore important that the treaty with the particular foreign country involved be researched when seeking the solution to a tax question involving the jurisdiction of the United States and the foreign country.

Non-Resident Alien

A non-resident alien is taxed only on income received from United States sources. All income that a non-resident alien receives from sources in the United States, other than certain investment income, is considered as being effectively connected with a trade or business in the United States. Only the profit portion of such income is subject to tax, and the tax is computed at graduated rates running up to a maximum rate of 50%.

The investment income excluded from treatment as effectively connected business income includes:

1. Fixed or determinable income (dividends, interest, rents, royalties, premiums, annuities, etc.).

2. Certain gains.

3. Capital gains and losses.

The tax on investment income except interest received by a non-resident alien is a flat 30% and is to be withheld at source. Tax treaties with certain countries provide for a lower rate of taxation. No deductions or credits are permitted against the investment income. The excess of capital gains over capital losses not connected with a business in the United States is taxed at 30% or at a lower treaty rate if the non-resident was present for 183 days or more in the United States during the taxable year. Gains or losses from the sale of a United States real property interest are subject to special treatment as explained later. Tax treaties with certain countries provide for the exemption of capital gains from taxation. In computing the capital gain subject to tax, no consideration is given to the 60% deduction ordinarily allowed for long-term gains, and there is no carryforward of capital loss from a prior year.

A non-resident alien who receives rental income may elect to have the business taxed as income from United States sources. Any capital gain resulting from the sale of the real property would then be taxable as capital gain (long-term if the real property was owned for more than a year). If the election is not made, then the gross rents would be subject to 30% withholding. Where a tax treaty exists that does not now permit the taxation of such gains, the tax of the gain from sale of interest in U.S. real property has been postponed until after December 31, 1984. Income that a non-resident alien receives from sources in the United States that is considered as being effectively connected with a trade or business in the United States is subject to tax at regular tax rates. Any gain resulting from the sale of capital assets, connected with such business, excluding inventory and certain receivables, will be taxed as capital gains (long-term capital gains if the assets were acquired before June 22, 1984, and have been held for more than six months). Any loss can be used to offset other business income or can be availed of as an unused net operating loss. (See the paragraphs on business income and capital gains losses, above.)

A non-resident alien who is a partner in a United States partnership is considered to have effectively connected business in the United States, even though he may not be physically present in the United States.

New York State and Local Income Taxes

A majority of the states of the United States, as well as cities located in those states, have income tax laws. New York State (together with New York City) rates are among the highest, while Florida, Nevada, South Dakota, Texas, Washington, and Wyoming have no income tax.

Both New York State and New York City impose tax on residents and non-residents. Residents must pay income tax on income earned both within and without the state and/or city. Taxable income for residents is determined in the same manner as for federal tax purposes, with few modifications. A taxpayer may claim an exemption for himself, for his spouse, and for each of his dependents. The sum of $800 is allowed for each exemption, and additional exemptions are allowed where the taxpayer or his spouse are blind or over the age of 65 years.

The income tax rates for New York State are graduated and begin at 2% on taxable income under $1,000 and rise to a maximum of 14% on taxable income over $23,000. Earned income is subject to a maximum tax rate of 10%.

The income tax rates for New York City are graduated and begin at 0.9% on taxable income under $1,000 and rise to a maximum of 4.3% on taxable income over $25,000. Exemptions for New York City income tax are identical with those allowed for New York State income tax. There is no maximum tax on earned income for New York City income tax.

Both the state and city impose a minimum tax on certain items of tax preference income which have received preferential treatment in computing regular taxable income. The minimum tax rate for New York State is 6% of minimum taxable interest in excess of $5,000 for unmarried taxpayers and taxpayers filing joint returns, and $2,500 for married taxpayers filing separately.

The tax rate for New York City minimum tax is $2\frac{1}{2}\%$ computed on the same basis as New York State.

New York City imposes an earnings tax on non-residents who work in New York City. The tax on wage earnings is $\frac{45}{100}$ of 1% after the granting of certain exclusions. The tax on self-employment earnings is $\frac{65}{100}$ of 1% after the granting of similar exclusions.

CONCLUSIONS

As stated at the beginning of this chapter, the purpose of the writers is to give the prospective immigrant to the United States an awareness of the complexity of the tax laws of the United States as they pertain to individuals. It is not intended that the chapter be used as a guide in tax planning or a solution of tax problems. If the reader, as a result of his reading this chapter, is alerted to the fact that consultation with knowledgeable tax counsel before a plan of action is adopted can result in material savings in both income tax and estate tax, then the chapter has served its purpose.

CHAPTER 18

Immigration Law

Prepared by Ann L. Ritter
Attorney at Law

As the international center of many of the world's activities, New York draws people from every continent, and for a multitude of reasons. But before foreigners can enter New York, they must become familiar with certain laws which are often very confusing to the newcomer. This chapter is intended to impart a general understanding of the complex United States immigration laws. The reader, however, should be aware that the laws and regulations frequently change, and should refer to this chapter only as a general guide.

VISAS

The first contact that any alien will have with United States immigration laws is in applying for a visa to enter the United States. All foreign non-immigrants are required to have visas, issued by United States consular offices overseas, before they can apply for entry into the United States. At the present time, consideration is being given to waiving the visa requirement for some countries, but, unless and until that is done, a visa is required unless you are a Canadian citizen crossing the border for a brief visit.

The issuance of a visa by a United States Consul, however, does not, in itself, guarantee entry. Upon arrival at a border of the United States, an officer of the Immigration Service will interview the entering alien and determine whether the purpose of the visit as indicated by the visa is the same as the purpose of the visit as indicated by the alien, and, if satisfied, will issue an official arrival and departure form (Form I-94) which will grant the alien a specified time to stay.

Depending upon the purpose of your visit, the Consul is authorized to issue one of the following visas:

"A" Diplomats. The A-1 visa is issued to an Ambassador, public minister, or career diplomat or consular officer accredited by a foreign government recognized by the United States, and to members of the applicant's immediate family. Other officials and diplomatic and consular employees, and members of their immediate families, are issued A-2 visas, and servants and personal employees are granted A-3 visas.

"B" Visitors. This visa is granted to visitors who are coming temporarily to the United States for business (B-1) or for vacation or pleasure (B-2). The business visa is issued to persons entering the United States for business meetings, conferences, and trade shows, but it is also used by regular household employees of executives transferred temporarily to the United States who will be accompanying their employers. A B-1 or B-2 visa holder, whether for business or pleasure, may not engage in employment for a United States employer. Prior to issuing a visitor's visa, a consular officer must determine that the visitor has a residence in a foreign country which he has no intention of abandoning, and may therefore require proof of assets overseas, proof of unrelinquished employment overseas, or proof of close family ties overseas, in determining whether or not this requirement has been met.

"C" Transit. Aliens who will be traveling through the United States either to another country or to a United Nations headquarters district or foreign consulate from overseas are granted "C" visas.

"D" Crewmen. Alien crewmen who wish to land temporarily in the United States and who intend to depart with the vessel or aircraft on which they arrived, or some other vessel or aircraft, are granted "D" visas.

"E" Treaty trader or Treaty investor. E-1 visas are granted to aliens entering the United States soley for the purpose of carrying on substantial trade between the United States and the foreign state of which they are nationals, under a treaty of commerce and navigation,

and to their spouses and minor children. An E-1 employer must show majority ownership by the nationals of the foreign country with which there is a treaty, and the E-1 employee must also be a national of that country. The E-1 visa is generally issued for four years and is valid only for the business activity for which it is granted, unless special permission to change employment is granted by the Immigration and Naturalization Service. The employee must hold an executive or managerial position or one requiring special qualifications.

E-2 visas are granted to aliens entering the United States to develop and direct enterprises in which they have invested or are in the process of investing a substantial amount of capital under a treaty of commerce and navigation, and to their spouses and minor children. For an E-2 visa, the alien must be a native of the foreign country with which the United States has a treaty and the majority ownership of the employer must be by nationals of that foreign country. While there is not a specific amount of capital specified for the granting of E-2 Treaty Investor visas, the Consul will determine whether the enterprise is substantial enough to employ persons other than the applicant and his immediate family. Many consulates overseas require a showing of an investment of approximately $250,000.

"F" Students. An F-1 student visa is issued to a *bona fide* and qualified student who wishes to enter the United States temporarily and solely to pursue a full course of study at an established institution of learning or other recognized place of study in the United States which has been accepted by the Immigration and Naturalization Service for accepting foreign students. The spouse and unmarried minor children of the student are issued F-2 visas. The student may not engage in employment in the United States, and the Consul, prior to issuing a visa, will endeavor to ascertain that the student has sufficient means to complete the course of study without requiring employment. Frequently, after entry, because of unforeseen circumstances, the student will wish to seek employment because of economic necessity. In that case, permission must be granted by the Immigration and Naturalization Service prior to the student's accepting employment. After graduating, he may be granted permission for up to one year's practical training employment, if that type of employment is not available to the student in his own country and if the school recommends that practical training in the United States is advisable to prepare the foreign student for a career abroad. On-campus employment after admission to the United States may also be granted if the school certifies that a United States resident will not be displaced. For some students on fellowships, scholarships, or assistantships, the

employment is considered part of their academic programs, and in such cases permission to accept employment is not required.

"G" Employees of international organizations. The G-1 visa is granted to a designated principal resident representative of a foreign government, recognized by the United States, to an international organization (including the United Nations), to his staff, and to members of his immediate family. The G-2 visa is granted to other accredited representatives of foreign governments and to members of their immediate families. The G-3 visa is granted to the representative of a government not recognized by the United States, or to one whose government is not a member of an international organization. The G-4 visa is granted to officers or employees of international organizations and to members of their immediate families, such as U.N. employees in New York. The G-5 visa is granted to attendants, servants, and personal employees of aliens holding G-1 through G-4 visas.

"H" Temporary workers. The H-1 visa is granted to aliens of distinguished merit and ability who are coming temporarily to the United States to perform services of an exceptional nature requiring such merit and ability. It is issued abroad by a United States Consul upon approval of a visa petition submitted to the Immigration and Naturalization Service by a United States employer. The H-1 visa is now valid for up to two years (formerly one year) and may be extended. This visa is generally used by professional workers such as engineers, scientists, university professors, etc. It is also used by models and entertainers who have exceptional qualifications.

The H-2 visa is granted to aliens who are coming to the United States temporarily to perform temporary jobs. Prior to the Consul issuing an H-2 visa, the intended employer must obtain, in addition to an approval of a visa petition by the Immigration and Naturalization Service, a temporary "labor certification" from the Secretary of Labor, which certifies that qualified persons in the United States are not available and that the employment of the beneficiary will not adversely affect the wages and working conditions of similarly employed United States workers.

H-3 visas are granted to non-immigrant aliens who enter the United States at the invitation of an organization to train or receive instruction which will then be used overseas.

"I" Journalists. "I" visas are granted to *bona fide* representatives of the foreign press, radio, television, or other foreign information media.

"J" Exchange visitors. "J" visas are granted to *bona fide* students, scholars, professors, research assistants, leaders in a specialized knowledge or skill, and others who enter the United States temporarily as participants in programs designated by the Secretary of State. The "J" visa is generally used by qualified foreign medical graduates to undergo graduate training. Persons accepting the "J" visa are generally required to depart from the United States upon completion of their programs and remain in their home countries for two years before becoming eligible to apply for immigrant visas, for "H" or "L" non-immigrant visas, or for permanent residence. This requirement may be waived in specific circumstances.

"K" Fiancés. The "K" visa is granted to an alien who is the fiancé of a United States citizen and who seeks to enter the United States solely to conclude a valid marriage within ninety days after entry.

"L" Intra-company transferees. The "L" visa is granted to aliens who, immediately preceding the time of an application for admission into the United States, have been employed by an overseas business continuously for one year, and who seek to enter the United States temporarily to continue rendering their services to the same employer or to a subsidiary or affiliate. The alien must be employed in a managerial or executive position, or in one requiring specialized knowledge. L-2 visas are granted to the accompanying spouses and unmarried minor children of L-1 visa holders.

CHANGING YOUR VISA STATUS TO ANOTHER NON-IMMIGRANT STATUS

Once a foreigner has entered the United States, he may discover that the visa issued by the Consul overseas is no longer appropriate. Frequently, an alien arrives with a visitor's visa, either for pleasure or for business, and determines that he would like to remain in the United States for more than a brief period and accept temporary employment with an "H" or "L" visa without leaving the country and obtaining a new visa overseas. So long as the alien is still "in status"—that is, the temporary permission to stay as indicated by the I-94 entry document has not expired—and so long as the new visa's requirements have been met, an application for a change of status may be submitted to the Immigration and Naturalization Service.

Employment generally should not be commenced, however, until the change of status is approved, or else the alien may find himself subject to deportation proceedings for violation of the original visa status which did not authorize employment.

A caution: When a visitor for pleasure applies for student status without having stated to the Consul overseas that he intended to study in the United States, this application generally will be denied, as it is the feeling of the Immigration and Naturalization Service that most students know prior to coming to the United States that they wish to study here and therefore should have submitted the required documentation to the Consul overseas prior to entry.

EMPLOYMENT FOR FOREIGNERS

While at present there is no federal law prohibiting an American employer from hiring an alien, only under certain circumstances are non-immigrant foreigners permitted to work in the United States without violating their non-immigrant status. The authorization for employment must be inherent in the type of visa granted, but, under special circumstances, employment authorization may be granted by the Immigration and Naturalization Service. Moreover, a Social Security card will not be issued for employment purposes unless either the visa itself or the Immigration and Naturalization Service authorizes employment.

If he becomes a permanent resident, of course, an alien may work at any occupation for which American citizenship is not specifically required.

For the non-immigrant, the "A," "E," "G," "H," "J," and "L" visas outlined previously allow employment for the term of the underlying visa and, if granted for a specific job, for only the job for which the visa is granted.

The immediate families of persons with non-immigrant visas which authorize the principal alien to work may not engage in employment. However, the immediate families of persons with "A" and "E" visas, although not granted specific authorization for employment by the Immigration Service, are not considered to be violating their immigration status if they work.

Additionally, refugees who file non-frivolous applications for political asylum will be granted employment authorization, and aliens who are able to apply for permanent residence will be granted employment authorization while their applications are pending.

Very frequently, a husband is granted an "L" visa when transferred to the United States by a multi-national corporation, and his wife, while not permitted to engage in employment by her L-2 visa, nevertheless discovers that she wishes to do so. If she has a profession or skills that would enable her to obtain a working visa, such as an H-1 or an H-2, she may wish to change her status to accept temporary employment.

BECOMING A PERMANENT RESIDENT

To become a permanent resident of the United States, an alien must meet the specific criteria of the Immigration and Naturalization Service. The number of aliens who may immigrate in any given year is subject to a world-wide quota. Within this quota, preference is given to certain categories of aliens who are close relatives of United States citizens or residents, or who have occupations which will either benefit the national economy and cultural interests of the United States, or who are needed by employers who cannot find similarly skilled workers in the United States.

Immediate relatives of United States citizens—spouses, unmarried minor children, and parents—are exempt from the quota system for acquiring permanent residence, as are certain other "special immigrants" and refugees. Everyone else must fit into the world-wide quota of 270,000 immigrants for any fiscal year.

The preference categories are as follows:

First preference: Unmarried sons and daughters of United States citizens (20%).

Second preference: Spouses and unmarried sons and daughters of permanent residents (26%).

Third preference: Members of the professions or persons of exceptional ability in the sciences or arts (10%).

Fourth preference: Married sons and daughters of United States citizens (10%).

Fifth preference: Brothers and sisters of United States citizens 21 years of age or over (24%).

Sixth preference: Skilled and unskilled workers in short supply (10%).

Non-preference: Investors, persons who do not intend to enter into the employment market, and certain other immigrants who do not fall into the first six categories.

Any alien may fall into one or more of these categories, and should determine the category in which an immigrant visa will be available in the shortest amount of time. The waiting period for an immigrant visa to become available varies, depending upon the preference category and sometimes upon the country in which the alien applicant was born. Up-to-date information can be obtained from the State Department Visa Office at 202–632–2919.

Many foreigners have some acquaintance with the investor immigrant visa category (non-preference), through which an alien theoretically could obtain permanent residence (that is, a "green card") through an investment of $40,000 or more in a business in the United States which would employ United States citizens. This category of visa theoretically still exists, but in practice it is not available, as the U.S. State Department estimates that no visas will be available in the non-preference category for many years.

Similarly, many aliens have brothers or sisters who are United States citizens, and, until just a few years ago, a petition by a brother or sister could be the basis for obtaining permanent residence in a relatively short period of time. At the present time, the fifth preference category has so many applicants waiting for immigration visas that it now takes several years to obtain residence through a brother or sister.

Aliens who could qualify for permanent residence in these two categories should consider first the other categories through which they could qualify, and they may find that the need of their profession or occupation by United States employers and their ability to qualify for the third or sixth preference categories will enable them to become permanent residents more quickly.

For most third and sixth preference occupations, a permanent "labor certification" (certification by the Secretary of Labor that United States workers are currently not available) is a prerequisite for a third or sixth preference visa petition approval. Some aliens do not require "labor certifications," such as those who were transferred to the United States in an executive or managerial capacity by an employer for whom they worked overseas for more than one year prior to coming to the United States. For certain professions, also, there is no need for individual labor certification.

No matter what preference an alien falls into, a proper visa petition must be approved for the preference category before the alien's individual application for permanent residence or an immigrant visa can even be considered.

Some aliens who are already in the country may qualify for a procedure known as "adjustment of status," whereby their temporary non-immigrant status is "adjusted" to permanent residence without their having to leave the United States. This procedure is available only to aliens who have legally entered the U.S. and who have not violated their non-immigrant visa status through unauthorized employment. Generally, all other aliens except refugees must obtain an immigrant visa from a United States Consul overseas.

THE LEGAL RIGHTS AND RESPONSIBILITIES OF FOREIGNERS LIVING IN THE UNITED STATES

Except for diplomats, all foreigners in the United States are subject to the laws of the United States, and it is their responsibility to familiarize themselves with these laws so that they do not unwittingly violate them. Aliens who violate the laws of the United States may be subject to deportation as well as to criminal penalties and imprisonment in the United States.

A resident alien has almost all of the rights accorded to United States citizens, the most notable exceptions being the right to vote and to hold positions for which United States citizenship is specifically required.

BECOMING AN AMERICAN CITIZEN

Five years after a foreigner has obtained permanent residence in the United States, he may (if he wishes) file an application for United States citizenship. For the wives and husbands of United States citizens, the period of residence required for citizenship is only three years.

The foreigner must actually have been physically present in the United States for at least 50% of the three- or five-year period and must intend to make the United States his permanent home.

To become a United States citizen, an alien must demonstrate good moral character and belief in the principles of the Constitution of the United States. Except in very limited cases, the alien must be able to read and speak English and know and understand the fundamentals of United States history and government.

PART VII

Recreation

CHAPTER 19

How To Join a Club

General Procedure for Joining a Private Club
What Is a Sponsor? Interview; Initiation Fee; Bond; Shares
Alternative Choice: Non-Membership Clubs
Private Clubs in Manhattan
Non-Membership Clubs in Manhattan

GENERAL PROCEDURE FOR JOINING A PRIVATE CLUB

THE CONCEPT of a private club is international. All over the world, members take advantage of "their club" for entertaining, discussing business, socializing, or merely for enjoying the facilities. New York has many private clubs. The choice, as with anything in New York, is limitless. But each club has its unique format and specific requirements for joining.

If you like to play golf or tennis, you may want to join a "country club." If you are interested in boating or sailing, you may want to join a "yacht club." There are many country clubs and yacht clubs scattered throughout Long Island, Westchester, Connecticut, and New Jersey. If you like this lifestyle, the first step is to visit several clubs, investigate their facilities, and inquire about their costs. If you call the membership offices of the clubs, they may be able to give you information and invite you to visit the premises. Some of the more "snobbish" clubs may require you to get all information through a member. At that point, you will need to know a member and ask him to propose and sponsor you.

WHAT IS A SPONSOR?

Many clubs are "private" clubs—members only. Not everyone can join. Each club has its own reputation and its own type of membership. It is "private," so legally they can do whatever they want.

To join a private club, you need to be sponsored. That means that one existing member must request a membership application for you and propose your name before a group of other existing members which comprise the Membership Committee. Afterwards, several other members must write letters of recommendation on your behalf, explaining who you are and why you would be an asset to the club. After all their papers are submitted, you will be called for an interview. That is the procedure if everything goes smoothly. But there may be some snags. Perhaps there is a waiting list, or perhaps you want to join not as an individual but as a part of a company. (Many clubs do not allow "companies" to join. Sometimes a membership may not be transferred to successors or colleagues.)

Some clubs may want a certain type of member, and, by nature of certain criteria, you may not fit the mold. Logically, however, the people you ask to sponsor you will tell you candidly if your applying is futile. No one wants to be embarrassed.

You will be interviewed by one member of the club or by a group of members. Some interviews are more formal than others. The members will ask you questions, and you, in turn, are expected to ask them questions.

During your interview, you should inquire about the financial aspects of becoming a member:
- What is the annual fee?
- Is there a separate initiation fee? Is this refundable when you terminate your membership?
- Do you have to buy a "bond" or "shares" in the club? Is this refundable, with interest, when you terminate your membership?
- Do you have to pay a separate, additional fee for tennis, golf, boating, swimming?
- Do you have to spend a minimum amount of money during the year at the restaurant and/or bar?

An *initiation fee* is a certain amount of money a new member pays for the privilege of joining the club. Usually, this is a one-time fee which is non-refundable.

A *bond* also is a certain amount of money a new member pays for the privilege of joining. Theoretically, this money is put into a savings account and earns interest. When you terminate your membership, you are returned the original sum plus the interest earned.

Shares for a club is the same concept as shares for a company or corporation. You invest money into the club, and you share in the expenses and profits. The details of the financial structure vary, but the general concept of profit-sharing is similar.

At the interview, ask the members of the committee about the club's rules for young children, spouse, guests, facilities, and availability of specific equipment (especially at yacht clubs, where slips, moorings, and launches are very desirable.)

ALTERNATIVE CHOICE: NON-MEMBERSHIP CLUBS

If for one reason or another you can't join a club of your choice, or you can't find a sponsor, then you should look for an alternative choice. Inquire through friends, neighbors, real estate agent, or the community center about which club in your area does not require you to be sponsored. There may be some new clubs which have less rigid membership rules. With a little investigation, you can find out which ones they are. There may also be some public clubs in your area that have excellent facilities for tennis or golf or boating. As a taxpayer of that community, you have the right to join. The Town Hall or Chamber of Commerce will have all this information.

PRIVATE CLUBS IN MANHATTAN

Manhattan has no country clubs (there is, however, a yacht club on the West 77th Street pier), but there are many clubs that are private and social and do require new members to be proposed and sponsored. All requests for information, application, and interviews must be made through an existing member.

Many of these clubs have luncheon and dining facilities, gyms, and saunas. Some even have swimming pools, tennis courts, racquet ball courts, and hotel accomodations. And others, like the New York Athletic Club, have supplementary facilities outside Manhattan such as yachting facilities, golf courses, tennis courts, and soccer fields.

The following is a list of some private clubs in New York City which require all prospective members to be proposed by a present member and then to be sponsored by several other members. Some of the clubs make joining rather difficult, as do the University Club, which requires five letters of recommendation, and the Century Club, which requires ten letters of recommendation from fellow members.

The Atrium Club. 115 East 57th Street. 826–9640.
Century Club. 7 West 43rd Street. 944–0090.
City Athletic Club. 50 West 54th Street. 247–0600.
Club at Citicorp. Citicorp Building (Lexington Avenue and 54th Street). 755–2455.
Cosmopolitan Club—"The Cosmo" (for women only). 122 East 66th Street. 734–5950.
Harmonie Club. 4 East 60th Street. 355–7400.
The Knickerbocker Club. 2 East 62nd Street. 838–6700.
Le Club. 313 East 58th Street. 355–5520.
The Marco Polo Club. 301 Park Avenue (Waldorf Astoria Hotel). 752–2244.
The Metropolitan Club. 1 East 60th Street. 838–7400.
The New York Athletic Club. Central Park South and Seventh Avenue. 247–5100.
River Club. 447 East 52nd Street. 751–0100.
The Sky Club. 200 Park Avenue. 867–9550.
The Town Club. 9 East 86th Street. 876–6020.
Union Club. 101 East 69th Street. 734–5400.
Union League Club. 38 East 37th Street. 685–3800.
University Club. 1 West 54th Street. 247–2100.

There are several advantages to joining a private club in Manhattan:

1. Belonging to a good club is a very civilized way to entertain and to discuss business.

2. Dining facilities are pleasant; service is good. You can usually get a reservation when you want it.

3. You can reserve a large, private room for receptions, special programs, and meetings.

4. All expenses for business entertaining are *bona fide* tax deductions.

Non-Membership Clubs in Manhattan

If you are interested in sports, New York City has an unending number of sports clubs which you can join *without* being sponsored. For a newcomer to the city who is not sure about which club to join, or who doesn't know whom to ask as a sponsor, the concept of joining a non-membership sports club is an appealing alternative.

There are several sports clubs that offer a wide variety of facilities:

Alzerreca's Gym. 1 East 28th Street. 683–1703.
Kounovsky Physical Fitness Center. 50 West 57th Street. 246–6415.
New York Health and Racquet Club. York Avenue and 76th Street. 737–6666. (They have several locations in Manhattan.)
Park Avenue Squash and Racquet Club. 3 Park Avenue, near 34th Street. 686–1085.
Rivereast Health Club. 614 Second Avenue at 34th Street. 689–4043.
The Manhattan Plaza Racquet Club. 484 West 43rd Street. 563–7001.
Turtle Bay Tennis and Swim Club. 1 United Nations Plaza. 355–3400.
Y.M.C.A. – Young Men's Christian Association. 224 East 47th Street. 755–2410.
Y.M.H.A. – Young Men's Hebrew Association. 92nd Street and Lexington Avenue. 427–6000.
Y.W.C.A. – Young Women's Christian Association. 53rd Street and Lexington Avenue. 755–4500.

This is just a sampling of some of the non-membership sports clubs that exist in Manhattan. The choice is unending.

If you are interested in a specific sport, there will certainly be a club or group in the New York area where you can practice it. New York City, in spite of its urban surroundings, offers as comparable a choice of activities and sports as a suburban town in Connecticut or New Jersey. In New York you can practice water skiing, fishing, scuba diving, sailing, downhill and crosscountry skiing, ice skating, horseback riding, soccer, etc., etc. All sports can be practiced in New York.

CHAPTER 20

Weekend and Seasonal Trips 1–2½ Hours from New York City

Summer
Autumn
Winter
Spring

No MATTER how much you are enjoying New York City, there will be moments when you feel you must get out—that you can't continue any longer—that you must cleanse yourself in nature and beauty—that you must return to the simple pleasures of life. This is not an uncommon feeling, even for the most ardent New Yorker. The city is difficult. Its competition, pressures, frustrations, and annoyances can take their toll, even for the very strong. When the first flakes of snow fall, or the song of a distant bird is heard, the New York visitor or resident wants to look beyond the skyscrapers and the concrete streets, to signs of nature and tranquility which only the country can offer. What makes New York's geographical location so ideal is that within 1–2½ hours you can find a tall mountain for downhill skiing or high seas for sailing. If you like the outdoor life, you can find beautiful paths to explore very near New York City. The following are suggested weekend trips in New York, New Jersey, and Connecticut for the four seasons.

SUMMER

New York — Long Island

Long Island, even before F. Scott Fitzgerald's day, was known as the playground of the New Yorkers. Long Island's beaches are wide and plentiful, the surf rough and picturesque, and the surrounding towns charming. But many New Yorkers think the same way, and unfortunately the roads from Long Island to New York City on a summer Friday night or late Sunday evening are extremely crowded. So just a word of caution: whenever you go for the weekend, make sure you reserve a place for the night at least one month in advance and give yourself extra time for traveling. A few nice beaches are:

1. *Fire Island.* From New York City, take the Triboro Bridge or Queens Midtown Tunnel to the Southern State Parkway. Take Route 111 South to 27A to Bayshore. From the town of Bayshore, you can take the ferry boat to one of the towns on Fire Island: Ocean Beach, Seaview, Davis Park, Kismet, Saltaire. You can also take your car from the Southern State Parkway directly to Fire Island's Robert Moses State Park. This area is more crowded but more easily accessible. Picnicing and fishing are allowed only in this area. If, however, you decide to take the ferry, you will enjoy a very beautiful ride. You have to park your car at the parking lot, for the ferry boats do not accommodate cars. The crossing takes about twenty minutes. There is never a problem getting a seat (no reservations allowed). The boat ride marks the transition between the reality of the mainland and the romantic aura of the island.

If you are not the house guest of a resident, you will find it difficult to spend the night on Fire Island. There are very few hotels, and reservations are difficult to find. However, as a day trip outside of Bayshore, the ferry ride, swimming in the refreshing ocean, sunning in the white dunes, and feasting on ice cream are very special ways to spend a summer day with a group of friends or family.

2. *The Hamptons.* From New York City, take the Long Island Expressway, Route 495, to the end. You will then take Route 27 to the specific town you want. The legendary Hamptons extend from Remsenburg and West Hampton on the west to Amagansett on the east (some people include Montauk). Many wealthy New Yorkers have summer residences here, and property values are extremely high. It's an area where people come to have fun and enjoy the gaieties of summer. Partying, beaching, fishing, and more partying are what summer New Yorkers enjoy about the Hamptons. It is best to visit these areas if you have friends you can join. There are some places to spend the night at

West Hampton, Tiana Bay, East Hampton, and Montauk, but you must reserve well in advance.

If you stay at an inn or motel, you will have the right to use its beach. If you join friends, you can profit from their car's sticker (each resident is allowed to park one registered car at the town beach). If you go for the day and do not have a car sticker, the best place is Montauk, where the beach is public. There is no problem parking a car, and Montauk has beautiful, wide beaches with dunes and some of the best deep-sea fishing on the eastern coast of the United States. Some places to stay are:

The Country Inn, Southampton: 516-283-4849.
The 1770 House, East Hampton: 516-324-1770.
The East Hampton House: 516-324-4300.
Driftwood Motel and Cottages, Montauk: 516-MO8-5744.
Gurney's Inn, Montauk: 516-668-2345 (Expensive).
Montauk Yacht Club & Inn, Montauk: 516-668-3100.

3. *Shelter Island* is a very special spot to visit. It is extremely different from any of the other communities on Long Island. Shelter Island is characterized by its maritime position and its sailing ambiance. There are many sections to this well-protected, hidden island, and each section has a different terrain, natural setting, and social status. Some spots are hilly, others rocky, and still others flat and beachy. Dering Harbor has a lovely inn, and Ram's Head is a very scenic spot. You can reach Shelter Island by taking the Long Island Expressway to Riverhead and then Route 25 East to Greenport. From Greenport you can get the ferry. Not many cars can fit on the ferry, so you have to wait your turn.

Some beautiful spots for dining and admiring the sunset are:

Dering Harbor Inn: 516-749-0900.
Ram's Head Inn: 516-749-0811.
Shelter Island Resort Motel: 516-749-2001.

4. *Long Beach* is another beach that has public parking and bathing. It is located on the Atlantic Ocean, and the beach is wide, white, and soft. To get there from New York City, take the Southern State Parkway past Lynbrook to Long Beach Road. At Long Beach Road, make a right, going south, to Long Beach. What is nice about this summer community is that it is accessible by car, is only one hour from New York City, and has many restaurants and accommodations for weary travelers. There is an old-fashioned boardwalk that is built parallel to the beach, and it is a favorite spot with children who enjoy amusement rides, games, and ice cream.

New Jersey

The "Jersey Shore" is very beautiful during the summer. There are boardwalks and amusement parks, boat rentals and fishing. In short, there is available all the summer pleasures for the entire family. You can spend a day, weekend, or weeks in this happy environment. From New York City, the driver takes the George Washington Bridge or the Lincoln or Holland Tunnel, depending on whether you are uptown or downtown. You ultimately want the Garden State Parkway to the Monmouth Beach exit at Route 36. Route 36 is the road that goes through all the towns and beaches of the "Jersey Shore," starting with Monmouth Beach and continuing to Long Beach Island. The "Jersey Shore" is the summer resort area for the residents of New Jersey.

Connecticut

Connecticut is beautiful in all seasons. During the summer, however, the day is longer and there are more hours in which to enjoy its beauty. All sports are possible in this area – canoeing on the Connecticut River in Maddan at Down River Canoes (203–388–4175), wind surfing at Elaine's Windsurfing School, Candlewood Lake in Danbury (203–281–7877), sailing on the Long Island Sound from Westport at Longshore Sailing (203–226–4646), golf in Stamford at Brennan's (203–324–4185) and Sterling Farms (203–322–8231), fishing on the Del-mar II in Greenwich (203–661–9166), tennis, swimming, and hiking on the coast.

For specific destinations try:

1. *Greenwich Point.* For the driver, take I-95 North from New York City's Bruckner Expressway to Exit 5 at Old Greenwich. From Old Greenwich make a right, going east toward the Long Island Sound. As you approach Greenwich Point, on the left side is a sandy beach where children can easily swim. There is a lifeguard and safe waters. As you continue on the main road and you drive into the park, there are areas for parking the car, picnicking, and hiking. If you want to dine at a fine French restaurant, the Café du Bec Fin at 199 Sound Beach Avenue in Old Greenwich is very good. Call for reservations at 203–637–4447.

2. *Sherwood Island State Park.* The driver continues on I-95 North to Norwalk. Take Exit 18 – "Sherwood Island State Park" – going to the right, toward the Long Island Sound. The fee is $8.00 per car per day. There are plenty of parking areas, barbecue grills for picnicing, and a long beach for swimming. The beach is not sandy as it is in Long Island, but the water is considerably calmer and warmer, especially pleasant for young children. There are a playground and snack bar and many conveniences to make your day's outing very pleasant. Nearby is

Westport, which is a charming town on the water, and it is interesting to explore as a side tour. They have their town beaches for which you usually need a car sticker, but you may be able to drive around for some scenic sights. An excellent restaurant for evening dining is the Chambord at 1572 Post Road East in Westport. Call and reserve a good table at 203-255-2654.

3. *Norwalk—Calf Pasture Park.* Off Gregory Boulevard. $15.00 per day for non-residents. Picnic area, bathhouse, playground, lifeguards, concessions, and fishing pier.

4. *Weed Beach in Darien.* I-95 to Darien Exit. Fishing and boating rentals, tennis courts, basketball, summer concerts, and lots of swimming.

5. *Westport—Compo Beach* off Compo Beach Road. $20.00 per car on weekends for non-residents. Lifeguards, concessions, picnic area, playground, and playing fields.

6. *Fairfield—Jennings Beach,* Fairfield Beach Road. $10.00 per car on weekends for non-residents.

Inns Nearby:

Stonehenge. Route 7, Ridgefield. 203-438-6511. 13 rooms. Pond, swimming pool.

The Elms. 500 Main Street, Ridgefield. 203-438-2541.

The Homestead Inn. 420 Field Point Road, Greenwich. 203-869-7500. 13 rooms. Free ferry boat ride to Captains Island for guests. Swimming and playground available. Restaurant serves outstanding continental cuisine.

West Lane Inn. 22 West Lane, Ridgefield. 203-438-7323. Near a lake, indoor and outdoor tennis.

AUTUMN

New York—Long Island

Autumn in Long Island is very special. Some people feel autumn is even nicer than summer, especially if the climate continues to be warm and September has an "Indian summer." On a sunny autumn day, you have less traffic, fewer crowds, fewer restrictions, and just as much beauty. Some suggested promenades are:

1. *Old Westbury Gardens and the Westbury House.* For the driver, take the Long Island Expressway to Exit 395 at Guinea Woods Road, South. Exit on ramp, continue parallel to the Expressway and follow the signs to the Gardens. There are eight different styles of garden, a luxurious Georgian mansion with museum furnishings, picnic areas, and superb trails for walking.

2. *Oyster Bay.* Take the Long Island Expressway to the Route 106

North exit for Oyster Bay. Go to Wolver Hollow Road to the State University Planting Fields. Turn right at Chicken Valley Road for:

"Planting Fields Arboretum," your first stop. You will see some of the finest collections of plantings in the East on this 409-acre Arboretum. There are 600 or more rhododendron and azalea plants, 400 different shrubs, and acres of plants listed alphabetically for serious students.

Sagamore Hill. Follow the signs from East Main Street to Theodore Roosevelt's grave and the Bird Sanctuary near the Oyster Bay Harbor. Sagamore Hill, dating to 1885, was the home of Theodore Roosevelt. Today you can take a tour of the house, visit the museum, and be a guest at some movies related to Theodore Roosevelt's life.

Oyster Bay Harbor. Lunch or a snack at this port will give you a feeling of Long Island's north shore sailing and boating community. The scenes are picturesque. Nearby Locust Valley is a very beautiful suburban community near the water.

New Jersey

1. *Great Adventure.* Take the New Jersey Turnpike South from the George Washington Bridge or Holland or Lincoln Tunnel. Exit at I-195 East to signs for Great Adventure on Route 537, in Jackson, 75 miles from New York City. In this 17,000-acre amusement park, there are a hundred rides, shows, and daily special attractions. Such rides as the roller coaster, parachute jump, and water slide will excite everyone. Especially interesting is the 450-acre safari park. Driving a car through an African-style jungle, you can marvel at more than two thousand wild animals in their natural habitats.

2. *Flemington.* For the driver, take U.S. 22 West to Somerville. Then take Route 202 for thirteen miles to Flemington. There are many places to visit and to stay. In Flemington's historical village, the restored nineteenth-century shops and houses will make you feel that you are returning to another era. Some other places to visit are:

Iorio Glass Company on Route 202. Watch skilled craftsmen at work.

Flemington Fur Company. Tour the storage vaults, the cleaning and processing areas, and, if you inquire, even the designing studios.

Turntable Junction. Built around an old railroad depot, there is a historical collection of specialty shops which are reproductions of historic buildings. Especially interesting for railroad enthusiasts.

Black River and Western Railroad. Rides on an original steam engine train for children.

Connecticut

One of the most beautiful spots in the world to see the fall foliage is New England. This section of the United States has the most beautiful colors from the end of September to late October. The reds and oranges and bright yellows bring visitors from all over. Within a hundred miles you can find yourself immersed in more beauty than you have ever dreamed possible. One envies those who walk through a Connecticut forest on a sunny mid-October afternoon for the first time. It is America at its best at a very special time.

1. An ideal spot to begin is *Old Lyme*. Take I-95 from Bruckner Expressway to Exit 70. Take Route 156 toward Hamburg and pass through the area of the Connecticut River. You will find yourself in tiny hamlets, in the midst of farms, forests, and picturesque country roads. If you like to bicycle ride, there is no better route to take than Highway 156 toward Hamburg. If you have time, take the car from Route 156 to Route 82 West. Go through Hadlyme and East Haddam toward Gillette Castle. Then take Route 9A South to Chester, Deep River, and Essex. Essex is the perfect spot for a snack and a stroll by the harbor. Tumble-downs Restaurant or the Griswold Inn are excellent spots for a drink or meal (203–767–0991).

2. The best spot to stop overnight is at one of Connecticut's finest inns, the *Old Lyme Inn* (203–434–2600) — Exit 70 off I-95 at Old Lyme. This inn is a prestigious nineteenth-century New England country house, restored and furnished with antiques of the period. There are only five rooms at the inn, so, for those who wish to stay overnight, it is most advisable to make reservations a long time in advance — maybe as much as one or two months. The best part of this elegant inn is the restaurant. Dining at the Old Lyme Inn is a culinary and aesthetic pleasure. The food is basically French. After a long hike or a challenging bicycle ride, or any other active means of relaxation, dinner at the Old Lyme is a pleasant reward.

3. *Rocky Neck State Park* offers many types of recreation. When it is not crowded, as in October, this park on Long Island Sound is one of Connecticut's most scenic salt-water beaches. Swimming, fishing, and camping are permitted, but the best part of this park is the wide choice of hiking trails. There is no better way to enjoy the fall foliage than by walking right into it.

4. *Mystic Seaport* is a very special visit, especially for children. In the fall it is less crowded than during the summer, and you can also profit from the beautiful fall foliage. Mystic is a little farther north than Old Lyme, off I-95 at Exit 90, and makes a very pleasant combination with a visit to Old Lyme. Mystic is known for its charming harbor, the Mystic Aquarium, and the re-created nineteenth-century Mystic Seaport. All are worth visiting, especially the seaport, which is done in excellent taste. Upon entering its large gates, you will find yourself in a town that

looks just like the whaling village Mystic was a hundred years ago. The reproduced shops and houses and ships are an endless treat for children of all ages. Various tours of Mystic and the surrounding area are offered. Call 203-572-0070 for information.

5. *Stonington,* the town to the north of Mystic, is a charming community to visit for some tranquility. If you have enough time and energy, a stroll through this fishing town is a delight, especially if you can find one of the Portuguese lobstermen at work. A fine place to have dinner is the Harborview in Stonington, where fish could not be fresher (203-535-2720). For the best lobster in Connecticut, Abbott's cannot be surpassed. On a sunny day, you can eat outdoors and admire the sailboats and power boats as they pass by or moor at the restaurant for some hearty vittles. This is a very scenic spot for lunch. It is America at its best. Abbott's is in nearby Noank at 203-536-7719.

WINTER

Within 2–2½ hours from New York City, we have skiing. Of course, it is nothing like that in Austria or Switzerland or France, but we do have some pleasant slopes.

New York

1. *Windham,* upstate New York in the Catskills, is a nice ski area, especially for families with children. Windham used to be a private mountain region for those residents who had homes and winter châlets in the Windham complex, but for financial reasons they opened the ski area to the public.

To get to Windham, you take the New York State Thruway from the Major Deegan and drive two hours. You will pass Newburgh and Woodstock. You take the exit to Cairo on Route 23 West to Windham. Just follow the signs through town and look westward for the slopes. The Windham Arms is a nice inn to patronize. But if you call the Windham Mountain Ski Area to verify prices and ski conditions, you can ask them to recommend other nearby inns. (During the ski season, it is always advisable to reserve at least a month in advance, especially for the Christmas and New Year's holidays. You may need to call more than one inn for a reservation.)

2. *Belleayre* has a 3,420-foot summit and is another lovely ski area. It has more demanding trails than Windham, and it also has cross-country ski trails. However, it may be a little more crowded than Windham.

Groups and buses patronize this ski center, but it is large enough to accommodate a lot of people. They have a good ski school and nursery. To get to Belleayre, you take the New York Thruway to the Kingston exit. You want Route 28 West to Highmount. An excellent inn is the French "Le Moulin," which is also a fine restaurant. They have very few rooms, so reserve in advance.

3. *Hunter Mountain,* with its 4,025-foot summit, in the same area, is popular and boasts a long season (November to April) due to the extensive snow-making facilities. They have some demanding slopes, such as "Hunter West," and even a true European skier has to pay attention. There are many German *Ratskellers* in the area, and Beck's beer and sauerbraten are popular with the Austrians who live in this community. Hunter's ski school is excellent, and their nursery is well-equipped. Hunter is midway between Bellayre and Windham. Take the New York State Thruway to the Catskill exit, Route 23A West. In the middle of town, follow the signs or the cars to the slopes.

4. *Catamount Mountain Range* is in another area worthy of skiers. It is located near Lake Copake and the Massachusetts border, neighboring on the Berkshire Mountains. The Swiss Hutte in Hillsdale, Route 23, is an excellent country-style inn six miles from Catamount. Call for reservations at 518–325–3333.

5. For the best cross-country skiing trails, there is an excellent area called *Mohonk Mountain House* in New Paltz. The trails are numerous and very well groomed. The main house is available for overnight accommodations. In this castle-like setting, the restaurant serves fine American food, and all baking and cooking is reminiscent of family fare. To get there, take the New York State Thruway to New Paltz. At the end of the town there are signs directing you to Mohonk Mountain House (914–255–1000).

New Jersey

1. *Great Gorge Ski Area.* This is the closest ski area to Manhattan that has some decent slopes. It is especially good for children. To get to Great Gorge, take the George Washington Bridge to the Garden State Parkway South. Go to Exit 154 to Route 46 West. Continue to Route 23 North until you reach Route 94 towards McAfee. Follow the signs to Great Gorge.

Connecticut

1. *Powder Ridge* in Connecticut is a very pleasant spot for day skiing. It is located a half-hour from New Haven and two hours from New York

City. They also have cross-country skiing, with well-groomed forest trails that take you deep into the woods. From New York City, you take the Connecticut Thruway, I-95, to New Haven. At the intersection of I-95 and I-91, take I-91 to Hartford. Continue to Route 147 to Middlefield, near Durham. The entrance is tricky, so watch your signs (1–800–622–3321).

2. There is also *Mohawk Mountain* in Cornwall off Route 4. They have the largest ski area in Connecticut. They have three double-chair lifts and several tow-ropes (203–672–6100).

3. For the lovers of cross-country skiing, Connecticut's natural hiking trails make excellent cross-country trails. All the state parks are beautiful, and nothing could be more pleasant than to glide on your skis through the freshly fallen snow in one of Connecticut's state forests. Particularly beautiful for cross-country skiing trails are:

White Memorial Foundation, Route 202 in Litchfield. 30 miles of flat trails.

West Hartford Reservoir Reservations. 40 miles of trails, flat and winding, for all levels. Located in West Hartford.

SPRING

New York

1. *Blue Mountain Reservation* in Peekskill, New York. Continue North on 9A from the Saw Mill River Parkway to Route 9A North to Peekskill. There are two very high peaks for mountain climbing. There are several horseback riding trails, swimming in a pond, and baseball fields.

2. *Home of Franklin D. Roosevelt,* Hyde Park, New York. From New York City, take the New York State Thruway or the Saw Mill River Parkway to the Taconic State Parkway North. After the Poughkeepsie exit, take the exit to Salt Point Road. Turn left and follow the signs to the F.D.R. Home. You can take a tour of the house, and with an "Acoustiguide" you can hear the voice of Mrs. Eleanor Roosevelt describing the paintings, furnishings, and rooms. The library is worth a visit, and don't forget to go downstairs to see the family cars.

3. *Old Rhinebeck Aerodrome,* Rhinebeck. From the Taconic State Parkway North to Route 9 North, go farther north on Route 9R to Rhinebeck. At Stone Church Road, you will see signs to the Old Rhinebeck Aerodrome. There are air shows of sixteen rare types of airplanes. A lot of fun for everyone.

New Jersey

1. *Washington Crossing State Park,* Delaware River. Leave New York to New Jersey via the Holland Tunnel or Lincoln Tunnel. Proceed by Route 3 or Route 95 toward Newark. Then take Route 22 West to Route 202 West to Lambertville. Cross into New Hope, Pennsylvania. Just over the bridge, take Pennsylvania 32 south. Continue three miles to Washington Crossing State Park in Pennsylvania. In the 293-acre park you will find a Memorial Arboretum, a Nature Center, and an Open Air Theatre which hosts a large summer festival of performing arts. (For schedules and details, write to Theatre Committee, Washington Crossing Association of New Jersey, Box 1776, Titusville, New Jersey 08560.) At the park there are tours, films, restored houses, and a reproduction of George Washington crossing the Delaware River.

2. *Princeton.* Nearby are Princeton University and the Princeton Museum of Natural History (take Route 95 to Princeton). A walk through the iron gates of this University town will give you the feeling that the American university life is very special. There are many inns nearby with excellent American cooking and hospitable accommodations. At Princeton University there are guided tours all year on Saturday and Sunday starting from the office in Stanhope Hall. But there are no tours on Saturday afternoons during the autumn football season.

The Peacock Inn, Route 206, Princeton, is well located near the University and very civilized (609-924-1707).

Cranbury Inn in Cranbury, 9 miles east of Princeton (609-395-0609).

Connecticut

1. *Essex* is special in all seasons. Take the Bruckner Expressway from New York City to I-95 North. Go 1½ hours until you reach Old Saybrook, then take Route 9 to Essex. During the spring in Essex, there is the usual activity of sailors getting ready for their summer season and their long trips to unknown sites. Essex is one of New England's oldest sailing communities. It is always fun to take a stroll down Main Street and peek into the piers and boatyards and observe the dreamy look of a bearded sailor as he paints and cleans, scrapes and shines, his beloved boat. In Essex, there are some charming antique shops and restaurants for New England chowder (Tumbledowns Restaurant is particularly colorful). If you want an excellent dinner and a historic inn in which to spend the night, there is the Griswold Inn (203-767-0991).

2. A nice side trip is to take the ferry from nearby East Haddam to *Gillette Castle.* Continue on Route 9N from Essex to Route 9A to Gillette Castle State Park. One of the few castles left in New England, it

is majestically built to overlook the Connecticut River. There are trails for hiking and picnicking. If you want to stay overnight, lovely accommodations and pleasant dining can be found nearby in Ivoryton at the Copper Beach Inn (203–767–0330) and the Inn at Chester (203–526–4961) in Chester.

3. Nearby is the *Goodspeed Opera House* in East Haddam (203–873–8668). If you have time to plan in advance, you may be able to get tickets for one of their musical revivals. Next door is the Gelson House, a pleasant restaurant with beautiful views overlooking the Connecticut River. A stroll in the area will take you back to another era.

4. Another part of Connecticut, the western part, near *Washington, Lake Waramaug, Roxbury,* and *New Preston,* is a very scenic and peaceful spot to visit. For those who enjoy hiking, antiquing, bicycle riding, or just strolling in nature, this part of the country is very special. Some pleasant inns are:

Lake Waramaug Inn, New Preston: 203–868–0563.
Boulders Inn, New Preston: 203–868–7918.
Hopkins Inn, New Preston: 203–868–7295.

CHAPTER 21

New York: A City for Children

Day Trips for Children Outside New York City
After-School, Weekend, and Summer Programs: Sports, Culture,
    Organized Activities
Summer Programs and Summer Camps: Day Camps in the Suburbs;
    Programs in the City; Sleep-Away Camps
Counseling for Camp Programs

DAY TRIPS FOR CHILDREN OUTSIDE NEW YORK CITY

THE FOLLOWING are in order of distance. No. 1 is the closest point to
New York City, No. 2 a little farther, etc.

New York
1. *Circle Line boat trips.* Pier 83 at West 43rd Street and Hudson
River. 563–3200. From April to October there are several sailings per
day. The cruise around Manhattan takes three hours. A recording points
out all the major sights of New York City as you pass by. There is also a
trip up the Hudson River to the Bear Mountain State Park. They give
you some free time to enjoy the park, its lake, hiking trails, and
playgrounds before the boat returns to New York City.
2. *Bronx Zoo.* 185th Street at Fordham Road and Southern Boulevard. 367–1010. This special children's zoo is one of the largest and
most intelligently created. There is an abundance of demonstrations,
lectures, exhibits, animals to pet, elephant rides, a monorail, train trips,
a "skyfari" train tour, and animals in natural habitats. This is a full day

of excitement, pleasure, and learning. From New York, less than half an hour.

3. *Rye Playland,* Rye, New York. 914-967-2040. Take the Bruckner Expressway from the F.D.R. Drive. Get onto I-95, New England Thruway, to Exit 11 and follow the signs to Rye Playland. This is an old-fashioned amusement park with modern, challenging amusements, rides, a roller coaster, and a ferris wheel. There are a special toddler section, a swimming pool, and a beach. From New York City, one-half hour.

4. *Sprain Road Riding Academy.* 341 Sprain Road, Scarsdale. 914-693-9742. Take the Bronx River Parkway north to Sprain Brook Parkway to the Jackson Avenue exit. Go left on Jackson Avenue and right on Sprain Road. There are horses, ponies, trails, corrals, lessons, and rides. From New York, half an hour.

5. *Rockland Lake State Park,* Nyack. 914-268-3020; 914-268-7598. On this 1,000-acre state park, you can have a wonderful day. The choice of activities is unending: fishing, swimming in pools, boating, hiking on nature trails, picnicking, and playing ball. It's a fun place for groups and large families. Take the George Washington Bridge to Palisades Interstate Parkway to Exit 4. Then take Route 9W north to the park. From New York, 45 minutes.

6. *Sterling Forest Gardens,* Tuxedo, New York. 914-351-2163. Take the Major Deegan from the F.D.R. Drive. Continue on the New York Thruway to Exit 15 and north on Route 17. At Route 210, continue to the Sterling Forest signs. You will find a lot to do here. There are porpoise and animal shows, a children's fishing area, animals, and playgrounds. There are many rides; favorites are the camel rides, boats, and trains. From New York City, 1 hour.

7. *Bear Mountain State Park,* Stony Point. 914-786-2701. Take the George Washington Bridge to Palisades Parkway and go north to the park. Just 5 miles south of West Point, this park is a nice place to visit in combination with your visit to West Point. There's a swimming pool, boat house, fishing, roller skating rink, and lots of hiking trails. From New York City, 1 hour.

8. *United States Military Academy at West Point.* 914-938-4011. Take the George Washington Bridge to the Palisades Parkway. Continue north to the Bear Mountain Bridge. Cross over and go north again on Route 9W. Follow the signs to West Point. On Saturdays there are parades; the cadets practice formation and marching. In the middle of all the fanfare, don't forget to visit the Military Museum. From New York City, 1 hour.

9. *Old Bethpage Village Restoration,* Old Bethpage, Long Island. 516-420-5280. Take the Long Island Expressway to Exit 48, then south

one-half mile on Round Swamp Road to Old Bethpage Village. This is a restored pre-Civil War farm village with reproduced inns, stores, church, homes, and shops. There are shows, demonstrations, and many activities. From New York City, 1 hour plus.

10. *Fruit and vegetable picking.* This type of day is a lot of fun. Depending on which farm you go to, you can combine it with another day trip. Hiking or picnicking in a nearby forest is also another pleasant way to supplement your outing. The best way to make arrangements is to call a central information number and find out where the farms are located and ask them for instructions. There are the Dutchess County Cooperative and the Putnam County Agricultural Service at 914–225–3641. The seasons are the following: asparagus in late April and May, strawberries and peas in June, blueberries in June and July, and apples in September and October. From New York, 1½–2 hours.

11. *The American Youth Hostel.* 75 Spring Street. 431–7100. They have bicycle trips for children and parents. Call to learn about their schedules and to reserve your place. If you are interested in hiking and camping, they organize these trips, too. In the winter they organize ski trips.

Connecticut

1. *Museum of Cartoon Art.* Comly Avenue in Port Chester. 914–939–0234. One of the largest collections of original cartoon art. Guest speakers on Sunday.

2. *Stamford Museum and Nature Center.* 39 Scofieldtown Road, Stamford. 203–322–1646. Planetarium shows. Observatory visits. Children can feed and pet many farm animals. There's a nature center with live animals and beautiful trails through the woods.

3. *Yale University,* New Haven. To get to Yale, give yourself a good 1½ hours from New York City. Take the Bruckner Expressway to I-95, the New England Thruway to Exit 47. At Exit 47 follow the winding trail to the Chapel Street exit. Park wherever you can. Yale is one of the oldest and best universities in the United States, dating back to the 1700s. The architecture is beautiful, reminiscent of Oxford and Cambridge in England. There are Saturday morning tours of the campus. Call 203–436–8330 or 203–436–4771 for information about these architectural tours. While you are there, visit the excellent museums of the Yale Center for British Art, 1080 Chapel Street (203–432–4594); the Yale University Art Gallery, 111 Chapel Street (203–436–2490); and Yale's Peabody Museum, 170 Whitney Avenue (203–436–0850) for dinosaurs.

4. *Children's Museum of New Haven.* 567 State Street, New Haven. 203-777-8002. Themes and exhibits about different neighborhoods and environments. Special programs. Weekend workshops for families.

5. *C & S Ranches.* Shaffer Road, Bethany. 203-393-2050. This is a visit to the Wild West with live steer and calves that are roped by cowboys on galloping horses. There are competitions, exhibitions, and plenty to see. To get to this modern cowboy-land, take the Bruckner Expressway to I-95, New England Thruway, to New Haven's Exit 47. Follow Route 63 to Bethany to the fire station. Make a left there at Peck Road to Johnson Road. Turn right to Pole Hill Road, then left to Shaffer Road, and right on Shaffer Road. Give yourself 2 hours from New York City.

A nice combination to this day's promenade is a trip to a very unusual "book farm." For those who love books, in nearby Bethany there is a converted farm which houses books — old books, new books, all languages, all subjects. The Whitlock Book Farm on Sperry Road in Bethany is a treat for anyone visiting the area. Call for directions at 203-393-1240. Nearby is a picturesque park where you can have an ideal picnic surrounded by a waterfall, stream, old trees, and beautiful country.

6. *Children's Museum of Hartford.* 950 Trout Brook Drive, West Hartford. 203-236-2961. There are planetarium shows, a marine aquarium with animals from all over the world, live animal demonstrations, and special exhibits.

7. *Valley Railroad in Essex.* Essex is a charming boating town on the Connecticut River. To visit the Valley Railroad and Essex together makes a wonderful day. You can arrange a boat tour of the Connecticut River, stroll in the town of Essex, and admire the sailing schooners. To get to Essex, take the Bruckner Expressway to I-95, the New England Thruway North, to the Essex exit. Go to Route 9 West and follow the signs. Give yourself a good 2 hours. Call 203-767-0103 for the schedule of the Valley Railroad. This railroad features an old-fashioned steam engine that takes a ten-mile trip along the Connecticut River. In the summer months, the train connects with several riverboats to continue the two-hour trip along the Connecticut River. This makes a lovely day for visitors of all ages and gives everyone the chance to see America and Connecticut at its most beautiful.

8. *Submarine tour* on the U.S.S. *Croaker* in Groton. This is a real submarine that was used during World War II in the Pacific. Tours are given, and you can see all the compartments and machinery of a real submarine. Take the Bruckner Expressway to I-95, New England

Thruway, and go north to Groton, Bridge Street exit. Follow the signs to Thames Street toward the water at the Long Island Sound. Give yourself 2 hours from New York City.

9. *Ocean Beach Park*. 203–447–3031. Take the Bruckner Expressway to I-95 to the New London exit. Follow the signs toward Long Island Sound. Ocean Beach Park has a long boardwalk with old-fashioned arcades, amusement rides, restaurants, and a beach. The amusement park has a lot of rides and games as well as a swimming pool, ocean swimming, a water slide, miniature golf, and an arcade. The Harkness Memorial State Park is nearby—an ideal setting for hikes, picnics, bike trips, and enjoying the beautiful surroundings.

10. *Bishop's Orchard*, Guilford. 203–453–6424. Take the Bruckner Expressway to I-95, the New England Thruway, to Guilford Exit 57 to Route 1A, Boston Post Road. Give yourself 2 hours from New York City. Every month from May to October you can spend a delightful day in beautiful country, picking the fruit of the month. Call for a schedule. If you like Connecticut's fall foliage, a perfect trip for a late September or early October day is to visit Bishop's orchards and pick apples and enjoy the fall foliage all at the same time.

New Jersey

1. *Turtle Back Zoo.* Northfield Avenue, West Orange. 201–731–5800. Take the George Washington Bridge or Lincoln Tunnel to the Garden State Parkway, Exit 147. Follow the service road to Park Avenue, then west to Main Street, south to Route 508. At Northfield Avenue, turn right and enter the South Mountain Reservation for the zoo. There are fifteen acres of live animals which can be fed. There is a restaurant and picnic facilities. From New York City, three-quarters of an hour for the trip.

2. *General Motors Assembly Plant.* 1016 Edgar Road, Linden. 201–474–4000. Take the George Washington Bridge or Lincoln Tunnel to the New Jersey Turnpike South. Go west to U.S. 1 and continue south on U.S. 1 to the buildings opposite Linden Airport. There are tours that show how General Motors cars are put together on the assembly line. Reservations are necessary. From New York City, 1 hour.

3. *Cranford Boat and Canoe Co.* Springfield and Orange Avenues, Cranford. 201–272–6991. Take the Garden State Parkway to Exit 137. Go west on North Avenue and again north at the second traffic light, which is Springfield Avenue. You can rent canoes. From New York City, 1 hour.

4. *Fairy Tale Forest,* Oak Ridge. 201–697–5656. Take the George

Washington Bridge and then go to Route 80. Continue west on Route 46 to Route 23. Go north on Route 23 to Oak Ridge Road. Then follow the signs. There are twenty acres of walks and forests where children unexpectedly meet famous fairy tale characters. There is a miniature Swiss village and a Christmas town. Also, some amusement-park rides are available for young children. From New York City, 1 hour.

5. *Wild West City.* Route 206, Netcong. 201–347–8900. Take the George Washington Bridge to Route 80. Go to Route 46 in Netcong. Continue north to Route 206. Wild West City is open from mid-June to Labor Day, every day during July and August and on weekends the other months. Wild West City is a miniature cowboy town with jail, covered wagons, Indian village, surprise gunfights, and a few sheriffs. From New York City, the trip is 1 hour.

6. *New Jersey State Fish Hatchery and New Jersey State Pheasant Farm,* Hackettstown. 201–852–3676 or 201–852–3790. Take the George Washington Bridge to Route 80. Then go on Route 46 to Hackettstown. Take Grand Avenue two miles south to the hatchery. For the Pheasant Farm, continue another two miles on Grand Avenue. There are organized tours, feedings, exhibitions, and demonstrations. From New York City, 1½ hours.

7. *Great Adventure,* Jackson. 201–928–2000. Continue to Exit 7A on the New Jersey Turnpike and then follow the signs. This is a superb amusement park with a very wide assortment of sophisticated and exciting rides. There is also a safari park where you can drive your car through a reproduction of an African jungle. Open April to September. An excellent day for the entire family. Plan to come early and leave late. From New York City, 1½ hours.

AFTER-SCHOOL, WEEKEND, AND SUMMER PROGRAMS: SPORTS, CULTURE, ORGANIZED ACTIVITIES

The following section has been categorized into topics. It is advisable to call the telephone numbers under each topic to get all information regarding type of program, age group, hours, fees, etc. After you get all your information, you can make an accurate decision based on your child's interests, level of accomplishment, schedule, and location.

Art
  Albert Pels School of Art. 226 West 26th Street. 807–6670.
  The Art Student's League. 215 West 57th Street. 247–4510.

The Children's Art Carnival. 62 Hamilton Terrace. 234-4093.

The Children's Art Gallery. 151 East 80th Street. 693-5453.

Greenwich House Pottery. 16 Jones Street, 6th Avenue near Bleecker Street. 242-4106. Classes in painting and pottery for children ages 4 and up.

Museum of Modern Art. 11 West 53rd Street. 708-9400. Courses for parent and child in painting.

events. During the week are classes in painting and drawing for parent and child.

Museum of Modern Art. 11 West 53rd Street. 245-3200. Courses for parent and child in painting.

92nd Street YM-YWHA. 1395 Lexington Avenue and 92nd Street. 427-6000. All types of art programs for children ages 3 and up, including pottery, ceramics, carpentry, and sculpture.

YWCA. 610 Lexington Avenue and East 53rd Street. 755-4500. Art workshops, stained-glass programs, and carpentry.

Astronomy

Hayden Planetarium. 81st Street and Central Park West. 873-1300.

Chess

Chess Center of New York. 69 West 14th Street. 924-7271.

Manhattan Chess Club. 155 East 55th Street. 223-9439.

Computers

Galanter Computer School. 222-3344. Tutoring is available in your home with your own computer. There are special Christmas and summer programs for children aged five years and up.

For summer programs, there is Computer Camps International. Campuses are located in Connecticut, Wisconsin, and Texas. For more information, write Computer Camps International, Suite D, 310 Hartford Turnpike, Vernon, Connecticut 06066.

Cooking

Cooking with Class. 226 East 54th Street. 355-5021. Classes for children ages 6-14 on Fridays 3:30-5:30 P.M.

Dance

American Ballet Center (Joffrey Ballet School). 434 Sixth Avenue, at West 10th Street. 254-8520. Classes of a serious type begin at age 6. There is also an excellent summer program that attracts many young people from all over the United States. This is one of the best ballet programs in New York City.

Ballet Academy East. 340 East 79th Street. 861-5204. Ballet and jazz instruction.

Ballet Arts. 61 Carnegie Hall, 154 West 57th Street. 582-3350. Ballet, jazz, and tap instruction.

Children's Dance Theatre. 133 West 21st Street. 242-0984. Classes in acting as well as dance, for the emphasis in this program is the emotional and creative development of the dancer. Ages 3 and up. Classes meet weekday afternoons and Saturdays. Tuition is not expensive. Students also put on shows.

Gelabert Studios. 255 West 86th Street. 874–7188. Ballet, modern dance, jazz, and tap instruction.

Harkness House for Ballet Arts. 4 East 75th Street. 570–1500. The Harkness Dance Theatre prepares ballet dancers as young as 5 years of age. There is also a summer program.

Martha Graham School of Contemporary Dance. 316 East 63rd Street. 838–5886. Programs for children ages 8–16. They learn Ms. Graham's dance techniques by instructors who are permanent faculty members of the school. Tuition is not expensive.

New York Academy of Ballet and Dance Arts. 667 Madison Avenue. 838–0822. Classes in ballet and jazz. A summer program is also available.

Neubert Ballet Institute. Carnegie Hall, 881 Seventh Avenue at West 56th Street. 685–7754. Eighty courses for children ages $3\frac{1}{2}$–20 at all levels of ballet. This program trains the young people for the Children's Ballet Theatre.

School of American Ballet. 144 West 66th Street. 877–0600. They are very selective about the students they accept, for this school prepares those students for professional performing careers in the New York City Ballet or other groups. For ages 8 and up. Classes after school and on Saturday. The students perform in *The Nutcracker* and other New York City Ballet performances. This is an outstanding program for serious students.

New York Conservatory of Dance. 226 West 56th Street. 581–1908. Ballet instruction.

YM–YWHA. 92nd Street Y, 1395 Lexington Avenue at East 92nd Street. 427–6000. Classes in folk dancing.

YWCA. Lexington Avenue at East 53rd Street. 755–4500. Classes in modern, tap, and ballet. Ages 5 and up.

Drama (Acting)

Academy of Dramatic Art. 184 Fifth Avenue. 243–8900. Classes in basic acting, scene study, speech, and improvisation.

Acting by Children Productions. YMCA at 5 West 63rd Street. 255–4968.

American Academy of Dramatic Arts. 120 Madison Avenue. 686–9244. Courses for teenagers.

The First All Children's Theatre. 37 West 65th Street. 873–6400. They have two groups of performers, ages 6–13 and ages 14–17, who participate in theatre productions. Call to find out details about an audition. In addition they have acting classes (ages 8–17) during the summer.

Herbert Berghof Studio. 120 Bank Street. 675–2370. For students ages 9–14 there is a 1½-hour per week program. For those ages 15–17 there is a 2-hour per week program. There are also classes in voice, dance, and speech.

New York Academy of Theatrical Arts. 184 Fifth Avenue. 243–8900. Courses for teenagers.

New York Pantomime Theatre. 242 West 27th Street. 242–4273. Instruction in mime and acting.

Weist-Barron School of Television. 35 West 45th Street. 840–7025. Programs for children who are interested in acting for television commercials and soap operas.

Fencing

The Fencers Club. 154 West 71st Street. 874–9800. Saturday morning program for children, ages 8 and up. Private lessons available.

Gymnastics

Alzerrecas. 1 East 28th Street. 683–1703. Programs for toddlers and up. Entirely equipped for Olympic training for ages 5–16.

MGC—Manhattan Gymnastic Center. 405 East 73rd Street. 737–2016. Excellent program for children of all ages at all levels. Extensive schedules to include after school, weekends, and summer camp.

New York School for Circus Arts. 1 East 104th Street. 369–5110.

92nd Street YM-YWHA. 1395 Lexington Avenue. 427–6000. Programs for tots of 17 months and on.

Great Shapes. 2291 Broadway at West 82nd Street. 362–6988. Programs for tots 3 months and on.

Walden School. 1 West 88th Street. 799–6269. After-school and summer programs. Equipped for Olympic programs.

YMCA. 5 West 63rd Street. 787–4400. Gymnastic summer day camp for children 8–14.

YWCA. 610 Lexington Avenue at East 53rd Street. 755–4500. Programs for children ages 4 and up.

Summer Camp

Woodward Gymnastics Camp. P.O. Box 93, Woodward, Pennsylvania 16882. 814–349–5634.

Horseback Riding

Claremont Riding Academy. 175 West 89th Street. SC4–5100. Riding and instruction are arranged. You can take a horse with or without an instructor and ride through the bridle paths of Central Park.

Pelham Bridge Riding Academy. City Island Road and Shore Road. 885–9848. Just twenty minutes from New York City either by car or bus. Call for instructions and particulars.

Ice Skating

Ice Studio. 1034 Lexington Avenue at East 73rd Street. 535–0304. After-school and weekend programs, September to June. Indoor ice skating rink. Private or group instruction.

Rockefeller Center Ice Skating. 1 Rockefeller Plaza at 50th Street. 757–6469. Group and private lessons. Outdoor ice skating rink.

Sky Rink. 450 West 33rd Street, 16th Floor. 695–6555. Olympic-size indoor rink open all year. This is the training rink for Olympic skaters. They have an excellent skate shop for repairs and purchases.

Wollman Memorial Rink. Central Park at 64th Street, west of Fifth Avenue. 397–3158. This is an outdoor rink which is not expensive.

Karate and Judo

Aikido of Uyeshiba. 142 West 18th Street. 242–6246. Free classes for children ages 6–13 every Saturday 12:15–1:15 P.M.

Richard Chun's Karate Tae Kwon Do Center. 163 East 86th Street. 722-2200. For children ages 4 and up.

S. Henry Cho's Karate Institute. 139 East 56th Street. 832-1660.

Language

China Institute of America. 125 East 65th Street. 744-8181.

French at the Alliance Française. 22 East 60th Street. 355-6100.

German at the Goethe House. 1014 Fifth Avenue. 744-8310. Saturday classes.

Hebrew at the Hebrew Language and Culture Association. 1841 Broadway. 581-5151.

Italian at the Italian Cultural Institute. 686 Park Avenue. 879-4242.

Russian at St. Sergius High School. 1190 Park Avenue at 93rd Street. 534-1725. This is a full-time private school, but you can arrange private after-school instruction in Russian.

Summer Camp Programs

Cardigan Mountain Summer Session. Cardigan Mountain School, Canaan, New Hampshire 03741. 603-523-4321. English as a Second Language is offered for a six-week program to foreign students, ages 10-15.

Choate-Rosemary Hall Foreign Programs. Choate-Rosemary Hall, Wallingford, Connecticut 06492. 203-269-7722. For those students, ages 15 and up, who are interested in traveling with a professor and students to France, Spain, or Greece for five weeks.

Experiment in International Living. Kipling Road, Brattleboro, Vermont. 802-257-7751. Programs that provide students ages 16-20 with the opportunity to combine travel and study in a choice of six countries. Two-week intensive language course is available prior to departure.

Music

Dalcroze School of Music. 161 East 73rd Street. 879-0316. Music appreciation courses for toddlers. Group and private instruction. Classes in theory.

Diller-Quaile School of Music. 24 East 95th Street. 369-1484. Famous for their toddler music appreciation and group courses. Private and group lessons for all instruments.

Hebrew Arts School. 129 West 67th Street. 362-8060.

The Juilliard School of Music. Lincoln Center. 799-5000. This is a school that has trained many of the great concert musicians.

Mannes College of Music. 150 West 85th Street. 580-0210.

92nd Street YM-YWHA. 1395 Lexington Avenue. 427-6000.

YWCA. 610 Lexington Avenue at East 53rd Street. 755-4500.

Summer Camp Programs

The Berkshire Center for the Performing Arts. Camp Wahconah, Potomac, Lake Pontoosuc, Pittsfield, Massachusetts 01201. This is a serious training program for students ages 13-18 in theatre, dance, or music.

Interlochen National Music Camp. Interlochen, Michigan. 616-276-9221. For students ages 8-21. This is an intensive music program with professional instruction given by a professional faculty. There is also an art, theatre arts, and dance program.

New York State Music Camp. Hartwick College, Oneonta, New York. 607-432-4200 or 607-432-4979. Campers perform in weekly concerts and attend daily rehearsals. Sports activities are also available on the campus.

Northeast Music Camp. Ware, Massachusetts. 413-477-6334 or 203-536-1483. Private instruction, workshops, concerts, and recitals. Located on a lake with water sports and recreational activities. Ages 11-18.

Navigation

Hayden Planetarium. Central Park West and 81st Street. 873-1300. All levels given during the week and early in the evenings.

Off-Shore Sailing School. 190 East Scofield, City Island. 885-3200. Navigation and sailing lessons in City Island. Programs on the weekends and during the summer every day.

United States Power Squadron. 608-3382. This is the most complete and well-organized course in navigation for enthusiasts of small craft, power boats, and sailboats.

Newspaper Journalism

Children's Express. 20 Charles Street. 243-4303. Those children who enjoy writing and journalism can become part of a children's newspaper that actually publishes their articles. It is a program of the nonprofit Children's Cultural Foundation.

New Youth Connections. 16 West 22nd Street. 242-3270. This is a monthly newspaper published by junior and senior high school students (ages 12-18). They also offer free weekly workshops in journalism and creative writing for children ages 12-20.

Photography

New York Institute of Photography. 211 East 43rd Street. 371-7050.

Puppetry

Wallace Lea Studio for Puppets. 123 Waverly Place. 254-9074.

Running

New York Road Runners Club. 9 East 89th Street. 860-4455 or 580-6880 or 580-2310. To participate in the New York Marathon, the minimum age is 16, but there is a Junior Marathon for younger children.

School Programs

The following programs are held in schools, for all children, regardless if they attend that school or not.

The After School Workshop. 122 East 83rd Street. 876-4428. Children can participate in arts and crafts, biking, carpentry, cooking, computer games, dramatics, hockey, roller skating, music, reading, tumbling, etc. Special Christmas and Easter workshops are also available.

Calhoun After School Program. 433 West End Avenue at West 81st Street. 877-1700. Programs for children ages 4-18 in drama, dance, singing, sewing, painting, music, chess, pottery, typing, woodworking, etc.

Friends Seminary. 222 East 16th Street. 477-9511. Classes are available to children ages 4-11. A wide gamut of choice. Private music instruction can also be arranged.

The Walden School. 1 West 88th Street. 877-7621. Programs available for children ages 1-16. They are especially good in gymnastics, art, and dance.

Soccer

The Auburndale Soccer Club: 358-0381.

Summer Camp Program

Winona. R.F.D. #1, Box 868, Bridgton, Maine. 207-647-3721. Facilities include three soccer fields as well as other sports and recreational activities.

Choate-Rosemary Hall. Wallingford, Connecticut 06492. 203-269-7722.

Sports Clubs

The following private groups arrange after-school sports activities in specific sports, all-day cultural trips on Saturdays, and special programs for vacations and summers. They arrange to pick up your child at school or home and deliver him home following the activity.

Billdave Sports Club. 206 East 85th Street. 535-7151.

Grunie's Superstars Sports Club. 251 West 97th Street. 316-0110.

Champions Sports Club. 1160 Fifth Avenue. 427-3800.

Swimming

Aerobics West Fitness Club. 131 West 86th Street. 787-3356.

Grand Central YMCA. 224 East 47th Street. 755-2410.

McBurney YMCA. 215 West 23rd Street. 741-9224.

92nd Street YM-YWHA. 1395 Lexington Avenue. 427-6000.

Topel Swimming School. 145 East 23rd Street, Hotel Kenmore. 674-4110.

Water Babies. 221 East 71st Street. 331 West 86th Street.

YWCA. 610 Lexington Avenue at East 53rd Street. 755-4500.

Summer Camp Program

Tangua Swim Camp. Kalkaska, Michigan. 616-258-9150 or 313-356-8527. Staff is comprised of current varsity swimmers. Special programs for serious swimmers.

Tennis

Midtown Tennis Club. 341 8th Avenue at West 27th Street. 989-8572.

Skip Hartman's Tennis Program. Winter telephone number 695-6883; summer number in Riverdale 884-1922. Summer and winter programs that specialize in children. Group instruction according to age and level.

Summer Camp Programs

Brian Eisner Tennis Camp. 3000 Park Ridge, Ann Arbor, Michigan. 313-665-7114. Ages 10-17.

Chase Golf and Tennis Camp. Bethleheim, New Hampshire. 603-869-5500; 617-526-7514. Ages 11-17.

John Gardiner's Tennis Camp at Carmel. P.O. Box 228, Carmel Valley, California. 408-659-2207. Ages 9-16.

John Gardiner's Tennis Camp at Sun Valley. P.O. Box 1558, Sun Valley, Idaho. 208-622-9281; 415-341-9717. Ages 9-17.

John Newcombe's Tennis Ranch. P.O. Box 469, New Braunfels, Texas. 512-625-9105. Ages 9-18.

The Julian Korinsky School of Tennis. Haverford College, Haverford, Pennsylvania. 215-642-9789; 215-265-6730. Ages 11-16.

New England Tennis Camp. Trinity Pawling School, Pawling, New York. 914-855-9650. Also at Lawrence Academy, Groton, Massachusetts (617-488-5508 or 914-835-3030). Ages 13-16.

Tamarack Tennis Camp. Easton Road, Franconia, New Hampshire. 603-823-5656. Ages 10-16.

Woodworking

The Woodsmith's Studio. 525 West 26th Street. 563-9317. For ages 5 and up there are after-school programs. On Saturdays there is a parent-child course. Classes also in cabinet-making, carving, finishing, and frame-making.

SUMMER PROGRAMS AND SUMMER CAMPS

Day Camps in the Suburbs

Breezemont Day Camp. 62 Cox Avenue, Armonk, New York 10504. 914-273-3162. 650 children ages 3-14. 18 acres, lake, two outdoor tennis courts, six swimming pools. Expensive. Transportation door-to-door.

Briarton Day Camp. 19 Bradhurst Avenue, Hawthorne, New York 10532. 914-793-2813. 250 children, ages 4-15. 10 acres, two swimming pools, good camper–counselor ratio. Reasonable price. Transportation door-to-door.

Camp Hillard. Box 155, Hartsdale, New York 10530. 914-949-8857. 600 children, ages 3-13. 17 acres, four swimming pools, horses, indoor and outdoor tennis. Excellent program for young children to teach them athletic skills and sports. Expensive. Transportation door-to-door. Hot lunches.

Mohawk Day Camp. Old Tarrytown Road, White Plains, New York 10603. 914-949-2635. 800 children, ages 3-13. Five heated pools, tennis courts, horses. There's a five-day, sleep-away program for 9–13-year-olds. This is a large camp, especially good for the older campers. Expensive. Transportation door-to-door. Hot lunch.

Mount Tom Day School Summer Program. 48 Mount Tom Road, New Rochelle, New York 10805. 914-636-8130. 375 children, ages 4-13. 8 acres, four swimming pools, two tennis courts, music rooms, low-key atmosphere. Reasonable to expensive price. Transportation door-to-door.

The 92nd Street YM–YWHA. 1395 Lexington Avenue and 92nd Street. 427-6000. Camp K'Ton-Ton, ages 3-5 (half day 9–12 A.M. or 12–3 P.M. or full day 9 A.M.–3 P.M.; camp is in the Y's building; indoor swimming pool). Camp Yomi, ages 5-11 (day camp outside the city, 9 A.M.-4 P.M.; located in Pearl River, New York; transportation to and from campground is provided daily from the 92nd Street Y). Teen Camp, ages 11-14 (facilities are used at the 92nd Street Y, with daily trips to supplement program).

The Riverdale Country School. 253rd Street and Fieldston Road. 549-8810. Summer day camp program for children ages 6-11. Transportation available. Pick up and delivery at child's home. Indoor swimming pool. Tennis courts. Twenty acres. In addition there is summer school for ages 12-17 and a tennis clinic for ages 12-17.

Tennis at Skip Hartman's Junior Tennis Camp. 341 West 246th Street, Riverdale. 293-2386 or 884-1922. At the ten outdoor tennis courts at Horace Mann School, children get 5-6 hours of daily tennis instruction. Ages 9-14. Swimming in the indoor pool. Expensive. Transportation door-to-door.

Programs in the City

The following New York City private schools offer summer programs. Call them for particulars regarding curriculum, program, time, bus service, and prices. Your children don't have to be students in these schools to participate in their summer programs.

All Souls School. 1157 Lexington Avenue. 861-5232. Ages 3-5.

Allen Stevenson School. 132 East 78th Street. 288-6710. Ages 6-14.

The Anglo-American School. 18 West 89th Street. 724-6360. Ages 11-15. Study skills course.

The Bank Street School for Children. 610 West 112th Street. 663-7200. Summer camps ages 2-9. Summer school ages 5-9.

Brearley School. 610 East 83rd Street. 744-8582. Typing course for children ages 10-17.

The Brick Church School. 62 East 92nd Street. 289-4400. Ages 5-11.

The Buckley School. 113 East 73rd Street. 535-8787. Ages 6-14.

The Chapin School. 100 East End Avenue. 744-2335. Language training workshop for ages 11-17. Study skills and writing workshop for ages 12-13.

Children's All Day School. 109 East 60th Street. 752-4566. Ages 3-6 years.

Christ Church Day School. 520 Park Avenue. 838-3036. Ages 3-6.

Convent of the Sacred Heart. 1 East 91st Street. 722-4745. Play-group ages 3-7. Gymnastics ages 4-17. Drama ages 12-17.

The Day School. 4 East 90th Street. 369-8040. Ages 4-13.

The Dalton School. 108 East 89th Street. 722-5160. Ages 3-15. General camp, sports programs, summer school for specific skills.

The Hewitt School. 45 East 75th Street. 288-1919. Ages 6-13.

International Play Group. 330 East 45th Street. 371-8604. Ages 18 months-5 years.

The McBurney School. 15 West 63rd Street. 362-8117.

Montessori Family School. 323 East 47th Street. 688-5950. Ages 3-7.

The Multimedia Preschool. 40 Sutton Place. 593-1041. Ages 3-7.

The Nightingale-Bamford School. 20 East 92nd Street. 289-5020. Ages 6-12.

Park Avenue United Methodist Church Day School. 106 East 86th Street. 289-6998. Ages 3-6.

The Rhodes School. 212 West 83rd Street. 787-4300. Summer school ages 12-17. Summer camp ages 9-17.

The Rodeph Sholom School. 7 West 83rd Street. 362-5441. Ages 3-5.

St. Bernard's School. 4 East 98th Street. 289-2878. Ages 6-14, boys.

St. David's School. 12 East 89th Street. 369-0058. Ages 8-13.

St. Luke's. 487 Hudson Street. 924-5960. Ages 4-11.

The Spence School. 22 East 91st Street. 289-5940. Ages 4-17, girls.

The Town School. 540 East 76th Street. 288-4383. Ages 3-13. Extensive offerings, tutorial program, week trips for children ages 8-13.

Trinity School. 139 West 91st Street. 873-1650. Ages 8-17.

Tutoring School of New York. 220 East 50th Street. 755-6666. Ages 14-17.

United Nations International School. 24-50 East River Drive. 684-7400. Ages 3-17. Enrichment courses, academic courses, language courses.

Walden School. 1 West 88th Street. 799-6269. Ages 3-11.

Sleep-Away Camps

Going away to sleep-away camp is more common among American children than among European children, and more sought after by children who live in an urban environment than suburban. The child who has the opportunity to go away from home for a few weeks or a couple of months is very fortunate. That child embarks on an adventure, early in life, and will certainly be exposed to a wide gamut of new situations. Summer experiences away from home broaden children's horizons. It teaches them independence from their families, self-sufficiency, and camaraderie with their peers. Some children, at the age of 9 or 10 or 11 or 12, have never been separated from their families. At sleep-away camp, in spite of supervised instruction and counselors at all activities and in living quarters, children must emotionally fare for themselves. They must share in cleaning their cabins or bunks, make their beds, perhaps cook for themselves. They must decide for themselves what clothes will be warm enough or appropriate for the climate, when and how much to eat, cleanliness, and hygiene. They must learn to live with children who may come from different backgrounds, speak different languages, and have different habits. Every day they must make decisions for themselves and experience the consequences of these decisions.

It is not unlikely that a young child, after living away from his family and with other children, will return home more mature and more responsible.

Summer camp also gives the child the opportunity to participate in a specific sport, or music, or dance, or camping, or traveling, or hiking, or canoeing—or any other activity in which the child cannot indulge during the school year. Some students are so busy with homework and school responsibilities during the year that they cannot play tennis or soccer or swim as much as they would like. Sometimes in New York City it is difficult to ride a horse every day or sail a sunfish or water ski. Some children want to play in an orchestra or perform in a show or dance in a ballet. Specialized summer camps offer these opportunities. In addition, children share with other children the same interests. If a child wants to practice the violin for several hours a day or play tennis non-stop, he will not feel "different" if there are other children doing the same. On the contrary, perhaps for the first time the child will find camaraderie.

There are many summer sleep-away camps in the New York-New England area. The preceding part of this chapter mentions a few specialized programs. The following section recommends several associations which are experts in the field of summer camps and will be able to consult with the family in making a choice appropriate for child and family.

If a family can afford sleep-away camp ($1,800–$3,000 for eight weeks) and the child wants the experience, both family and child will enjoy a unique summer of learning and enjoying.

COUNSELING FOR CAMP PROGRAMS

For information about sleep-away camps and day camps, the following organizations arrange programs and slides and private consultations. Call for specific details.

American Camping Association. 225 Park Avenue South.

Association of Private Camps. 55 West 42nd Street.

AWS—American Welcome Services: 794-1024. Excellent listings and information about all types of summer programs in New York City and/or the suburbs.

Catholic Camp Guide. 225 Park Avenue South. They offer a directory of Catholic-affiliated day and sleep-away camps in and near New York City.

Community Council of Greater New York. 225 Park Avenue South. They have a directory of summer camps that are located in New York City as well as a list of nonprofit camps (those that are reasonably priced).

Jewish Camp Information Services. Box 35, Cooper Station. They have a directory of Jewish camps for children ages 6-17.

Parents League. 115 East 82nd Street. 737-7385. They have information and files on all types of summer programs, sports programs, and foreign programs. Annual membership fee of $18 entitles you to the use of all their services.

CHAPTER 22

More Than Thirty Different Sports You Can Practice in New York City

————— ☆ —————

MANY PEOPLE who come to New York City for the first time have preconceived images of New Yorkers working and living in cubicles, one on top of the other, piled as high as the sky, without the opportunity to practice sports, admire nature, or notice the change in seasons. After you spend some time in this city, you soon realize that this does not necessarily have to be true—especially in regard to the opportunity to practice sports. More than half of New Yorkers practice at least one sport weekly, and they do so in New York.

Where do they go? The following list will give you an idea. There are more than thirty sports you can practice in or near New York City.

Airplane Flying

In order to fly a plane in the New York area, you must have a single- or multi-engine license. You can rent a plane at one of the following small private airports. If you don't have a license, you can arrange lessons and fulfill the requirements to apply for one.

Academics of Flight. 43–49 45th Street, Sunnyside, Queens. 937–5716.
Safair Flying School at Teterboro Airport in Teterboro, New Jersey. They have one of the oldest and best flying schools in the tri-state area.

Bicycles

You can rent bicycles in many bicycle stores throughout New York City. A small sampling is the following:

Columbus Avenue and 61st Street
Columbus Avenue and 84th Street
Lexington Avenue and 87th Street
Third Avenue and 85th Street
Second Avenue and 14th Street

Come prepared with identification and/or driver's license and enough money for a deposit.

Boating

To rent boats:

A & S Boatiques. 735 John Fitch Blvd., South Windsor, Connecticut. 203-528-8682. Rentals of sailboats, canoes, and water skis.

Colvin Yachts, Inc. Hammock Dock Road, Westbrook, Connecticut. 203-399-9300. Sailboats of all sizes for the day and for overnight use.

Housatonic Marina, Inc. Sniffen's Lane, Stratford, Connecticut. 203-375-1840. Boats and motors for rent.

Lighthouse Marina Boat Rentals. Old Town Highway, East Haven, Connecticut. 203-467-7325. Motorboats for rent.

Longshore Sailing School. Westport, Connecticut. 203-226-4646. Hobiecats and Windsurfers for rent.

Boxing

Bobby Gleason's Gym. 252 West 30th Street. 947-3744. They have training and workout sessions, rings, and all equipment for rental.

Canoe Trips and Lessons

Clarke Outdoors in Cornwall, Connecticut on Route 7. 203-672-6365. They offer guided day trips on Connecticut's Housatonic River. They supply the canoes. They also offer instruction for half-day or full day.

Down River Canoes in Haddam, Connecticut on Route 82. 203-388-4175. Near Essex on the Connecticut River. They, too, supply the canoes and arrange instruction and trips.

North American Canoe Tours in Niantic, Connecticut. 203-739-0791. Trips are conducted each weekend from April through September starting on Friday evenings at Middletown, Connecticut. Groups canoe down the Connecticut River to Saybrook by Sunday afternoon. The trips pass by the Goodspeed Opera House, Gillette Castle, and Essex. Equipment and food provided.

For renting canoes:

Great World. Route 10 North, Riverdale Farms, Avon, Connecticut. 203-674-1755. Reservations recommended.

Main Stream Outfitters. Route 44, Canton, Connecticut. 203-693-6353.

Marineland. 120 Old Town Park Road, New Milford, Connecticut. 203-354-3929.

Croquet

New York Croquet Club. 635 Madison Avenue. 688–5495. They use the croquet field in Central Park near 69th Street on the west side of the park.

Fencing

New York Fencer's Club. 154 West 71st Street. 874–9800, evenings. Established in 1883, this club offers private and group lessons and organizes tournaments.
George Santelli. 40 West 27th Street. 684–2823.

Fishing

For fresh-water fishing in the New York area, you need a New York State fresh-water fishing license. You can obtain an application from any tackle store or the Department of Environmental Conservation at 488–2755. This is the sort of fishing you would do in lakes and rivers.

For salt-water fishing, no license is required. Surfcasting can be done year round from any beach in the New York area without a license.

The Friday *Daily News* has a good section on fishing to tell you what fish are plentiful that week and where some good spots are.

For salt-water fishing, some popular spots are on Long Island, especially Montauk, City Island, and Brooklyn, and in nearby Connecticut. The following list may prove helpful:

Jack's Bait and Tackle. 551 City Island Avenue. 885–2042. City Island, Bronx.
Rosenberg's Boat House. 663 City Island Avenue. 885–3453. City Island, Bronx.
The Lucky Star. 597–8603. City Island, Bronx.
Twin Craft Co. 557 City Island Avenue. 885–1798. City Island, Bronx.
Ms. City Island. 824–4234. City Island, Bronx.
Betty W. 769–9815. Sheepshead Bay, Brooklyn.
Dorothy B. 646–4057. Sheepshead Bay, Brooklyn.
Bill's Fish at Bill Herold, Waterways Inc., Cos Cob, Connecticut.

Golf

There are thirteen public golf courses in the five boroughs and even more in Westchester, Long Island, and New Jersey. For information about the public courses in New York City, call the Department of Parks at 472–1003.

You no longer need a city golf permit to play at a public course. Just go to the public golf course of your choice and pay the greens fee. It is recommended that before you go you call the course to find out whether it is crowded.

You can also call the Department of Parks to find out how crowded the course is and if you can find instruction. There are two places in the city for instruction:

Al Lieber's World of Golf. 147 East 47th Street. 242-2895. Astroturf putting green and instant replay on TV.

Richard Metz's Golf Studio. 35 East 50th Street. 759-6940. Practice greens and sand traps.

In the suburban areas such as Westchester, Long Island, and New Jersey, there are many putting greens where you can just hit golf balls and practice teeing off.

In Connecticut there are two excellent public golf courses:

Brennan Golf Course, Stamford: 203-324-4185.
Sterling Farms Golf Club, Stamford: 203-322-8231.

Gymnastics

Alzerreca's Gym. 1 East 28th Street. 683-1703. Well-equipped gym for private and group lessons and classes.

McBurney YMCA. 215 West 23rd Street. 741-9216. Class lessons; co-ed classes.

Kounovsky Physical Fitness Center. 50 West 57th Street. 246-6415.

Handball

There are 2,000 public handball courts in the New York area. Call the Department of Parks 472-1003 for the location nearest you. To play is free.

For a private handball court, the 92nd Street YMHA at 92nd Street and Lexington Avenue (427-6000) has five, four-walled courts.

Health Clubs

New Yorkers are obsessed with keeping fit. Perhaps they feel sensitive about living in an urban environment and not having as much time as they would like to practice sports. In any event, there are many health clubs located throughout the city. The following is a very small list, but it is a good start for your investigation.

Metrofit. 305 East 47th Street. 838-5451. Sauna, sunlamps, and weightlifting equipment. Co-ed.

Rivereast Health Club. 614 Second Avenue, at 34th Street. 689-4043. Swimming pool, sauna, and whirlpool.

YMCA. 224 East 47th Street. 755-2410. Gym, pool, sauna, and indoor track.

Apple, Health and Sports Club. 88 Fulton Street. 227-7450. Pool, sauna, calisthenics, karate, racquetball, and yoga.

St. George Health & Racquet Club. 43 Clark Street. 625–0500. Racquetball and squash clubs, swimming pool, child care center, and full exercise center.

New York Health & Racquet Club. 24 East 13th Street. 924–4600. Swimming, squash, racquetball, and exercise programs. They have many centers throughout the city.

Hiking

Mohawk Mountain House. This is near New Paltz, upstate New York. 914-225-1000. You can spend the weekend here or travel two hours each way, for the day. In the summer they have a beautiful lake for swimming, canoeing, peddalo, and rowboats. In the spring and fall they are famous for their nature hikes and mountain climbing. Mountain climbers from all over the Eastern Coast come here to climb the steep cliffs. The beautiful main house resembles a castle. Reservations for the weekend are recommended.

Bear Mountain and West Point in New York.

Sherwood Island in Westport, Connecticut.

The Westwoods, Peddlars Road in Guilford, Connecticut. 2,000 acres of wilderness and marked trails. A real paradise for people who love woods and hiking.

Hockey

Metropolitan Junior Hockey Association. 1133 Broadway, near West 25th Street. They have a hockey team for boys 16-20 years old.

Horseback Riding

Claremont Riding Academy. 175 West 89th Street. 724–5100. Instruction and classes are arranged. Riding trails are in Central Park.

Ice Skating

Rockefeller Center. Fifth Avenue near 51st Street. 757-6230. Private lessons available. Rental of all skates and free checking. Only open during cold months such as November to March.

Sky Rink. 450 West 33rd Street, 16th Floor. 695–6555. Year-round ice skating, early morning to late at night. Many of the Olympic and competing skaters practice here. Excellent instruction and skate shop. Rentals available. Coffee shop. Friday and Saturday are disco ice skating evenings.

The Ice Studio. 1034 Lexington Avenue at 75th Street. 535-0304. They specialize in children's groups. Saturday and after-school programs available.

Karate

Eastern Karate Center. 1487 First Avenue, near 77th Street. 628-0661. Classes and private lessons.

New York Karate Club. 2121 Broadway, near 74th Street. 874–9868.

Lacrosse

New York Lacrosse Club, 111 West 57th Street. This is a club that plays in nationwide competitions.

Paddleball

This is a sport which has become very popular in the past several years. There are more than 400 paddleball courts in the New York area. Call the Department of Parks at 472–1003 to find out which court is near you. In addition, many of the YMCAs have paddleball courts indoors.

Polo

Unlike Florida and other parts of the United States, there is only one polo club in the New York area:

Meadowbrook Polo Club. 50 East 42nd Street. 687–3939. This is the main office, but the field is in Westbury, Long Island. This is the oldest polo club in the U.S. They have practice sessions two evenings a week and on Saturday. Formal games are held from May to October at Bethpage State Park Polo Fields in Bethpage, Long Island. For all other information regarding membership, practice, and lessons, call the New York telephone number or the Long Island number (516–626–9790).

Racquetball

There are many racquetball clubs in the New York area. A popular club is:

Manhattan Plaza Racquet Club. 450 West 43rd Street. 594–0554. A private club open to the public by appointment as well as to members. They have two racquetball courts, a tennis court, and a swimming pool.

Roller Skating

A simple way to roller skate is to rent skates and go on your own through the City or in Central Park. On Saturdays and Sundays, Central Park is closed to cars and traffic, and it becomes a safe area for joggers, skaters, cyclists, and strollers. You can rent roller skates at:

Goodskates. Central Park West and 69th Street. 535–1080. They are open seven days a week during the warm months and on weekends during the winter.

Rugby

New York Rugby Club. 501 Fifth Avenue. 953–9054.

Running

To get the calendar of events for marathons, call the New York Road Runners Club at 9 East 89th Street (860–4455). They also have programs, clinics, classes, and road maps for runners.

Sailing

The closest sailing area for New Yorkers is City Island in the Bronx. The two big sailing schools at City Island which offer group lessons are:

> Offshore Sailing School: 885–3200
> City Island Sailing School: 885–0776

There is also Port Washington on Long Island, a lovely spot for sailing in the Manhasset Bay. The best people to contact in Port Washington for lessons and sailboat rentals are:

Sigsbee Marina: 516–PO7–0944.

Connecticut's section of the Long Island Sound offers beautiful scenery and challenging seas. Some sailing schools to contact are:

Colvin Yachts Sailing School. Hammock Dock Road, Westbrook, Connecticut. 203–399–9300. You can rent large sailboats for overnight trips.

Longshore Sailing School. Westport, Connecticut. 203–226–4646.

Orbit Marine Sports Center. 3272 Fairfield Avenue, Fairfield, Connecticut. 203–333–DIVE.

Yale University Sailing Center. Clark Avenue, Short Beach, Branford, Connecticut. 203–432–4940. For children ages 10–17 they have two series of four-week clinics during the summer.

Scuba Diving

Aqua Lung School of New York. 582–2800. They have classes for certification and private lessons.

Ski and Scuba Shop. Stratford Marina, Stratford, Connecticut. 203–377–6969. They provide rental of equipment and instruction.

Skiing

The nearest downhill skiing in New York is at Cortlandt Park in the Bronx near Jerome Avenue and Holly Lane (543–4595). The slopes are good for novices. Instruction and classes are available. They also have some short cross-country trails.

For those who are interested in going for a day or weekend with an organized tour (lessons and rental of equipment included), you can inquire with the following groups:

Scandinavian Ski: 757-8524
Sporthaus: 734-7677

For those who want to go downhill skiing without a group, the following ski centers are located within 2-2½ hours from New York City. (For more detailed information, refer to Chapter 20.)

Windham, New York
Belleayre, New York
Hunter Mountain, New York
Catamount Mountain Range, New York
Great Gorge Ski Area, New Jersey
Powder Ridge, Connecticut
Mohawk Mountain, Connecticut

For those who like cross-country skiing, there are several spots, also within 2-2½ hours from New York City:

Mohonk Mountain House, New Paltz, New York
West Hartford Reservoir Reservation, Connecticut
White Memorial Foundation, Litchfield, Connecticut

Soccer

Cosmos Soccer Club, Inc. 44 East 50th Street. 308-1410. They have programs for adults and children.

Squash

Park Place Squash Club. 25 Park Place near Church Street. 964-2677.
Park Avenue Squash and Racquet Club. 3 Park Avenue near East 34th Street. 686-1085.

Swimming

Several of the Y's have indoor pools, and they are excellent. They have superb programs for children and adults. The best ones are the YWCA at 53rd Street and Lexington Avenue (755-2700) and the YMHA at 92nd Street and Lexington Avenue (427-6000).

Several of New York's hotels have indoor swimming pools, and you can arrange directly with them to pay on a daily basis when you go:

The Sheraton City Squire. 790 Seventh Avenue near 51st Street. 581-3300.
The United Nations Plaza Hotel. 44th Street and First Avenue. 355-3400.

Several of New York City's health clubs have indoor swimming pools:

The Sheffield Club. 322 West 57th Street. 247-2088.
The Morad Club. 84th Street and York Avenue.
New York Health and Racquet Club. York Avenue and 76th Street.
737-6666. They have other locations as well.

Some excellent children's programs for swimming instruction, group or private, are at the YMCA at 53rd Street (755-2700), the 92nd Street YMHA (427-6000) and the McBurney YMCA at 23rd Street (741-9224).

Tennis

There are many public tennis courts in the public parks of the five boroughs. In order to play there, it is necessary to get a tennis permit. You can acquire a permit at Fifth Avenue and 64th Street in the arsenal building at the entrance to the Central Park Zoo. It costs $27.50 for the permit, and you must give them two snapshots of yourself. They are open Monday to Friday, 9:00 A.M. to 4:00 P.M. (360-8204).

For the use of the public parks' tennis courts, the system is a "first come, first served, sign-up basis." The courts in Central Park have a reservation system, and you can inquire about this at the tennis house in Central Park, West 97th Street entrance.

If you are interested in playing on a private court at a specific time, there are many such tennis courts in New York City. The following represent a sampling:

Wall Street Racquet Club. Wall Street and the East River. 952-0760.
Midtown Tennis Club. 341 Eighth Avenue (27th Street). 989-8572.
Village Courts. 110 University Place. 989-2300.
Turtle Bay Tennis and Swim Club. 1 United Nations Plaza. 355-3400.
Gramercy Tennis and Racquet Club. 708 Sixth Avenue (23rd Street). 764-1701.
Sutton Tennis Club. 488 East 60th Street. 751-3452. Indoor courts open only October through May.
Sterling Tennis. Roosevelt Avenue at 126th Street in Corona, Queens. 446-5619. They have reserved courts for employees of the United Nations. In warm months they take the bubble down for outdoor playing.
East River Tennis Club. 44-02 Vernon Boulevard, Long Island City, Queens. 937-2381. 22 courts, minibus service to Manhattan.

Tennis Port Inc. 51-24 Second Street near Borden Avenue, Long Island City. 392-1880. 16 indoor courts, 14 outdoor courts. Members only.

Water Skiing

Post Ski and Sport Shop. 1323 Third Avenue at 76th Street. 744-5104. They arrange one-day water-skiing trips to a lake in New York State. The cost of the trip includes the rental of equipment.

A & S Boatiques. 735 John Fitch Blvd., South Windsor, Connecticut. 203-528-8682.

Windsurfing

Elaine's Windsurfing School. Candlewood Lake in Danbury, Connecticut. 1-800-228-7225.

APPENDIX A

Housing Price Ranges for Eighty-Two Communities

RENTAL APARTMENTS IN NEW YORK CITY

The rental market for apartments in New York City is very volatile and highly unpredictable. Prices for renting a two-bedroom apartment can fluctuate from one unit to another in the same building depending upon such criteria as how many leases have been signed for that particular apartment, the layout and design of rooms, hours of sunlight, exposure, floor, view, etc. Rents vary from one building to another, even on the same block, depending upon age of building, financial status of the building, number of employees and amenities. Neighborhoods also contribute to differences in rents for the exact same apartment of equal square footage. Proximity to parks, recreational facilities, public transportation, shopping, security, and schools all influence the price of a rental. Clearly the Upper East Side, Sutton Place, Central Park South, and Central Park West will be more expensive than Murray Hill, Greenwich Village, and Lincoln Center. But, again, there can always be the exception depending upon the particular building, the specific apartment.

There is no clear-cut rule that predicts what exact price you could expect to pay for an apartment in New York City. The same apartment can cost $2,000 per month in one building and $4,500 in another building. And this is not unusual. There is no explanation, there is no logic. Just be prepared for the reality. However, there are certain guidelines that can be used and we will list what you can expect to pay for an "average" two-bedroom, two-bathroom, dining alcove apartment in Manhattan. The same apartment will vary in price according to the following neighborhoods in which the apartment is located. (These figures are to be used as a guideline. Undoubtedly, you can find an apartment in a particular neighborhood for less rent than we mention. But these prices represent the average price you would have to expect to pay.)

1. The Upper East Side $2,000–$5,000
2. Sutton Place $2,000–$5,000

285

3. The United Nations	$2,000–$5,000
4. Murray Hill	$1,700–$2,500
5. Gramercy Park	$2,000–$3,000
6. Greenwich Village (East)	$1,200–$2,000
Greenwich Village (West)	$1,500–$3,000
7. SoHo	$1,500–$4,000
8. Chelsea	$1,400–$2,500
9. Lincoln Center	$1,500–$4,000
10. The Upper West Side	$1,400–$4,000
11. Columbia University	$1,200–$2,500
12. Yorkville	$1,500–$3,500
13. Ukrainian	$ 900–$1,800
14. Little Italy	$1,200–$2,000
15. Chinatown	$1,000–$1,700

CO-OPERATIVE APARTMENTS IN NEW YORK CITY

In discussing prices for co-op apartments in New York City, one must remember what was mentioned about the rental market. There is a very great fluctuation in price for the same apartment depending upon the specifics and location of the apartment. For a co-op or a condominium apartment, there is an even greater variance in price than for a rental apartment because there can be many extras due to decoration, design, addition of rooms, deletion of walls, etc. One may be asked to pay for the previous owner's changes. Therefore, when we list the asking prices for a two-bedroom, two-bathroom co-op or condominium apartment, the price must be looked upon as a very general guideline.

When one owns a co-op apartment, one must pay the designated monthly maintenance charges. The maintenance remains the same for a year but can be increased each year from between 5 and 15%. (Refer to Chapter 2 for more detailed information.) The monthly maintenance charges differ greatly from one building to another. Factors such as age of building, type of mortgage, number of employees, special assessments, and real estate taxes all influence the wide variance in determining a precise monthly rate. However, for a two-bedroom co-op apartment, one can expect to pay maintenance charges of $800–$1,300 per month.

1. The Upper East Side	To buy: *$275,000–$500,000*
2. Sutton Place	To buy: *$275,000–$550,000*
3. The United Nations	To buy: *$275,000–$550,000*
4. Murray Hill	To buy: *$275,000–$400,000*

5. Gramercy Park   To buy: *$300,000–$475,000*
6. Greenwich Village (East)   To buy: *$200,000–$450,000*
    Greenwich Village (West)   To buy: *$175,000–$450,000*
7. SoHo   To buy: *$180,000–$300,000*
8. Chelsea   To buy: *$175,000–$350,000*
9. Lincoln Center   To buy: *$275,000–$600,000*
10. The Upper West Side   To buy: *$225,000–$500,000*
11. Columbia University   To buy: *$150,000–$350,000*
12. Yorkville   To buy: *$225,000–$400,000*

CONDOMINIUM APARTMENTS IN NEW YORK CITY

There are several differences between a co-op apartment and a condominium apartment which would warrant that a condominium is generally more expensive to purchase in New York City than the same sized co-op apartment. (Chapter 2 elucidates these points.) In addition to monthly maintenance fees, the owner of the condominium pays real estate taxes. All these expenses can be calculated at the beginning of the calendar year, allowing for a 5 to 15% annual increase. Real estate taxes are billed to each owner by the City of New York.

Monthly maintenance charges are calculated according to the building's common charges and expenses as determined by such factors as employees' salaries, security, maintenance fees, etc. This amount varies greatly from one building to another. However, for a two-bedroom condominium apartment one can expect to pay monthly common charges of $350–$800.

1. The Upper East Side   To buy: *$380,000–$650,000*
2. Sutton Place   To buy: *$380,000–$750,000*
3. The United Nations   To buy: *$380,000–$800,000*
4. Murray Hill   To buy: *$300,000–$500,000*
5. Gramercy Park   To buy: *$400,000–$550,000*
6. Greenwich Village (East)   To buy: *$300,000–$550,000*
    Greenwich Village (West)   To buy: *$250,000–$550,000*
7. SoHo   To buy: *$300,000–$500,000*
8. Chelsea   To buy: *$250,000–$400,000*
9. Lincoln Center   To buy: *$350,000–$650,000*
10. The Upper West Side   To buy: *$325,000–$600,000*
11. Columbia University   To buy: *$225,000–$400,000*
12. Yorkville   To buy: *$325,000–$450,000*

RENTALS IN QUEENS

Many newcomers to New York forget that there are five boroughs that make up New York. Manhattan is not the only borough in which to live. Queens, a borough that has 197 miles of shoreline, 16,000 acres of park grounds, and is located within thirty minutes commuting distance from mid-town Manhattan, is an ideal place in which to live. 1.9 million New Yorkers think so, and that represents a quarter of the city's total population. There are many spacious, attractive, and affordable apartments to choose from as well as one- and two-family homes with a very low tax structure in comparison to neighboring suburban Long Island. Queens offers the resident the option of living very near to public transportation and city facilities, within close proximity to Manhattan, yet in a countrified setting.

The following communities in the four boroughs correspond to the map in Chapter 3. The price range is based on what one would spend to rent a two-bedroom apartment and/or a three-bedroom house.

1. *Roosevelt Island*
   Apartment: $1,500
2. *Long Island City*
   Apartment: $600–$650
3. *Astoria*
   Apartment: $600–$650
4. *Sunnyside*
   Apartment: $600–$650
5. *Flushing*
   a. Apartment: $600–$750
   b. House: $900–$1,000
6. *Rego Park*
   a. Apartment: $600–$700
   b. House: $900
7. *Forest Hills*
   a. Apartment: $700–$1,200
   b. House: $1,000–$4,000
   Forest Hills Gardens is the expensive section.
8. *Kew Gardens*
   a. Apartment: $650
   b. House: $1,000–$1,500
   Kew Gardens Hills is the expensive section.

9. *Bayside*
   a. Apartment: $650–$800
   b. House: $1,200–$1,400
Bay Terrace is a desirable area.
10. *Little Neck*
   a. Apartment: $650
   b. House: $1,100–$1,400
11. *Whitestone*
   a. Apartment: $650–$700
   b. House: $1,200–$3,500
Malba Proper, Douglaston Manor, and areas near the water are expensive.

HOUSING IN THE BRONX

The Bronx has some beautiful sections in which to live. Proximity to the Hudson River offers water views of sailboats, the New Jersey cliffs, and the George Washington Bridge. Proximity to Westchester County affords rolling hills, varying terrain, and a suburban feeling in an urban environment.

As with all our lists, prices for a two-bedroom apartment vary greatly according to building, precise street, and proximity to an endless number of conveniences and amenities.

The following information will give you an idea of the Bronx's real estate market and what a two-bedroom apartment would cost to rent and/or buy.

1. *Riverdale*
   a. To rent an apartment: $800–$1,000
   b. To buy a co-op: $49,500–$150,000
   c. To buy a house: $120,000–$450,000
Fieldston is a very expensive section; annual property taxes can be $6,000.
2. *North-east*
   To rent an apartment: $450
3. *Pelham*
   a. To rent an apartment: $500–$1,400
   b. To rent a house: $1,500–$3,000
Pelham Manor is an expensive section for renting and buying homes.

City Island, located on Long Island Sound, is a charming place in which to live and slightly less expensive than Pelham Manor.

4. *Tremont Avenue*
   a. To rent an apartment: $500–$600
   b. To buy a house: $80,000–$180,000

HOUSING IN BROOKLYN

In the past several years Brooklyn has been rediscovered. Once a very independent and autonomous community (in 1833 Brooklyn refused to join the city as a borough, claiming it had "nothing in common" with Manhattan), Brooklyn is now attracting a large number of Manhattanites. Young home owners are attracted to Brooklyn's historic neighborhoods of Brooklyn Heights, Park Slope, and Cobble Hill. They are restoring the old world charm of elegant townhouses and landscaped brownstones. Other neighborhoods located nearer to the ocean are also being sought after for their 200 miles of shoreline and their fishing and boating facilities.

The following information will give you an idea of Brooklyn's real estate market and what a two-bedroom apartment would cost to rent and/ or buy.

1. *Brooklyn Heights*
   a. To rent: $900–$1,600
   b. To buy: $150,000–$200,000
2. *Carroll Gardens*
   To rent: $500–$1,000
3. *Cobble Hill*
   a. To rent: $500–$1,000
   b. To buy: $120,000–$200,000
4. *Prospect Park*
   a. To rent: $650–$900
   b. To buy: $100,000–$150,000
5. *Park Slope*
   a. To rent: $750–$1,000
   b. To buy: $125,000–$190,000

HOUSING ON STATEN ISLAND

Staten Island is not so far away from Manhattan as many people may think. With 25¢ in your pocket and thirty minutes to spare for a romantic ferry crossing, you can go from St. George to Battery Park with little aggravation. Staten Island is a relaxing place to live for those people who work in the Wall Street area or downtown Manhattan, or for those who work in Brooklyn and enjoy commuting by car over the Verrazano Bridge.

Staten Island is the Marin County of the East Coast, the Shelter Island of the five boroughs. Contrasting sections of St. George, Stapleton Heights, Todt Hill, West Brighton, Emerson Hill, and Shore Acres offer a wide choice of residential architecture in addition to community ambiance.

For our example of real estate value we are listing St. George. At the foot of the Staten Island ferry on the Bay Landing side, St. George is the largest populated community of Staten Island and the most accessible to New York City.

1. *St. George*
   a. To rent an apartment: $500–$600
   b. To buy a house: $75,000–$125,000

HOUSING IN WESTCHESTER COUNTY

Westchester County is separated into four general areas: upper Westchester in the north, lower Westchester in the south, Hudson River vicinity in the west, and Long Island Sound area in the east. (Refer to map in Chapter 4 for locations of the following communities in the tri-state area.)

Again there is a great variance in prices. Proximity to the water, age of house, style of architecture, design of property, closeness to the town and the town's facilities, shopping, and transportation all influence the price of each house.

In this listing we present a general guideline for the range of: an average three-bedroom, two-bathroom "starter house" on a half-acre of land; annual taxes on that particular house; and the monthly rental for that particular house.

1. *Chappaqua*
   a. To buy: $160,000–$180,000
      Taxes: $3,800–$4,000
   b. To rent: $1,200

This price range is for houses on ⅓- and ¼-acre lots. Lawrence Farms East is an excellent area.

2. *Edgemont*
   a. To buy: $150,000–$160,000
      Taxes: $3,300–$3,500
   b. To rent: $1,300–$1,500

3. *Rye*
   a. To buy: $175,000–$190,000
      Taxes: $3,400–$3,700
   b. To rent: $1,800–$2,000

This price range is for houses on ⅓- and ¼-acre lots. Rye Brook is an excellent area.

4. *Scarsdale*
   a. To buy: $150,000–$200,000
      Taxes: $3,500–$4,000
   b. To rent: $1,300–$1,800

5. *Harrison*
   a. To buy: $140,000–$160,000
      Taxes: $4,200
   b. To rent: $1,800

The most dramatic residential area, and the most expensive, is located near the Westchester Country Club.

6. *Port Chester*
   a. To buy: $150,000–$160,000
      Taxes: $2,500–$3,000
   b. To rent: $1,500

The area near the Ridge Street schools is the most desirable residential area of Port Chester.

7. *Hastings-on-Hudson*
   a. To buy: $145,000–$190,000
      Taxes: $3,000–$3,500
   b. To rent: $1,300–$1,500

Water views on the Hudson River can be dramatic—and costly.

8. *Katonah:*
   a. To buy: $160,000–$175,000
      Taxes: $3,000
   b. To rent: $1,200

The areas in the John Jay High School district are the best.

9. *Pound Ridge*
   a. To buy: $180,000–$250,000
      Taxes: $3,200–$3,500
   b. To rent: $1,400–$2,500
10. *North Salem*
   a. To buy: $125,000–$140,000
      Taxes: $2,300–$2,500
   b. To rent: $1,100

Peach Lake area has had recent troubles with their waste disposal. It would not be the most desirable section of North Salem.

11. *Pelham*
   a. To buy: $155,000–$200,000
      Taxes: $3,000–$4,000
   b. To rent: $1,200–$1,500

Pelham Manor, Pelham Heights, and those sections affording views of Long Island Sound are very beautiful.

12. *Pleasantville*
   a. To buy: $120,000–$250,000
      Taxes: $2,600
   b. To rent: $1,100–$1,300

The sections of Rolling Fields and Thornwood are both to be recommended.

13. *Bronxville*
   a. To buy a house or townhouse: $225,000–$275,000
      Taxes: $3,200–$3,500
   b. To rent: $1,500–$1,800
   c. To buy a two-bedroom co-operative apartment:
      $130,000–$150,000
      Monthly maintenance: $500–$550
   d. To buy a two-bedroom condominium apartment:
      $115,000–$125,000
      Taxes: $1,000–$1,200
      Monthly maintenance: $130–$150
   e. To rent a two-bedroom apartment: $1,500–$1,800
14. *Hartsdale*
   a. To buy: $150,000–$160,000
      Taxes: $3,500
   b. To rent: $1,300–$1,500
15. *New Rochelle*
   a. To buy: $150,000–$160,000
      Taxes: $3,500
   b. To rent: $1,300–$1,500

16. *Tuckahoe*
   a. To buy: $140,000–$160,000
      Taxes: $2,500–$3,000
   b. To rent: $900
17. *White Plains*
   a. To buy: $125,000–$160,000
      Taxes: $2,500
   b. To rent a house: $1,100–$1,300
   c. To rent a two-bedroom apartment: $900–$1,300

The sections in the Ridgeway School area are good. Hillaire Circle and Highlands area are both excellent. The Battle Hill School District is not as good.

HOUSING ON LONG ISLAND

There are many private homes on Long Island. The opportunity to rent a house is not as complicated or difficult as it would be if you were looking to rent a house in Rockland County, Westchester County, or Connecticut. It is not possible, however, to give precise dollar value for each community. The parameter and criteria vary greatly. The ranges we list are indicative and can serve as a valuable guideline when comparing all the eighty-two communities in the tri-state area that are discussed in *Welcome To New York*.

The following list will elucidate those prices on: an average three-bedroom, two-bathroom "starter house" on a half-acre; annual taxes on that particular house; and monthly rental price on that particular house.

1. *Great Neck*
   a. To buy: $200,000+
      Taxes: $2,500–$3,500
   b. To rent: $2,000–$3,000

Expensive communities are: Kings Point, Great Neck Estates, and Saddle Rock.

2. *Roslyn*
   a. To buy: $175,000–$225,000
      Taxes: $3,000–$4,000
   b. To rent: $1,500–$2,000

Expensive areas are Roslyn Harbor, Roslyn Country Estates, Norgate, and Roslyn Heights.

3. *Woodmere*
   a. To buy: $185,000–$225,000

Taxes: $3,500–$4,200
   b. To rent: $1,200–$2,000
Woodsburg and Old Woodmere are the expensive sections.
 4. *Manhasset*
   a. To buy: $225,000–$250,000
      Taxes: $2,500–$3,000
   b. To rent: $1,500–$2,500
Taxes are relatively low because of the high commercial tax revenue from the shopping center "Miracle Mile." Plandome Heights, Flower Hill, and Plandome are the expensive areas.
 5. *New Hyde Park*
   a. To buy: $130,000–$200,000
      Taxes: $2,500
   b. To rent: $1,200–$1,400
Taxes are relatively low because of the strong commercial tax revenue.
 6. *Syosset*
   a. To buy: $125,000–$175,000
      Taxes: $2,500–$3,500
   b. To rent: $1,000–$1,400
 7. *Port Washington*
   a. To buy: $200,000
      Taxes: $2,500
   b. To rent: $1,500–$2,000
The expensive sections are located on the water at Sands Point.

HOUSING IN ROCKLAND COUNTY

Real estate in Rockland County may be slightly less expensive than in Westchester County. However, commuting and transportation from Rockland County is more complicated in comparison with Westchester. (Appendix B gives more information on that subject.)

The following list will give the general parameter for: buying a "starter house"—an average three-bedroom, two-bathroom house on a half-acre; the annual taxes you would pay on that particular house; and the monthly price, if you were to rent that same house.

 1. *South Orangetown*
   a. To buy: $95,000–$175,000
      Taxes: $3,500
   b. To rent: $1,000

2. *Orangeburg*
   a. To buy: $125,000–$150,000
      Taxes: $3,500
   b. To rent: $1,000
3. *Tappan*
   a. To buy: $150,000–$175,000
      Taxes: $3,500
   b. To rent: $1,000
4. *Palisades*
   a. To buy: $200,000
      Taxes: $3,500
   b. To rent: $1,000–$2,000

Sneden's Landing is the expensive community.

5. *Sparkill*
   a. To buy: $155,000–$350,000
      Taxes: $3,500–$4,500
   b. To rent: $1,000–$2,500

Houses are very large in this area, especially near Piermont.

6. *Nyack*
   a. To buy: $95,000–$175,000
      Taxes: $3,500
   b. To rent: $1,000–$1,500

HOUSING IN NEW JERSEY

New Jersey is not so far away from New York as many people would think. In fact, many New Jersey residents were once New Yorkers and many New Yorkers consider New Jersey as a sixth borough.

The following list will serve as a parameter for: a three-bedroom, two-bathroom "starter house" on a half-acre of land; the annual taxes for that particular house; and the monthly rental on the same house. We have listed communities in Bergen County and Essex County, for they are both within commuting distance to and from Manhattan.

1. *Franklin Lakes*
   a. To buy: $200,000+
      Taxes: $2,500
   b. To rent: $1,200–$2,000

Real estate value is very high in this community. Summer living and outdoor life are extensive and community oriented.

2. *Ridgewood*
   a. To buy: $137,500
      Taxes: $3,200
   b. To rent: $1,000–$1,400
3. *Tenafly*
   a. To buy: $125,000–$250,000
      Taxes: $3,000–$3,500
   b. To rent: $1,000–$2,000

Real estate value is high in this community. Proximity to Manhattan and good public schools contribute to its stable investment value.

4. *Montclair*
   a. To buy: $110,000–$150,000
      Taxes: $1,000–$1,400
   b. To rent: $1,000–$1,400
5. *Millburn*
   a. To buy: $120,000–$175,000
      Taxes: $2,500
   b. To rent: $1,100–$1,500

Short Hills section is the expensive area.

6. *Fort Lee*
   a. To buy a house: $140,000–$175,000
      Taxes: $1,500
   b. To buy a two-bedroom co-operative apartment: $120,000
      Maintenance: $750 per month
   c. To buy a two-bedroom condominium: $190,000
      Maintenance: $190 per month
      Taxes: $2,500
   d. To rent a two-bedroom apartment: $1,100–$1,300
7. *Summit*
   a. To buy: $110,000–$200,000
      Taxes: $2,400–$3,000
   b. To rent: $1,000–$1,500

Short Hills is the expensive section.

8. *Upper Saddle River*
   a. To buy: $150,000
      Taxes: $2,500
   b. To rent: $1,000–$1,500
9. *Westfield*
   a. To buy: $110,000–$190,000
      Taxes: $2,400–$3,000
   b. To rent: $1,000–$1,500

10. *Teaneck*
    a. To buy: $92,000–$100,000
       Taxes: $2,200
    b. To rent: $1,000

HOUSING IN CONNECTICUT

Fairfield County in Connecticut has a good number of residents who commute to New York. The most civilized way is with the New Haven Line of Metro-North Commuter Railroad. Within one hour the commuter can travel from station to station; whereas by car, the commute is considerably longer and more tedious. Fairfield County offers true suburban living in all its glorious colors.

The following list represents those communities in Fairfield County that can be found on the map in Chapter 4. The prices we mention are to be used as a "very" general guideline. The closer the house is located to Long Island Sound, the more expensive will be the real estate. We are listing information for: a three-bedroom, two-bathroom "starter house" on a half-acre of land and the annual taxes for that particular house. House rentals are hard to find. If you are looking specifically to rent a house you will need a good deal of patience and a lot of investigating skills.

1. *Darien*
   To buy: $210,000–$250,000
   Taxes: $2,000–$2,200
2. *Greenwich*
   To buy: $300,000–$350,000
   Taxes: $1,700–$2,500
   Old Greenwich is extremely expensive.
3. *New Canaan*
   To buy: $215,000–$275,000
   Taxes: $1,600–$1,700
4. *Norwalk*
   To buy: $140,000–$160,000
   Taxes: $1,500–$2,500
5. *Westport*
   To buy: $250,000–$275,000
   Taxes: $1,900–$2,100

Green Farms and the area near the Saugatuck River are expensive sections. Wilton and Weston can be more reasonably priced.

6. *Stamford*

To buy: $175,000–$200,000

Taxes: $1,350–$2,300

Taxes are considerably lower in Stamford because of the large number of Fortune 500 companies who pay substantial commercial real estate taxes.

APPENDIX B

Commuting Options for Forty-Five Suburban Communities Outside New York

WESTCHESTER

Train

1. *Harlem Line of Metro-North Commuter Railroad.* General information telephone number is 212–532–4900 or 800–522–5624. The station in New York City is Grand Central Terminal at 42nd Street and Lexington Avenue. Monthly commutation ticket available, goes on sale ten days in advance. Connects the following communities on our list: Katonah, Chappaqua, Pleasantville, White Plains, Hartsdale, Scarsdale, Tuckahoe, Bronxville.

2. *Hudson Line of Metro-North Commuter Railroad.* General information telephone number is 212–532–4900 or 800–522–5624. The station in New York City is Grand Central Terminal, 42nd Street and Lexington Avenue. Monthly commutation ticket available, goes on sale ten days in advance. Connects the following communities of our list: Hastings-on-Hudson.

3. *New Haven Line of Metro-North Commuter Railroad.* General information telephone number is 212–532–4900 or 800–522–5624. The station in New York City is Grand Central Terminal at 42nd Street and Lexington Avenue. Connects the following communities of our list: Port Chester, Rye, Harrison, New Rochelle, Pelham.

Bus

Liberty Line buses service the following communities to and from Manhattan: White Plains, Hastings-on-Hudson, Port Chester, Rye, New Rochelle, Pelham Manor, Scarsdale, Bronxville, Tuckahoe. There are many routes available depending upon your destination in Manhattan—east side, west side, uptown, mid-town, Wall Street. For exact information call 914–682–2020. Fares are $3 each way; senior citizens and disabled persons half fare on buses other than rush-hour buses. For those who commute each day by bus there is a "Golden Passport" commutation fare of $100 for each month.

Car

To commute to and from New York by car, there is a wide choice of routes:

1. The Henry Hudson Parkway
2. The Connecticut Thruway I-95
3. The New York Thruway and Major Deegan Expressway I-87
4. The Hutchinson River Parkway
5. Saw Mill River Parkway
6. Bronx River Parkway
7. Sprain Brook Parkway
8. Taconic State Parkway
9. Route I-684

There are tolls for the parkways, thruways, and bridges. Special fares and options exist. For example, the Triboro Bridge offers discount tokens. You can buy one roll of twenty tokens for $26, for a savings of 20¢ each trip. A single crossing of the bridge is $1.50 per car.

For more information call 360–3000.

1. *Chappaqua*
   a. Harlem Line, Metro-North Commuter Railroad, $117 monthly commutation ticket; 1-hour, 7-minute train trip.
   b. Liberty Lines bus, $3 each way, $100 monthly commutation ticket.
   c. Chappaqua Transportation Company: 914–238–4404.
   d. Chappaqua Minibus service.
2. *Rye*
   a. New Haven Line, Metro-North Commuter Railroad; $108 monthly commutation ticket; 45-minute train trip.
   b. Liberty Lines bus, $3 each way, $100 monthly commutation ticket.
3. *Scarsdale*
   a. Harlem Line, Metro-North Commuter Railroad; $98 monthly commutation ticket; 36-minute train trip.
   b. Liberty Lines bus, $3 each way, $100 monthly commutation ticket.
   c. Scarsdale Bus Corporation: 914–725–2044.
   d. Scarsdale "Surrey" bus service
4. *Harrison*
   a. New Haven Line, Metro-North Commuter Railroad; $99 monthly commutation ticket; 41-minute train trip.

5. *Port Chester*
   a. New Haven Line, Metro-North Commuter Railroad; $108 monthly commutation ticket; 47-minute train trip.
   b. Liberty Line bus, $3 each way, $100 monthly commutation ticket.
6. *Hastings-on-Hudson*
   a. Hudson Line, Metro-North Commuter Railroad; $100 monthly commutation ticket; 40-minute train trip.
   b. Liberty Lines bus, $3 each way, $100 monthly commutation ticket.
7. *Katonah*
   a. Harlem Line, Metro-North Commuter Railroad; $131 monthly commutation ticket; 1-hour, 21-minute train trip.
   b. Liberty Lines bus, $3 each way, $100 monthly commutation ticket.
8. *Pound Ridge*
   a. Up-County Express Bus of the Scarsdale Bus Corporation: 914–725–2044.
9. *North Salem*
   a. Harlem Valley Express.
10. *Pelham*
   a. New Haven Line, Metro-North Commuter Railroad; $90 monthly commutation ticket; 28-minute train trip.
   b. Liberty Lines bus, $3 each way, $100 monthly commutation ticket.
11. *Pleasantville*
   a. Harlem Line, Metro-North Commuter Railroad; $117 monthly commutation ticket; 1 hour, 3-minute train trip.
   b. Pleasantville Bus Line, 914–769–0616.
   c. Pleasantville "looper" bus service.
12. *Bronxville*
   a. Harlem Line, Metro-North Commuter Railroad; $91 monthly commutation ticket; 30-minute train trip.
   b. Liberty Lines bus, $3 each way, $100 monthly commutation ticket.
   c. Bronxville Bus line: 914–965–0733.
13. *Hartsdale*
   a. Harlem Line, Metro-North Commuter Railroad; $98 monthly commutation ticket; 40-minute train trip.
   b. Hartsdale Bus Company: 914–965–0733.
14. *New Rochelle*
   a. New Haven Line, Metro-North Commuter Railroad; $90 monthly commutation ticket; 31-minute train trip.
   b. Liberty Lines bus, $3 each way, $100 monthly commutation ticket.
15. *Tuckahoe*
   a. Harlem Line, Metro-North Commuter Railroad; $91 monthly commutation ticket; 30-minute train trip.

b. Liberty Lines bus, $3 each way, $100 monthly commutation ticket.
16. *White Plains*
a. Harlem Line, Metro-North Commuter Railroad; $105 monthly commutation ticket; 42-minute train trip.
b. Liberty Lines bus, $3 each way, $100 monthly commutation ticket.
c. White Plains Bus Company: 949–2085 and 769–0616.

LONG ISLAND

Train

The Long Island Rail Road. General information telephone number is 212–739–4200 or 516–222–2100. Station in New York City is Pennsylvania Station at Eighth Avenue and 34th Street. Weekly and monthly commutation tickets are available. You can have your monthly ticket mailed to your home. Call 212–657–6464 for more information. There is also a group rate for more than thirty people. Parlor car service is available on some trains. Reservations are necessary and a fee is required. The LIRR connects the following communities from our list: Port Washington Branch—Port Washington, Manhasset, Great Neck; Port Jefferson Branch—Syosset, New Hyde Park; Oyster Bay Branch—Roslyn; Far Rockaway Branch—Woodmere.

Bus

Metropolitan Suburban Bus Authority. For general information call 516–222–1000. A "Uniticket," which combines the MSBA bus fare to the suburban train station and LIRR fare to Penn Station in New York City, is available. There is a monthly and weekly program. For more information call 212–739–4200, 516–222–2100, or 516–222–1000.

Car

To commute to and from New York by car, there is a wide choice of routes:

1. The Long Island Expressway, I-495
2. The Northern State Parkway
3. Jericho Turnpike, Route 25
4. Hempstead Turnpike, Route 24
5. The Southern State Parkway
6. Sunrise Highway, Route 27

Most routes lead to the Triboro Bridge. For commuters there is the option of buying a discount role of twenty tokens for $26, a savings of 20¢ on every toll. Each single crossing of the bridge costs $1.50 per car. For more information call 360–3000.

Those commuters traveling downtown follow the signs to the Queens Midtown Tunnel. This toll is $1.50 at each crossing. There are no special programs for commuters. For more information call 360–3000.

There is also the Queensboro Bridge, which will take you to 59th Street and the East Side. No toll is required to cross this bridge, which can make traffic difficult during rush hour.

1. *Great Neck.* Long Island Rail Road; $97 monthly commutation ticket; 34-minute train trip.

2. *Roslyn.* Long Island Rail Road; $109 monthly commutation ticket; 49-minute train trip.

3. *Woodmere.* Long Island Rail Road; $97 monthly commutation ticket; 52-minute train trip.

4. *Manhasset.* Long Island Rail Road; $97 monthly commutation ticket; 37-minute train trip.

5. *New Hyde Park.* Long Island Rail Road; $97 monthly commutation ticket; 31-minute train trip.

6. *Syosset.* Long Island Rail Road; $109 monthly commutation ticket; 53-minute train trip.

7. *Port Washington.* Long Island Rail Road; $97 monthly commutation ticket; 44-minute train trip.

Rockland County

Train

From Nanuet and Suffern the commuter can take the Pascack Valley Line of the New Jersey Transit Company to Hoboken, New Jersey. From Hoboken there is the PATH train, which goes into New York's World Trade Center and/or into Journal Square at 33rd Street and Sixth Avenue. For more information call the New Jersey Transit Company at 201–762–5100. Call PATH at 212–466–7649 or 201–963–2558.

Bus

1. *Red and Tan Bus Company* services all the communities on our list. From Orangeburg, South Orangetown, and Tappan there is a direct bus to New York's Port Authority Building. From Palisades, Sparkill, and Nyack

the bus only goes to the New York side of the George Washington Bridge; the commuter can then take the bus or the Eighth Avenue subway to downtown Manhattan. For more information call 914–356–0877.

2. *Tour Bus of Rockland County* connects different points of all Rockland County; the bus costs 60¢. For more information call 914–634–1100.

Car

To commute to and from New York by car there is the choice of crossing the George Washington Bridge or the Tappan Zee Bridge. Both options should be tested to determine which is the best route.

1. *The George Washington Bridge* offers special rates for commuters: (a) monthly ticket book for $20, which represents a 50% savings—each single crossing is $2; (b) carpool book for each car that has at least three people in the car; sixty-ticket book for six months at $30; (c) "toll script program," a booklet of twenty-five tickets that does not have an expiration date—you are not obliged to consume the tickets within one month. For more information call 800–221–9903 or 201–867–9095.

2. *The Tappan Zee Bridge* also offers special rates for commuters: (a) monthly ticket book for $15, issued to be used by the same car—this represents a 50% savings, for a single crossing is $1.50; (b) carpool book for each car that has at least three people in the car; $10 for the month's twenty trips; (c) $18 booklet for twenty trips to be used within thirty-five days by any vehicle. For more information call 914–631–6262.

1. *Orangeburg.* Red and Tan Bus; $2.75 one-way; $49 for 20-trip commuter ticket; trip is 1 hour, 10 minutes to Port Authority Building.

2. *South Orangetown.* Red and Tan Bus; $2.75 one-way; $49 for 20-trip commuter ticket; trip is 1 hour, 10 minutes to Port Authority Building.

3. *Tappan.* Red and Tan Bus; $2.60 one-way; $46.10 for 20-trip commuter ticket; trip is 1 hour, 2 minutes to Port Authority Building.

4. *Palisades.* Red and Tan bus to the George Washington Bridge; $2.30 one-way; $41.45 for 20-trip commuter ticket; trip is 36 minutes to Bridge.

5. *Sparkill.* Red and Tan Bus to the George Washington Bridge; $2.45 one-way; $44.45 for 20-trip commuter ticket; trip is 36 minutes to Bridge.

6. *Nyack.* Red and Tan Bus to George Washington Bridge; $2.70 one-way; $48 for 20-trip commuter ticket; 48 minutes to Bridge.

NEW JERSEY

Train

1. *PATH (Port Authority Trans-Hudson Corporation)*. Each trip costs 75¢; 20–25-minute trip. In New Jersey the commuter can use the Newark Station and/or the Hoboken Station. In New York the commuter can use the World Trade Center Station and/or the Journal Square Station at 33rd Street and Avenue of the Americas. To travel to Newark from the communities of our list, the commuter can use the local trains of the New Jersey Transit Company and/or Amtrak. For more information for PATH call 212–466–7649 or 201–963–2558; for New Jersey Transit Company call 201–762–5100; for Amtrak call 800–USA–RAIL.

2. *Amtrak*. There are many direct trains between Newark Station and the Pennsylvania Station at Eighth Avenue and 33rd Street, New York City. The trip costs $1.50 each way and is only 12 minutes. For more information call 800–USA–RAIL.

3. *New Jersey Transit Company*. There are direct trains from Ridgewood, Montclair, Millburn, Summit, and Westfield to Pennsylvania Station, Eighth Avenue and 33rd Street in New York City. There are local trains from other communities to Newark, and from Newark the commuter can take the PATH trains or Amtrak into New York City. For more information call 201–762–5100.

Bus

1. *Lakeland Bus* services Millburn and Summit to the Port Authority Building at Seventh Avenue and 41st Street. For more information call 201–366–0600.

2. *Short Line Bus System* services Upper Saddle River to the Port Authority Building at Seventh Avenue and 41st Street. For more information call 201–262–0800.

3. *DeCamp Bus Line* services Montclair to the Port Authority Building at Seventh Avenue and 41st Street. For more information call 201–783–7500.

4. *Leisure Line Bus Company* services Franklin Lakes to the Port Authority Building at Seventh Avenue and 41st Street. For more information call 201–529–4070.

5. *New Jersey Transit Bus Company* services Ridgewood, Tenafly, Fort Lee, Westfield, and Teaneck to the Port Authority Building at Seventh Avenue and 41st Street. For more information call 201–762–5100.

Car

To commute to and from New York by car there is a wide choice of routes. All routes will meet at one of four points in order to cross into New York. They are in order from south to north points of New York: Verrazano Narrows Bridge, Holland Tunnel, Lincoln Tunnel, and George Washington Bridge.

1. *Verrazano Narrows Bridge.* There are special discount tokens that Staten Island residents can purchase. Twenty tokens cost $24. This represents a savings from the $1.50 toll for each crossing. Staten Island residents should send a photocopy of their car's registration to TBTA, Randall's Island, New York, New York 10035. They will send you a sticker verifying that you are a Staten Island resident. Take the sticker to the Verrazano toll for your discount tokens. For more information call 981–2443.

2. *Holland Tunnel* and *Lincoln Tunnel.* Special rates for commuters: (a) monthly ticket book for $20, which represents a 50% savings—a single crossing is $2; (b) carpool book for each car that has at least three people in the car; sixty-ticket book for six months at $30. For more information call 800–221–9903 or 201–867–9905.

3. *George Washington Bridge.* Points (a) and (b) above are also applicable to commuters crossing the George Washington Bridge, but in addition there is: (c) "toll script program"—a booklet of twenty-five tickets without an expiration date. You are not obliged to consume the tickets in one month. For more information call 800–221–9903 or 201–867–9905.

1. *Franklin Lakes.* Leisure Line Bus; ten-trip ticket at $38.10, forty-trip ticket at $115.75; 1-hour, 30-minute trip to Port Authority Building.

2. *Ridgewood.* New Jersey Transit Bus Company; $73 monthly commutation ticket; 1-hour trip to Port Authority Building.

3. *Tenafly.* New Jersey Transit Bus Company; $60 monthly commutation ticket; 55-minute trip to Port Authority Building.

4. *Montclair.* DeCamp Bus; thirty-trip ticket at $81.85; 35-minute trip to Port Authority Building.

5. *Millburn.* Lakeland Bus; weekly commutation ticket at $31; 35-minute trip to Port Authority Building.

6. *Fort Lee.* New Jersey Transit Bus Company; $54 monthly commutation ticket; 35-minute trip to Port Authority Building.

7. *Summit.* Lakeland Bus; weekly commutation ticket at $31; 45-minute trip to Port Authority Building.

8. *Upper Saddle River.* Short Line Bus; ten-trip book at $40.05, forty-trip book at $121.50, 50-trip book at $167.50; 45-minute bus trip to Port Authority Building.

9. *Westfield*. New Jersey Transit Bus Company; $98 monthly commutation ticket; 45-minute trip to Port Authority Building.

10. *Teaneck*. New Jersey Transit Bus Company; $60 monthly commutation ticket; 55-minute trip to Port Authority Building.

CONNECTICUT

Train

New Haven Line, Metro-North Commuter Railroad. General information telephone number is 212–532–4900 or 800–532–4900. Station in New York City is Grand Central Terminal at 42nd Street and Lexington Avenue. Monthly commutation ticket is available, and goes on sale ten days in advance. It connects the following communities from our list: Darien, Greenwich, New Canaan, Norwalk, Westport, and Stamford.

Bus

Greyhound Bus. For general information call 635–0800. Bus departs from and arrives at the Port Authority Building in New York City at Seventh Avenue and 41st Street. Route is Stamford–New York.

Limousine Service

Connecticut Limousine services all the following towns to and from Manhattan as well as to and from New York's airports. One-way to midtown Manhattan costs $18 to $20, round trip costs $35 to $39.

Car

To commute to and from New York by car there is a choice of using the Merritt Parkway or the New England Thruway, I-95.

1. The Merritt Parkway services those communities from our list that are not on the coast near the Long Island Sound. The Merritt Parkway has two lanes for traveling; if there is an accident or construction, rush hour commuting can be very difficult. There is, however, a financial advantage for rush-hour commuters: Monday–Friday, during 6 A.M.–9 A.M. and 3 P.M.–6 P.M., there is a free toll for three people or more in a car. "Three for free" is the slogan to encourage commuter carpools. For Connecticut residents who have a Connecticut license plate, you can purchase at your community's Department of Motor Vehicles for $40 per year a "Merritt Parkway toll plate." Attach it to your license plate and you won't have to stop to pay the 35¢ toll at Greenwich. General information telephone number is 203–869–4511.

2. The New England Thruway, I-95, offers those Connecticut residents the same "toll plate" program, but not the "three for free" carpool. I-95 has more tolls than the Merritt Parkway and for New York license plate owners it may be advantageous to buy a roll of forty tokens for $7 rather than to pay 35¢ for each toll. I-95 has three lanes for traveling and a service road. Traffic can get heavy at times, especially as you approach the toll booths, but it is not as lethal as the Merritt Parkway. General information telephone number is 203–869–8844.

1. *Darien.* New Haven Line, Metro-North Commuter Railroad; $130 monthly commutation ticket; 51-minute train trip.

2. *Greenwich.* New Haven Line, Metro-North Commuter Railroad; $126 monthly commutation ticket; 52-minute train trip.

3. *New Canaan.* New Haven Line, Metro-North Commuter Railroad; $134 monthly commutation ticket; 1-hour, 5-minute train trip.

4. *Norwalk.* New Haven Line, Metro-North Commuter Railroad; $137 monthly commutation ticket; 55-minute train trip.

5. *Westport.* New Haven Line, Metro-North Commuter Railroad; $145 monthly commutation ticket; 1-hour train trip.

6. *Stamford.* a) New Haven Line, Metro-North Commuter Railroad; $130 monthly commutation ticket; 1-hour train trip; b) Greyhound Bus; $7 one-way; 1-hour, 20-minute trip to the Port Authority Building in New York.

APPENDIX C

Public High Schools in the Suburbs

The forty-five communities listed in Appendix B are also categorized in this appendix. Our purpose is not to give a subjective opinion or an evaluation about a specific high school. Instead we will list objective criteria for each school which will offer the reader an overall picture of the tri-state area's suburban high schools.*

The following information is provided:
a. Number of graduates in the class of 1984
b. Percentage of graduates who continue on to a 4-year college
c. Mean SAT scores in English (Verbal scores)
d. Mean SAT scores in math
3. Student-faculty ratio

WESTCHESTER

1. *Chappaqua*
   Horace Greeley High School
   70 Roaring Brook Road
   Chappaqua, New York 10514
   914–238–4908
   914–238–3911
   a. 277
   b. 85%
   c. 496
   d. 550
   e. 14 to 1
2. *Rye*
   Rye Neck Union Free School
   District High School

Rye (cont.)
   310 Hornidge Road
   Mamaroneck, New York 10543
   914–698–6171
   a. 106
   b. 50%
   c. —
   d. —
   e. 10 to 1
3. *Scarsdale*
   Scarsdale High School
   Post Road
   Scarsdale, New York 10583
   914–723–9593

*Information for each school has been compiled and submitted by the faculty members of the particular school. If there is missing data in our listing, it is at the request of the school. The SAT scores are from 12th graders who took the tests in 1983 or 1984.

310

Scarsdale (cont.)
   a. 400
   b. 89.9%
   c. 508
   d. 547
   e. 14 to 1

   Edgemont High School
   White Oak Lane
   Scarsdale, New York 10583
   914–725–1500
   a. 147
   b. 87%
   c. 530
   d. 590
   e. 10 to 1
4. *Harrison*
   Harrison High School
   Union Avenue
   Harrison, New York 10528
   914–835–3300
   a. 235
   b. 58%
   c. 443
   d. 498
   e. 11 to 1
5. *Port Chester*
   Port Chester High School
   Tamarack Road
   Port Chester, New York 10573
   914–939–7300
   a. 203
   b. 40%
   c. —
   d. —
   e. 19 to 1
6. *Hastings-on-Hudson*
   Hastings High School
   Sarragut Avenue
   Hastings-on-Hudson,
   New York 10706
   914–478–2903, 914–478–2902

Hastings-on-Hudson (cont.)
   a. 126
   b. 72%
   c. 512
   d. 531
   e. 15 to 1
7. *Katonah*
   John Jay Senior High School
   Katonah, New York 10536
   914–763–3126
   a. 273
   b. 80.6%
   c. 452
   d. 484
   e. —
8. *Pound Ridge*
   Fox Lane High School
   P.O. Box 390
   Bedford, New York 10506
   914–666–6731
   a. 304
   b. 56%
   c. 471
   d. 527
   e. 10 to 1
9. *North Salem*
   North Salem High School
   Old Route 124
   North Salem, New York 10560
   914–669–5414
   a. 80
   b. 40–45%
   c. 450
   d. 470
   e. —
10. *Pelham*
   Pelham High School
   Colonial & Corlears Drive
   Pelham, New York 10803
   914–738–2555
   a. 220
   b. 70.6%

Pelham (cont.)
- c. 482
- d. 514
- e. 13 to 1

11. *Pleasantville*
Pleasantville High School
Romer Avenue
Pleasantville, New York 10570
914–769–8000
- a. 110
- b. 85%
- c. 500
- d. 471
- e. 12 to 1

12. *Bronxville*
Bronxville High School
Pondfield Road
Bronxville, New York 10708
914–337–5600
- a. 99
- b. 98%
- c. 532
- d. 574
- e. 12 to 1

13. *Hartsdale*
Edgemont High School
White Oak Lane
Scarsdale, New York 10583
914–725–1500
- a. 147
- b. 87%
- c. 530
- d. 590
- e. 10 to 1

Woodlands High School
475 West Hartsdale Avenue
Hartsdale, New York 10530
914–761–6000
- a. 200
- b. 60%
- c. 422

Hartsdale (cont.)
- d. 459
- e. 10 to 1

14. *New Rochelle*
New Rochelle High School
265 Clove Road
New Rochelle,
New York 10801
914–632–9000
- a. 699
- b. 50%
- c. 474
- d. 508
- e. 4 to 1

15. *Tuckahoe*
Tuckahoe High School
65 Siwanowy Boulevard
Eastchester, New York 10707
914–337–5376
- a. 45
- b. 80%
- c. 460
- d. 470
- e. 15 or 17 to 1

16. *White Plains*
White Plains High School
550 North Street
White Plains, New York 10605
914–997–2182
- a. 417
- b. 74%
- c. 421
- d. 458
- e. 25 to 1

LONG ISLAND

1. *Great Neck*
Great Neck High School
(South)
341 Lakeville Road
Great Neck, New York 11020
516–482–8650
   a. 263
   b. 79.1%
   c. 455
   d. 511
   e. 12.4 to 1

Great Neck High School
(North)
35 Polo Road
Great Neck, New York 11023
516–482–8650
   a. 257
   b. 88%
   c. 490
   d. 544
   e. 10 to 1

2. *Roslyn*
Roslyn High School
Round Hill Road
Roslyn Heights,
New York 11577
516–621–4900
   a. 244
   b. 88%
   c. 477
   d. 520
   e. 12 to 1

3. *Woodmere*
Hewlett High School
(Woodmere)
60 Everitt Avenue
Hewlett, New York 11557
516–374–5200

Woodmere (cont.)
   a. 350
   b. 75%
   c. 480
   d. 520
   e. 23 to 1

4. *Manhasset*
Manhasset High School
200 Memorial Place
Manhasset, New York 11030
516–627–4400
   a. 192
   b. 75%
   c. 480
   d. 520
   e. 23 to 1

5. *New Hyde Park*
Memorial High School
500 Leonard Boulevard
New Hyde Park,
New York 11040
516–328–4654
   a. 246
   b. 51%
   c. 430
   d. 450
   e. 16 to 1

6. *Syosset*
Syosset High School
Southwoods Road
Syosset, New York 11791
516–921–5500
   a. 549
   b. 70%
   c. 487
   d. 537
   e. 12 to 1

7. *Port Washington*
   Paul D. Schreiber High School
   Campus Drive
   Port Washington,
   New York 11050
   516–883–4000

   a. 415
   b. 67%
   c. 460
   d. 510
   e. 14 to 1

ROCKLAND COUNTY

1. *Orangeburg, Tappan,*
   Palisades, Sparkill
   Tappan Zee High School
   Dutchhill Road
   Orangeburg, New York 10962
   914–359–3320
   a. 313
   b. 60–80%
   c. 437
   d. 493
   e. 25 to 1

2. *Nyack*
   Nyack Senior High School
   Midland & Fifth Avenue
   Nyack, New York 10960
   914–358–7505
   a. 240
   b. 57%
   c. 419
   d. 450
   e. 10 to 1

NEW JERSEY

1. *Franklin Lakes*
   Ramapo High School
   George Street
   Franklin Lakes,
   New Jersey 07417
   201–891–1500
   a. 1,350
   b. 70%
   c. 494
   d. 537
   e. 12 to 1

2. *Ridgewood*
   Ridgewood High School
   627 East Ridgewood Avenue
   Ridgewood, New Jersey 07451
   201–670–2600

Ridgewood (cont.)
   a. 450
   b. 77.7%
   c. 504
   d. 554
   e. 14 to 1

3. *Tenafly*
   Tenafly High School
   Columbus Drive
   Tenafly, New Jersey 07670
   201–569–4400
   a. 240
   b. 82.1%
   c. —
   d. —
   e. 10 to 1

4. *Montclair*
Montclair High School
100 Chestnut Street
Montclair, New Jersey 07042
201-783-4000
   a. 439
   b. 62%
   c. 433
   d. 455
   e. 18 to 1
5. *Millburn*
Millburn High School
462 Millburn Avenue
Millburn, New Jersey 07041
201-376-3600
   a. 293
   b. 90%
   c. 482
   d. 537
   e. 13 to 1
6. *Fort Lee*
Fort Lee High School
3000 Lemoine Avenue
Ft. Lee, New Jersey 07024
201-592-3707
   a. 228
   b. 60%
   c. 421
   d. 476
   e. 22 to 1
7. *Summit* ·
Summit High School
129 Kent Place Boulevard
Summit, New Jersey 07901
201-273-1494
   a. 334
   b. 66%
   c. 459
   d. 517
   e. 10 to 1

Summit (cont.)
Governor Livingston High
School
Watchung Boulevard
Berkeley Heights,
New Jersey 07922
201-464-3100
   a. 219
   b. 65%
   c. 481
   d. 524
   e. 20 to 1
8. *Upper Saddle River*
Northern Highlands High
School
Hillside Avenue
Allendale, New Jersey 07401
201-327-8700
   a. 298
   b. 75%
   c. 471
   d. 512
   e. 10 to 1
9. *Westfield*
Westfield High School
550 Dorian Road
Westfield, New Jersey 07090
201-654-6400
   a. 499
   b. 74%
   c. 548
   d. 605
   e. 22 or 25 to 1
10. *Teaneck*
Teaneck High School
100 Elizabeth Avenue
Teaneck, New Jersey 07666
201-837-2882
   a. 420
   b. 70%
   c. 444
   d. 480
   e. 14.5 to 1

CONNECTICUT

1. *Darien*
   Darien High School
   High School Lane
   Darien, Connecticut 06820
   203–655–3981
   a. 351
   b. 75%
   c. 464
   d. 506
   e. —

2. *Greenwich*
   Greenwich High School
   10 Hillside Road
   Greenwich, Connecticut 06830
   203–625–8000
   a. 764
   b. 66%
   c. 460
   d. 508
   e. 12 to 1

3. *New Canaan*
   New Canaan High School
   Farm Road
   New Canaan,
   Connecticut 06840
   a. 321
   b. 70%
   c. 466
   d. 522
   e. —

4. *Norwalk*
   Norwalk High School
   County Street
   Norwalk, Connecticut 06851
   203–838–4481
   a. 478
   b. 52%
   c. 410
   d. 440
   e. 25 to 1

5. *Westport*
   Staples High School
   70 North Avenue
   Westport, Connecticut 06680
   203–222–1209
   a. 486
   b. 81%
   c. 478
   d. 495
   e. 10 to 1

6. *Stamford*
   Stamford High School
   55 Strawberry Hill Avenue
   Stamford, Connecticut 06902
   203–358–4223
   a. 396
   b. 45%
   c. 390
   d. 411
   e. 9 to 1

APPENDIX D

Public High Schools in the Five Boroughs

Each borough is divided into many different school districts. Each school district has at least one elementary school, one junior high school, and one senior high school. Some communities may fall into the jurisdiction of two school districts, but your specific address will only be in one district. There will be a time when it may be very important for you to know in which school district your residence is located. This information may be crucial to have even before you choose your housing. You can call the Board of Education at 596–5953 or 596–6066 with your inquiry. They will check their "School Attendance Area Directory" to identify your residence with the schools of your district.

In the following listing we present information about the high schools in the five boroughs that correspond to the map in Chapter 3.* In some cases we list two high schools. Your specific address will determine which of the two high schools is in your district. If you are not sure, you can call the high school directly.

Note that starting on page 323 there is information on "special" public high schools.

The following information is provided:
a. Students in graduating class
b. Percentage of graduates attending 4-year colleges
c. Pupil-teacher ratio
d. Average class size
e. Mean math grade for 12th grade in New York City testing
f. Mean reading grade for 12th grade in New York City testing

---

*The source for the data in this appendix comes from *Public Schools Rated*, 1983 edition, compiled by the Board of Education, Educational Statistics Office, 110 Livingston Street, Brooklyn, New York.

317

PUBLIC HIGH SCHOOLS

Manhattan
  1. *The Upper East Side*
     Julia Richman High School
     317 East 67th Street
     879–6866
     a. 361
     b. 43.2%
     c. 20.1 to 1
     d. 33.7
     e. 10.1
     f. 10.7
  2. *Sutton Place*
     Julia Richman High School
     317 East 67th Street
     879–6866
     a. 361
     b. 43.2%
     c. 20.1 to 1
     d. 33.7
     e. 10.1
     f. 10.7
  3. *The United Nations*
     Julia Richman High School
     317 East 67th Street
     879–6866
     a. 361
     b. 43.2%
     c. 20.1 to 1
     d. 33.7
     e. 10.1
     f. 10.7
  4. *Murray Hill*
     Washington Irving High School
     40 Irving Place
     674–5000
     a. 335
     b. 41.5%
     c. 17.9 to 1
     d. 31.7

Murray Hill (cont.)
     e. 10.3
     f. 10.3
  5. *Gramercy Park*
     Washington Irving High School
     40 Irving Place
     674–5000
     a. 335
     b. 41.5%
     c. 17.9 to 1
     d. 31.7
     e. 10.3
     f. 10.3
  6. *Greenwich Village (West)*
     Charles Evans Hughes High
     School
     351 West 18th Street
     675–5350
     a. 247
     b. 28.7%
     c. 15.5 to 1
     d. 27.7
     e. 9.5
     f. 9.4
Greenwich Village (East)
     Washington Irving High School
     40 Irving Place
     674–5000
     a. 335
     b. 41.5%
     c. 17.9 to 1
     d. 31.7
     e. 10.3
     f. 10.3
  7. *SoHo*
     Seward Park High School
     350 Grand Street
     674–7000
     a. 567
     b. 38.8%

SoHo (cont.)
   c. 16.9 to 1
   d. 29.5
   e. 10.6
   f. 9.9
8. *Chelsea*
   Charles Evans Hughes High
   School
   351 West 18th Street
   675–5350
   a. 247
   b. 28.7%
   c. 15.5 to 1
   d. 27.7
   e. 9.5
   f. 9.4
9. *Lincoln Center*
   Martin Luther King Junior
   High School
   122 Amsterdam Avenue
   874–1202
   a. 283
   b. 35.3%
   c. 16.5 to 1
   d. 30.7
   e. 10.3
   f. 10.8
10. *The Upper West Side*
    Louis D. Brandeis High School
    145 West 84th Street
    799–0300
    a. 638
    b. 31.5%
    c. 15.6 to 1
    d. 31.9
    e. 10.0
    f. 10.3
11. *Columbia University*
    A. Philip Randolph High
    School
    Convent Avenue & 140th
    Street
    926–0113

Columbia University (cont.)
   a. —
   b. —
   c. —
   d. 16.2 to 1
   e. 11.4
   f. 12.0
   Louis D. Brandeis High School
   145 West 84th Street
   799–0300
   a. 638
   b. 31.5%
   c. 15.6 to 1
   d. 31.9
   e. 10.0
   f. 10.3
12. *Yorkville*
    Julia Richman High School
    317 East 67th Street
    879–6866
    a. 361
    b. 43.2%
    c. 20.1 to 1
    d. 33.7
    e. 10.1
    f. 10.7
13. *Ukrainian*
    Washington Irving High School
    40 Irving Place
    674–5000
    a. 335
    b. 41.5%
    c. 17.9 to 1
    d. 31.7
    e. 10.3
    f. 10.3
14. *Little Italy*
    Seward Park High School
    350 Grand Street
    674–7000
    a. 567
    b. 38.8%
    c. 16.9 to 1

Little Italy (cont.)
   d. 29.5
   e. 10.6
   f. 9.9
15. *Chinatown*
   Seward Park High School
   350 Grand Street
   674–7000
   a. 567
   b. 38.8%
   c. 16.9 to 1
   d. 29.5
   e. 10.6
   f. 9.9

Queens
 1. *Long Island City, Astoria,*
   Sunnyside
   Long Island City High School
   28-01 41st Avenue
   937–1610
   a. 588
   b. 48.1%
   c. 19.3 to 1
   d. 34.5
   e. 11.3
   f. 11.9

   William C. Bryant High School
   48-10 31st Avenue
   721–5404
   a. 672
   b. 36.2%
   c. 18.7 to 1
   d. 34.3
   e. 10.4
   f. 10.4
 2. *Flushing*
   Flushing High School
   35-01 Union Street
   762–8360
   a. 404
   b. 57.4%

Flushing (cont.)
   c. 16.5
   d. 34.7
   e. 10.7
   f. 10.7

   Bayside High School
   32nd Avenue & 208th Street
   229–7600
   a. 693
   b. 54.7%
   c. 18.4 to 1
   d. 33.6
   e. 11.9
   f. 11.9
 3. *Rego Park, Forest Hills,*
   Kew Gardens
   Forest Hills High School
   67-01 110th Street
   268–3137
   a. 541
   b. 51.2%
   c. 18.4 to 1
   d. 34.7
   e. 12.2
   f. 12.1
 4. *Bayside*
   Bayside High School
   32nd Avenue & 208th Street
   229–7600
   a. 693
   b. 54.7%
   c. 18.4 to 1
   d. 33.6
   e. 11.9
   f. 11.9

   Benjamin Cardozo High School
   57-20 233rd Street
   631–4880
   a. 598

Bayside (cont.)
  b. 49.5%
  c. 17.7 to 1
  d. 35.1
  e. 11.0
  f. 11.4
 5. *Little Neck*
  Benjamin Cardozo High School
  57-20 233rd Street
  631–4880
  a. 598
  b. 49.5%
  c. 17.7 to 1
  d. 35.1
  e. 11.0
  f. 11.4
 6. *Whitestone*
  Bayside High School
  32nd Avenue & 208th Street
  229–7600
  a. 693
  b. 54.7%
  c. 18.4 to 1
  d. 33.6
  e. 11.9
  f. 11.9

  Francis Lewis High School
  58-20 Utopia Parkway
  357–7740
  a. 518
  b. 49.4%
  c. 18.5 to 1
  d. 35.7
  e. 11.3
  f. 11.0

Bronx
 1. *Riverdale*
  John F. Kennedy High School
  99 Terrace View Avenue
  562–5500
  a. 1,140

Riverdale (cont.)
  b. 28.6%
  c. 19.0 to 1
  d. 33.1
  e. 10.7
  f. 10.6
 2. *North-east*
  Evander Childs High School
  800 East Green Hill Road
  547–7700
  a. 739
  b. 28.7%
  c. 20.4 to 1
  d. 31.2
  e. 10.9
  f. 11.2

  Harry S. Truman High School
  750 Baychester Avenue
  320–2300
  a. 464
  b. 45.7%
  c. 18.9 to 1
  d. 33.6
  e. 10.9
  f. 10.3
 3. *Pelham*
  Christopher Columbus High
  School
  925 Astor Avenue
  231–5000
  a. 530
  b. 47.4%
  c. 18.9 to 1
  d. 34.1
  e. 10.6
  f. 10.4

  Harry S. Truman High School
  750 Baychester Avenue
  320–2300
  a. 464
  b. 45.7%

Pelham (cont.)
   c. 18.9 to 1
   d. 33.6
   e. 10.9
   f. 10.3
4. *Tremont Avenue*
   Christopher Columbus High School
   925 Astor Avenue
   231–5000
   a. 530
   b. 47.4%
   c. 18.9 to 1
   d. 34.1
   e. 10.6
   f. 10.4

   Herbert H. Lehman High School
   3000 East Tremont Avenue
   824–0500
   a. 604
   b. 33.6
   c. 20.1 to 1
   d. 33.7
   e. 10.5
   f. 10.8

Staten Island
1. *St. George*
   Curtis High School
   Hamilton Avenue & St. Mark's Place
   273–3210
   a. 326
   b. 65.0%
   c. 17.0 to 1
   d. 35.1
   e. 10.7
   f. 10.9

Brooklyn
1. *Brooklyn Heights, Carroll Gardens, Cobble Hill, Prospect Park, Park Slope*
   John Jay High School
   237 7th Avenue
   788–1514
   a. 393
   b. 45.5%
   c. 18.2 to 1
   d. 29.7
   e. 10.0
   f. 10.5

SPECIAL PUBLIC HIGH SCHOOLS

The following high schools are "special" high schools that are under the jurisdiction of the Board of Education of New York City.* They are public high schools, which means that theoretically they are available to the students who live in one of the five boroughs. But they are "special," which means that the student must take a test or present a portfolio or proof of talent for admission. There are specific requirements for admission and specific dates to demonstrate these qualities. It may be necessary to apply as much as one year in advance. Call the Office of Admissions of the particular school for exact information.

Manhattan

School of Fashion Industries *(cont.)*

Chelsea Vocational High
School
131 Sixth Avenue
925–1080
a. 133
b. 29.3%
c. 17 to 4
d. 30.4
e. 10.6
f. 10.9

High School of Art and Design
1075 Second Avenue
752–4340
a. 398
b. 48.2%
c. 16 to 2
d. 30.3
e. 11.2
f. 12.2

School of Fashion Industries
225 West 24th Street
255–1235
a. 336

b. 28.9%
c. 16 to 5
d. 32.4
e. 10.2
f. 11.3

Hunter High School
Park Avenue and 94th Street
860–1267
a. 181
b. 99%
c. 20 to 1
d. 24
e. SAT verbal scores: 600
f. SAT math scores: 600

New York School of Printing
439 West 49th Street
245–5925
a. 202
b. 50.5%
c. 14 to 9
d. 27.7
e. 11.3
f. 11.8

*The following data has been compiled by the Board of Education, Educational Statistics Office.

Manhattan *(cont.)*

Stuyvesant High School
345 East 15th Street
673–9030
a. 631
b. 93.2%
c. 19 to 5
d. 38
e. SAT verbal scores: 600
f. SAT math scores: 600

Bronx

Bronx High School of Science
75 West 205 Street
295–0200
a. 698
b. 86%
c. 18 to 1

Bronx High School of Science *(cont.)*

d. 32
e. SAT verbal scores: 350–780
f. SAT math scores: 350–780

Brooklyn

Brooklyn Technical High
School
29 Fort Greene Place
858–5150
a. 835
b. 66.8%
c. 19 to 3
d. 31
e. SAT verbal scores: 442
f. SAT math scores: 517

APPENDIX E

Private High Schools in New York City

The key for the following list* is as follows:

a. Number of graduates in the class of 1984
b. Percentage of those graduates who went on to a 4-year college
c. Median SAT score in English (verbal scores)
d. Median SAT score in math
e. School's total student-faculty ratio
f. Tuition for the 12th grade

1. *Anglo-American School*
   18 West 89th Street
   New York, New York 10024
   724–6360
   a. 45
   b. 100%
   c. 550
   d. 560
   e. 14 to 1
   f. $6,600

2. *Baldwin School of New York*
   160 West 74th Street
   New York, New York 10023
   873–4900
   a. 27
   b. 85%
   c. —
   d. —
   e. 7 to 1
   f. $6,798

3. *Barnard School*
   554 Fort Washington Avenue
   New York, New York 10033
   795–1050
   a. 3
   b. 100%
   c. 500
   d. 400
   e. 8–15 to 1
   f. $4,000

4. *Birch-Wathen School*
   9 East 71st Street
   New York, New York 10021
   861–0404
   a. 42
   b. 100%
   c. 560
   d. 580
   e. 8 to 1
   f. $6,425

*Information for each school has been compiled and submitted by the Office of Admissions of the particular school. If there is missing data in our listing, it is at the request of the school. The SAT scores are from 12th graders who took the tests in 1983 or 1984.

5. *Brearly School*
   610 East 83rd Street
   New York, New York 10028
   744–8582
   a. 47
   b. 100%
   c. 630
   d. 620
   e. 8 to 1
   f. $6,700

6. *Browning School*
   52 East 62nd Street
   New York, New York 10021
   838–6280
   a. 37
   b. 100%
   c. 520
   d. 590
   e. 8 to 1
   f. $6,700

7. *Calhoun School*
   433 West End Avenue
   New York, New York 10024
   724–2308
   a. 35
   b. 99%
   c. 550
   d. 550
   e. 12 to 1
   f. $6,250

8. *Chapin School*
   100 East End Avenue
   New York, New York 10028
   744–2335
   a. 41
   b. 100%
   c. 580
   d. 580
   e. 6 to 1
   f. $6,500

9. *Collegiate School*
   241 West 77th Street
   New York, New York 10024

Collegiate School (cont.)
   873–0677
   a. 45
   b. 99.9%
   c. —
   d. —
   e. 9 to 1
   f. $5,900

10. *Columbia Grammar &
    Preparatory School*
    5 West 93rd Street
    New York, New York 10025
    749–6200
    a. 46
    b. 100%
    c. 610
    d. 600
    e. 8 to 1
    f. $5,616

11. *Convent of the Sacred Heart*
    One East 91st Street
    New York, New York 10028
    722–4745
    a. 36
    b. 100%
    c. 510
    d. 537
    e. 8 to 1
    f. $6,400

12. *Dalton School*
    108 East 89th Street
    New York, New York 10028
    722–5160
    a. 96
    b. 100%
    c. 608
    d. 625
    e. 7 to 1
    f. $7,300

13. *Dwight School*
    402 East 67th Street
    New York, New York 10021
    737–2400

Dwight School (cont.)
   a. 64
   b. 100%
   c. 550
   d. 500
   e. 11 to 1
   f. $6,100
14. *Fieldston School*
   Fieldston Road
   Bronx, New York 10471
   543–5000
   a. 121
   b. 100%
   c. 640
   d. 590
   e. 8 to 1
   f. $6,975
15. *Friends Seminary*
   222 East 16th Street
   New York, New York 10003
   477–9500
   a. 47
   b. 90%
   c. 540
   d. 530
   e. 9 to 1
   f. $5,840
16. *Hewitt School*
   45 East 75th Street
   New York, New York 10021
   288–1909
   a. 17
   b. 100
   c. —
   d. —
   e. 6 to 1
   f. $6,300
17. *Horace Mann–Barnard Schools*
   231 West 246th Street
   Bronx, New York 10471
   548–4000
   a. 158
   b. 100%

Horace Mann–Barnard Schools (cont.)
   c. 630
   d. 680
   e. 10 to 1
   f. $6,500
18. *Lenox School*
   170 East 70th Street
   New York, New York 10021
   288–4778
   a. 22
   b. 100%
   c. 560
   d. 550
   e. 15 to 1
   f. $6,425
19. *Elisabeth Irwin High School*
   40 Charlton Street
   New York, New York 10014
   477–5316
   a. 15
   b. 100%
   c. 550
   d. 550
   e. 6 to 1
   f. $5,500
20. *Loyola High School*
   980 Park Avenue
   New York, New York 10028
   288–6200
   a. 45
   b. 96%
   c. 530
   d. 520
   e. 15 or 18 to 1
   f. $4,175
21. *Lycée Français de New York*
   3 East 95th Street
   New York, New York 10028
   369–1400
   a. 50
   b. 64% attend a 4-year
      American college; 100%
      attend either a 4-year

Lycee Français de New York (cont.)
   American or a foreign
   college
c. —
d. —
e. 6 to 1
f. $4,200

22. *McBurney School*
15 West 63rd Street
New York, New York 10023
362–8117
a. 65
b. 100%
c. 470
d. 460
e. 9 to 1
f. $6,150

23. *Marymount School*
1026 Fifth Avenue
New York, New York 10028
744–4486
a. 31
b. 100%
c. 510
d. 500
e. 8 to 1
f. $6,200

24. *New Lincoln School*
210 East 77th Street
New York, New York 10021
879–9200
a. 36
b. 92%
c. 490
d. 500
e. 9 to 1
f. $6,100

25. *Nightingale-Bamford School*
20 East 92nd Street
New York, New York 10028
289–5020
a. 35

Nightingale-Bamford School (cont.)
b. 100%
c. —
d. —
e. 8 to 1
f. $6,600

26. *Professional Children's School*
132 West 60th Street
New York, New York 10023
582–3116
a. 55
b. Many of these students
   continue on to specific
   professions that may not
   require students to be
   college-bound
c. —
d. —
e. 10 to 1
f. $5,280

27. *Ramaz School*
60 East 78th Street
New York, New York 10021
787–4300
a. 87
b. 100%
c. 591
d. 606
e. 6 to 1
f. $6,000

28. *Rhodes School*
212 West 83rd Street
New York, New York 10024
787–4300
a. 45
b. 95%
c. —
d. —
e. 6 to 1
f. $5,800

29. *Riverdale Country School*
5250 Fieldston Road
Bronx, New York 10471
549–8810
a. 110
b. 99%
c. 600
d. 600
e. 10 to 1
f. $7,200

30. *Robert Louis Stevenson School*
24 West 74th Street
New York, New York 10023
787–6400
a. 21
b. 99%
c. 500
d. 500
e. 4 to 1
f. $9,500

31. *Rudolf Steiner School*
15 East 79th Street
New York, New York 10021
535–2130
a. 22
b. 100%
c. 600
d. 550
e. 4 to 1
f. $5,075

32. *St. Hilda's & St. Hugh's School*
619 West 114th Street
New York, New York 10025
666–9645
a. 23
b. 100%
c. 530
d. 490
e. 10 to 1
f. $4,675

33. *Searing School*
127 East 59th Street
New York, New York 10022
755–5626
a. 9
b. 100%
c. 500
d. 500
e. 3 to 1
f. $10,800

34. *Spence School*
22 East 91st Street
New York, New York 10028
289–5940
a. 28
b. 100%
c. 590
d. 610
e. 11 to 1
f. $6,740

35. *Trinity School*
139 West 91st Street
New York, New York 10024
873–1650
a. 90
b. 100%
c. 620
d. 620
e. 7 to 1
f. $7,545

36. *United Nations International
School*
24-50 East River Drive
New York, New York 10010
684–7400
a. 116
b. 99%
c. —
d. —
e. 10 to 1
f. $5,500

37. *Walden School*
    1 West 88th Street
    New York, New York 10024
    787-5315
    a. 34
    b. 95%
    c. 510
    d. 500
    e. 18 to 1
    f. $6,300

38. *York Preparatory*
    116 East 85th Street
    New York, New York 10028
    628-1220
    a. 64
    b. 100%
    c. 510
    d. 440
    e. 10 to 1
    f. $6,300

Bibliography of Useful Books

Adams, Robert Lang. *The Metropolitan New York Job Bank*. New York: Bob Adams Publishing, 1981.

American Express Pocket Guide to New York. New York: Simon and Schuster, 1983.

Appleberg, Marilyn J. *I Love New York Guide*. New York: Collier, 1981.

Ardman, Harvey and Perri Ardman. *The Complete Apartment Guide*. New York: Collier, 1978.

Berlitz: New York Travel Book. New York: Berlitz, 1983.

Berman, Eleanor. *Away for the Weekend: Great Getaways Less Than 200 Miles from New York City*. New York: Crown, 1982.

Blumberg, Richard E. and James R. Grow. *The Rights of Tenants*. New York: Avon, 1978.

Boyer, Richard and David Savageau. *Places Rated Almanac: Your Guide to Finding the Best Places to Live in America*. Rand McNally.

Britchky, Seymour. *Best Restaurants in New York*. New York: Random House, 1983.

Cohen, Marjorie Adoff. *The Shopper's Guide to New York for International Visitors and United States Visitors*. New York: E.P. Dutton, 1981.

Fishchler, Stan. *Uptown, Downtown: New York on the Subways*. New York: Hawthorn, 1976.

Fodor's New York City. New York: Fodor, 1983.

Frank, Gerry. *Where To Find It, Buy It, Eat It in New York*. Salem, Oregon: Gerry's Frankly Speaking, rev. 1983.

Freeman, Darlene and Virginia Stuart. *Resources for Gifted Children in the New York Area*. Trillum Press.

Goldberger, Paul. *New York: Guide to the Architecture of Manhattan*. New York: Vintage, 1979.

Goldsmith, Alice and Adrienne Lansing. *Summer Camps and Programs.* Harmony Books.

Hammel, Faye. *Fromer's 1982-83 Guide to New York.* New York: Simon & Schuster, 1981.

Hauser, Joan. *Manhattan Epicure.* New York: Peanut Butter Publishing, 1983.

Lawrence, Peter. *A Kid's New York.* New York: Avon, 1981.

McDarrah, Fred W. *Museums in New York.* New York: Simon & Schuster, 1983.

Madison, Richard. *The Greencard Book.* New York: Visa Publishing Corp., 1981.

Michelin's New York City. New York: Michelin Tire Corp., 1979.

Newberry, Lida. *One Day Adventure by Car.* New York: Hastings House, 1971.

New York in Your Pocket. New York: Barrons, 1983.

New York Visitor's Bureau has many brochures and guides about New York. 2 Columbus Circle. 397–8222.

Petersen's Annual Guide to Independent Secondary Schools. Petersen's Guides.

Petersen's Annual Guide to Undergraduate Studies: Four-Year Colleges and Two-Year Colleges. Petersen's Guides.

Quik Finder New York: Easy-to-Use-Map Guidebook. New York: Geographia Map Co., 1983.

Schuberth, Christopher. *New York Walk Book.* New York: Doubleday, 1971.

Sheraton, Mimi. *Best Restaurants in New York.* New York: New York Time Press, 1983.

Stern, Zelda. *The Complete Guide to Ethnic New York.* New York: St. Martin's, 1980.

Tauranac, John. *Essential New York: A Guide to the History and Architecture of New York.* New York: Holt, Rinehart, and Winston, 1979.

Thomas, Bill and Phyllis Thomas. *Natural New York: Guide to Parks.* New York: Holt, Rinehart, and Winston, 1983.

White, Norval. *A.I.A. Guide to New York City* (American Institute of Architects). New York: Collier, 1978.

Wiener, Solomon. *Questions and Answers on American Citizenship.* New York: Regents Publishing Co., 1970.

Wolfe, Gerald R. *New York: A Guide to the Metropolis, Walking Tours.* New York: New York University Press, 1975.

W.P.A. Guide to New York. New York: Pantheon, 1982.

Yeadon, Anne and David Yeadon. *Free New York*. New York: Free City Books, 1983.

Zuesse, Eric. *Bargain Finder: The Encyclopedic Money Saving Guide to New York City*. Golden Lee Books, 1983.

Index

335

apartments *(continued)*
  directory of residents (lobby), 23
  fixtures, 16
  heat, 17
  leases: *see* leases
  moving into, 20–24
  painting of rooms, 23
  professional use of, 27
  rentals *versus* co-ops, 26–27
  renting agencies: *see* renting agencies
  sharing, 12–13
  staff, 13, 196, 197
  sublets, 15, 18, 20
  suburban, 58, 63
appliances, electrical
  stores for, 91
  voltage converters for, 86
Arizona State University, 145
artists visiting U.S., visa status of, 233
art schools and classes, 263
Asian Studies, Institute for, 151
Astoria section of Queens, 40
audio equipment stores, 92
automobiles, use of, 48, 52
  accidents involving, 105
  driver's license, 77
  garaging of, 107
  gasoline credit cards, 76
  insurance, 87, 104, 105
  limousines, 108
  parking, 105, 106
  parking and traffic violations, 105
  purchase of, 104
  registration of, 104
  rental of, 87, 102–4
  theft of, 105
  towaway of, 106, 107
  traffic signs, 106
autumn vacations and trips, 250–53

B

babysitters, 78, 196
banking services, 71–73
  checking accounts, 72
  commercial *versus* savings banks, 72
  currency exchange services, 76–77
  loans for co-ops, 27, 30
  safe deposit vaults, 73–74

banking services *(continued)*
  savings accounts, 72–73
  travelers' checks, 76
Barnard College, 145, 148
Bayside section of Queens, 41, 42
beaches
  Connecticut, 249–50, 252, 262
  Jersey Shore, 249
  Long Island, 247–48
beauticians, tipping of, 196–97
"bedroom community" defined, 60
Belleayre, N.Y., winter visits to, 253–54, 281
Bergen County, N.J., residential communities, 52–53, 59–60, 66–67
Bethany, Conn., recreational attractions, 261
Better Business Bureau, 21
bicycling
  A.Y.H. activities, 260
  stores and rentals, 91, 274–75
binder payment, 30
birth control services, 167
birthday celebrations and gifts, 195
Bishop's Orchard, 262
Bloomingdale's department store, 5
Blue Mountain Reservation, spring visits to, 255
boating, 152, 241, 249, 262
  canoeing lessons, 275
  navigation courses, 152, 268
  rentals, 275
  sailboating schools, and rentals, 280
boat trips
  Circle Line, 258
  Essex, 261
botannical gardens: *see* plant and animal preserves
Bowery section of Manhattan, 92
Brazilian communities, Scarsdale, 58
bridges
  Brooklyn, 44
  George Washington, 9, 42, 52, 58, 60, 66
  Queensboro, 39
brokerage services, 73
Bronx borough of New York, 64
  E.S.L. programs in, 204–5
  hospitals, 160, 162

About the Author

Roberta Seret, Ph.D. has lectured widely on how newcomers to New York can understand and adapt to their new environment. As president and founder of the AMERICAN WELCOME SERVICES, she has appeared on nationwide television programs and has been interviewed on foreign and American radio shows. Dr. Seret has given orientation courses, seminars, workshops, and consultations to newcomers who come to live and work in New York City. By answering their questions, allaying their fears, and assisting them with their problems, she has helped many foreigners and Americans to understand New Yorkers and to become part of the city.

Her philosophy is that if newcomers can understand the mentality and customs of New Yorkers, as well as the mechanism and system of the city, their acclimation will be easier.

In her book *Welcome to New York,* she offers practical advice, shortcuts, and valuable insights. *Welcome to New York* provides names and addresses, hidden secrets, and all types of information that one usually learns after years of living in New York. *Welcome to New York* helps all newcomers to *Settle and Survive in New York,* and to enjoy it as well.